Johnson Re-Visioned

The Bucknell Studies in Eighteenth-Century Literature and Culture

General Editor: Greg Clingham, *Bucknell University*

Advisory Board: Paul K. Alkon, *University of Southern California*
Chloe Chard, *Independent Scholar*
Clement Hawes, *The Pennsylvania State University*
Robert Markley, *West Virginia University*
Jessica Munns, *University of Denver*
Cedric D. Reverand II, *University of Wyoming*
Janet Todd, *University of Glasgow*

The Bucknell Studies in Eighteenth-Century Literature and Culture aims to publish challenging, new eighteenth-century scholarship. Of particular interest is critical, historical, and interdisciplinary work that is interestingly and intelligently theorized, and that broadens and refines the conception of the field. At the same time, the series remains open to all theoretical perspectives and different kinds of scholarship. While the focus of the series is the literature, history, arts, and culture (including art, architecture, music, travel, and history of science, medicine, and law) of the long eighteenth century in Britain and Europe, the series is also interested in scholarship that establishes relationships with other geographies, literatures, and cultures of the period 1660–1830.

Titles in This Series

http://www.departments.bucknell.edu/univ_press

Johnson Re-Visioned

Looking Before and After

Edited by

Philip Smallwood

Lewisburg
Bucknell University Press
London: Associated University Presses

Associated University Presses
2010 Eastpark Blvd.
Cranbury, NJ 08512

The paper used in this publication meets the requirements of the American National Standard for Permanence of Paper for Printed Library Materials Z39.48-1984.

Library of Congress Cataloging-in-Publication Data

Johnson re-visioned : looking before and after / edited by Philip Smallwood.
    p.   cm. — (The Bucknell studies in eighteenth-century literature and culture)
Includes biographical references and index.
ISBN 0-8387-5494-5 (alk. paper)
    1. Johnson, Samuel, 1709–1784 — Criticism and interpretation.   2. Literature and history — Great Britain — History — 18th century.   3. Literature and society — Great Britain — History — 18th Century.   3. Johnson, Samuel, 1709–1784 — Political and social views.   5. Johnson, Samuel, 1709–1784 — Knowledge — History.   I. Title: Johnson revisioned.   II. Smallwood, Philip.   III. Series.
PR3534.J66   2001
828'.609 — dc21   2001025983

First paperback edition 2009
ISBN 978-0-8387-5742-0 (paperback)
PRINTED IN THE UNITED STATES OF AMERICA

Detail from James Barry's mural of 1783 *The Distribution of Premiums in the Society of Arts*. Johnson is depicted between the Duchesses of Rutland and Devonshire. Reproduced courtesy of the Royal Society for the Encouragement of Arts, Manufactures and Commerce.

Contents

Preface

PHILIP SMALLWOOD

One might say: " 'I know' expresses *comfortable* certainty,
not the certainty that is still struggling."
—Ludwig Wittgenstein, *On Certainty*

THE EFFECT OF LITERARY SCHOLARSHIP ON LITERARY REPUTATION, and of what we know of the past upon the fluctuating perceptions of volatile literary value, was once beautifully evoked by Samuel Johnson in the opening pages of his "Preface to Shakespeare" of 1765:

> The poet, of whose works I have undertaken the revision, may now begin to assume the dignity of an ancient, and claim the privilege of established fame and prescriptive veneration. He has long outlived his century, the term commonly fixed as the test of literary merit. Whatever advantages he might once derive from personal allusions, local customs, or temporary opinions, have for many years been lost; and every topick of merriment or motive of sorrow, which the modes of artificial life afforded him, now only obscure the scenes which they once illuminated. The effects of favour and competition are at an end; the tradition of his friendships and his enmities has perished; his works support no opinion with arguments, nor supply any faction with invectives; they can neither indulge vanity nor gratify malignity, but are read without any other reason than the desire of pleasure, and are therefore praised only as pleasure is obtained; yet, thus unassisted by interest or passion, they have past through variations of taste and changes of manners, and, as they devolved from one generation to another, have received new honours at every transmission.
>
> But because human judgment, though it be gradually gaining upon certainty, never becomes infallible; and approbation, though long continued, may yet be only the approbation of prejudice or fashion; it is proper to inquire, by what peculiarities of excellence Shakespeare has gained and kept the favour of his countrymen. (*Shakespeare*, 7:61)

What is here stated of Shakespeare by Johnson, with its pregnant "turn" as the reasoning moves resistlessly from the first to the second paragraph, overcomes many less complex explanations of the relevance,

immediacy, or "presence" of the literary past. Similar criteria can apply
to our relations with Johnson nearly 250 years later. Samuel Johnson
has "long outlived" the eighteenth century, the term according to his
own standards "fixed as the test of literary merit." Yet many readers,
critics, and scholars continue to "know" Johnson with unhindered certainty only by means of a totalizing label or classificatory system—as a
"neoclassic," a "preromantic" on the cusp of a cultural divide, an "Enlightenment rationalist" or English nationalist with archetypally narrow, elitist, or conservative opinions on everything from the laws of
poetry to colonial subordination and the rights of women.

By questioning unadvised assumptions in the matter of Johnson's
current value, contributors to this volume are accepting responsibility
for defining the quintessence of a future description. *Johnson Re-Visioned*
attempts a critical reappraisal of past Johnsonian scholarship conceived
in the company of fresh scholarly determinations. Recapitulating their
subject from the brink of a new century, the essays look "before and
after" in that their emphasis is divided between historically recuperative
approaches to Johnson on the one hand, and on the other emergent
directions in Johnsonian studies. Within the range of opinion represented here the reader will find a fuller account of what Johnson's contemporaries actually thought of his most inexplicably controversial
critical judgments (on Shakespeare and other writers), and a suggestion
of the status of Johnsonian judgments as literary—even "poetic"—
artifacts in their own right. Contributors examine the role of his writings in the historical formation of a self-consciously national and
international literary culture, Johnson's unequivocally abolitionist
views on slavery and the quality (as well as the fact) of his contemporary relations with eighteenth-century literary women. In exploring
these subjects, the essays herein embrace, or more fundamentally reex-
amine, a wide range of Johnson's work and of work on Johnson—his
conversations, contemporary anecdotes, and reports of his views; the
Lives of the Poets and the Shakespearean criticism; *Rasselas* and the
poems and periodical essays of Johnson's middle career; his *Letters*, political, and travel writing, as well as some of the lesser-known pamphlets, reviews, and miscellaneous studies yet to appear in modern
editions. By drawing together new thinking based on references to
these and other topics under a common head, the essays organize a connected exchange of current voices on Johnson and mark out significant
trends in Johnsonian studies for forthcoming years. The volume combines fresh treatments of traditional issues such as biography, historiography and aesthetics, with aspects of the politics of empire, culture,
race, gender, and theory.

By attention to continuities and contrasts between older and newer ways of reading Johnson, the initial essay by Greg Clingham, "Resisting Johnson," surveys the state of opinion on Johnson in the closing years of the twentieth century. The essay highlights disparities between the text, language, history, and mind of Johnson and the persistence even within academic circles of a "Minimized" account of Johnsonian thought. Clingham argues that the late or aging generation of Johnson scholarship has been excessively unreceptive to wider cultural movements, and his essay in this way opens central questions about the limits and legitimacy of established Johnsonian study. In the system of resistances is to be found *both* the cutting edge of Johnsonian thought in its application to present concerns *and* a sharper instrument for probing the eighteenth-century past from our present situation. Subsequent essays respond to the questions raised by this claim. The immediately following discussion by Clement Hawes bridges a gap between interdisciplinary approaches to Enlightenment and the Johnsonian text. In "Johnson's Cosmopolitan Nationalism," Hawes locates Johnson within the politics and textuality of Enlightenment nationalism and internationalism and reveals the subtlety of Johnson's cultural, critical, and human stance. Focusing on Johnson's treatment of the "Bard" of Thomas Gray, the notorious "Ossian" affair, and Johnson's suspicion of "national genealogies," Hawes shows how Johnson's conception of the public sphere is both multifaceted and underdetermined, paradoxically inward and rooted, yet unusually detached. Johnson offers a political wisdom unconfined to the genre of the political tract, and embracing issues that our daily experience of the morality of national and international perspectives leaves unresolved.

In "Multicultural Perspectives: Johnson, Race, and Gender," the next essay in this collection, James G. Basker develops a reading of Johnson which again brings current social and cultural priorities to the center of Johnsonian scholarly concerns. Basker systematically refutes traditional charges of racism and misogyny in Johnson while revealing the recoverable values a modern age might take from Johnson on the organization of society, racial and sexual equity, and ethics. A more particular exploration of this revisionary "Samuel Johnson" is continued in the following essay where Jaclyn Geller considers the role of Johnson's close but multifarious personal and writing relations with women friends and associates, and pursues the implications of a feminized Johnsonian consciousness in the history and development of the novel. Linking Johnsonian insights into human nature and human institutions with those of Jane Austen, her investigation reinforces how much recent feminist anti-Johnsonianism remains an anachronistic reaction to Boswell.

The last three essays in the collection apply versions of the "turn to history" to Johnsonian study. In "Thinking of Italy, Making History: Johnson and Historiography," Danielle Insalaco examines Johnson's conception of history in relation to contemporary historical practice. She explores the "microhistory" and "local history" of Johnson's neglected biographical portrait of Paul Sarpi as elements within Johnson's latent theory of history. Then, in "Ironies of the Critical Past: Historicizing Johnson's Criticism," my own essay seeks to contrast the philosophy of a twentieth-century historicization of Johnson's criticism with a Johnsonian model of the critical-historical process and to assimilate this to the terms of modernity's temporal hermeneutics. By revising one's "idea of history," and by resisting the reductive definitions of criticism implicit in the narrative of "classic to romantic," I argue that Johnsonian judgments and emotional agency could play a fuller part than hitherto in living the critical and scholarly life of the present.

Finally, in " 'Looking Before and After'? Reflections on the Early Reception of Johnson's Critical Judgments," Tom Mason and Adam Rounce return the reader historically to the first responses in the eighteenth and early nineteenth centuries to some of Johnson's most eccentric-seeming critical decisions and to the interplay between the context of Johnson's early reception as a critic and his actual and potential importance today. They argue that Johnson's criticism at its best struck its admirers as indistinguishable from literature itself, and that Johnson appears to have wished to place his critical judgments beyond the vicissitudes of his time. Thus comprehended, Johnson's judgments may begin to count for more than they have done in the immediate past.

To realize this program, as several essayists suggest, is not to abandon the scholarship of this past in thrall to its false dichotomy with "Critical Theory," but to try in effect to transform a "comfortable certainty" into "a certainty that is still struggling." In recognizing the role of the traditions of Johnsonian scholarship as a constituent element within this struggle, this volume works cooperatively with, but is not governed by, contemporary theoretical change. All contributors have attempted to keep past and present in reciprocal play. But the essays also respond to a new definition of the "historical" in the meaning of "literary history" that is not in any formulaic sense "New Historical." Its aspiration to progressive adequacy implies the combination of permanent incompleteness and rediscoverable sameness in our image of Johnson which is the sign of its subject's continuing life.

Acknowledgments

I AM GRATEFUL TO SUSAN BENNETT, CURATOR AT THE ROYAL SOCIETY for the encouragement of Arts, Manufactures and Commerce, and to Natasha McEnroe, Curator of Dr. Johnson's House, Gough Square, for their knowledgeable assistance in securing transparencies for the illustrations to this volume. I should like to express my gratitude to the authors of all the essays for their patience and responsiveness throughout the editorial process. I should particularly like to thank Professor Greg Clingham, National Endowment for the Humanities Professor of Humanities at Bucknell University, for his inspiration and support at all stages from the first conception to the final evolution of this volume, and Professor Pauline Fletcher, Acting Director of Bucknell University Press, for her good editorial advice.

Short Titles and Abbreviations

THE YALE EDITION OF THE WORKS OF SAMUEL JOHNSON, GENERAL Editor: John H. Middendorf (New Haven and London: Yale University Press, 1958–). References to this edition are cited parenthetically throughout in abbreviated form as follows:

Diaries	*Diaries, Prayers, and Annals*, ed. E. L. McAdam Jr., with Donald and Mary Hyde (1958).
Idler	*The Idler* and *The Adventurer*, ed. W. J. Bate, John M. Bullitt, and L. F. Powell (1963).
Poems	*Poems*, ed. E. L. McAdam Jr., with George Milne (1964).
Rambler 3–5	*The Rambler*, ed. W. J. Bate and Albrecht B. Strauss, 3 vols. (1969).
Shakespeare	*Johnson on Shakespeare*, ed. Arthur Sherbo, introduction by Bertrand H. Bronson, 2 vols. (1969).
Journey	*A Journey to the Western Islands of Scotland*, ed. Mary Lascelles (1971).
Politics	*Political Writings*, ed. Donald J. Greene (1977).
Rasselas	*Rasselas and Other Tales*, ed. Gwin J. Kolb (1990).

Other references are abbreviated as follows:

Letters	*The Letters of Samuel Johnson*. The Hyde Edition, ed. Bruce Redford, 5 vols. (Princeton: Princeton University Press, 1992). Cited parenthetically throughout.
Life	*Boswell's Life of Johnson*, ed. George Birkbeck Hill, revised by L. F. Powell, 6 vols. (Oxford: Clarendon Press, 1934–64). Cited parenthetically throughout.
Lives	*Lives of the English Poets*, ed. George Birkbeck Hill, 3 vols. (Oxford: Clarendon Press, 1905). Cited parenthetically throughout.

Miscellanies	*Johnsonian Miscellanies*, ed. George Birkbeck Hill, 2 vols. (Oxford: Clarendon Press, 1897). Cited parenthetically throughout.
AJ	*The Age of Johnson: A Scholarly Annual*
BJECS	*The British Journal for Eighteenth-Century Studies*
ECS	*Eighteenth Century Studies*
ELH	*English Literary History*
HLQ	*Huntington Library Quarterly*
PMLA	*Publications of the Modern Language Association of America*
TLS	*Times Literary Supplement*

Johnson Re-Visioned

Resisting Johnson

Greg Clingham

IN A PARTICULARLY ELOQUENT PASSAGE IN THE "LIFE OF DRYDEN,"
Johnson reflects on the cultural significance of Dryden's "Essay on
Dramatick Poesy" as follows:

> He who, having formed his opinions in the present age of English literature,
> turns back to peruse this dialogue, will not perhaps find much increase of
> knowledge or much novelty of instruction. . . . A writer who obtains his full
> purpose loses himself in his own lustre. Of an opinion which is no longer
> doubted, the evidence ceases to be examined. Of an art universally prac-
> tised, the first teacher is often forgotten. Learning once made popular is no
> longer learning: it has the appearance of something which we have bestowed
> upon ourselves, as the dew appears to rise from the field which it refreshes.
> (*Lives*, 1:411)

As I take it, Johnson is praising Dryden here for having so convincingly articulated views and positions about the nature of drama—
especially Shakespeare's—that they have become classic, have changed
and penetrated the collective imaginative experience, so that in 1779—
when the "Life of Dryden" was written—it is no longer possible to distinguish what one knows from what one has been taught. There is
something deeply and attractively natural about such knowledge—
making for an experience larger than the self and more than merely
subjective or personal—and this larger sense is suggested by Johnson's
metaphor of the dew and the grass.

Johnson continues the passage under consideration by saying that
"To judge rightly of an author we must transport ourselves to his time,
and examine what were the wants of his contemporaries, and what were
his means of satisfying them" (*Lives*, 1:411), and this reminder to consider the historical context when assessing a work of the past is obviously what we expect from a literary scholar. Yet that is not what
Johnson actually gives us; rather than embarking on archival work—
what we would describe as placing Dryden in his historical context—he
mounts an entirely more general and almost lyrical form of recollection
of Dryden's thought.

19

Although, as one would expect, the *kind* of knowledge offered by Dryden's "Essay" in 1669 (when it was published) is different from that characterizing scholarship in the late eighteenth century, the retrospective glance of Johnson's critical judgment clearly and deliberately frames its own particular narrative. The work of time in this narrative not only encompasses the appearances of nature, and the fantasy of knowledge as self-begetting; it also envisages the prospect — apparently inevitable — by which history eclipses or erases the trace of even the great and successful writer.[1]

This erasure or absence — or, in Dryden's case, this having been swallowed up in his own luster — is one of the great subjects of Johnson's *Lives of the Poets* and its general narrative, as distinguished from the many smaller particular narratives of individual lives and moments within those individual lives. This overarching, general narrative might be said to make it possible to continue to see and remember those vanished subjects when time and history and human judgment would have determined otherwise. Memory, that is, is central to meaning for Johnson, in the *Lives* as elsewhere, for, as he says in *Idler* 44, "Memory is the primary and fundamental power, without which there could be no other intellectual operation" (2:137). In its peculiar memorableness and use of memory, the mini-narrative of Dryden's critical erasure is paradigmatic of the structure of the *Lives* as a whole, as it is of a central strand of all of Johnson's writing about human experience and institutions. However, there is, also, something suggestive in this vignette on time and knowledge, of Johnson's *own* situation, and of our late-twentieth-century relation to the knowledge represented in *his* writings. It is altogether too easy to forget that he has taught us much of what we already seem to know, and to assume that scholarship has taken his measure. It is, thus, not only the case that we need to "transport ourselves to [Johnson's] time," reconstructing as best we can the terms and the parameters of the worlds in which he lived, in order to grasp *and to benefit from* his contribution to knowledge; but we need also to attempt to remember or to historicize Johnson's writing in a more comprehensive and differential way, indicative of his own stance on Dryden. But what might it mean to historicize our reading of Johnson? What, in any case, characterizes existing scholarship on Johnson? How much of this work makes Johnson excitingly available to students and to nonspecialists? What kinds of work remain to be done?

This moment,[2] at the beginning of the new millennium, at a time of considerable confidence and optimism among eighteenth-century scholars, when the canon has been very broadly enlarged and diversified, and the number of new doctoral students attracted to the period is growing, is an appropriate occasion on which to reflect on the institution of Johnson studies. Certainly, in Johnson studies, much significant work has recently been done—addressing the interpretation of specific works as well as the reconceptualization of Johnson's life and the basic structure of his thought. One would be hard pressed to offer even a brief overview of these achievements in recent Johnson scholarship and criticism. For this purpose I would refer the reader to Jack Lynch's "A Bibliography of Johnson Studies, 1986–1997," and to Steven Lynn's essay on "Johnson's Critical Reception" in the *Cambridge Companion to Samuel Johnson*.[3]

In general, however, one might notice the large body of recent work. There have been monographs published on *Rasselas*, on Johnson's Shakespeare work, on his psychological theory, on his understanding of greatness, on his view of history, on his attitude to romance, on Johnson and medical science, on his religious and philosophical work, on his political thought, on his cultural politics, on his feminism, on the *Dictionary*, on his poetry, on Johnson's practice of reading, and on the whole oeuvre.[4] Two biographies have recently been published.[5] There has been a recent edition of Johnson's Latin and Greek poems and a new edition of the *Journey to the Western Islands*, in addition to the continuation of the Yale Works.[6] Of particular significance are the steps that have been taken toward rethinking the place of gender and women in Johnson's writing in Charles Hinnant's special issue of the *South Central Review* (9, no. 4 [1992]), in essays by Isobel Grundy and James Basker,[7] and in Kathleen Kemmerer's *Samuel Johnson's Sexual Politics* (1998). And essays by James Basker, Clement Hawes, and John Wiltshire have begun to explore the many connections between Johnson's political and cultural thought and postcolonial perspectives.[8]

Less obviously successful have been the various attempts by Jonathan Clark and Howard Erskine-Hill to redefine the emphases of Johnson's national and constitutional politics in terms of Jacobitism,[9] although their arguments have called forth thoughtful and more adequate responses to the question of the nature of Johnson's political thought from Steven Scherwatzky, Thomas Curley, and the contributors to the extended discussion on Jacobitism in the *Age of Johnson* (7 [1996] and 8 [1997]) and the special issue of *ELH* (64, no. 4 [1997]), all edited or organized by Paul Korshin.[10]

This enormous body of work indicates, among other things, how substantial has been the recent interest in Johnson's life and writing. And this interest has been reflected in the publishing world: Harvard, Duke, Princeton, Georgia, Penn, St. Martin's, Greenwood, Barnes & Noble, Leicester, Blackwell, Oxford, Bucknell, Delaware, Fairleigh Dickinson, Kentucky, Wisconsin, Southern Illinois, Missouri, Johns Hopkins, and Cambridge have all published books on Johnson in the last decade

or so. The *Age of Johnson*—the only scholarly journal devoted to Johnson and his age—has, after ten volumes, published some five thousand
pages of discussion on Johnson and related concerns!

Notwithstanding this level of interest, more work remains to be done.
It is not just, following Frank Kermode's suggestion, that Johnson's
classic status spawns and sustains new interpretations of his writing;
nor that, as Donald Greene remarks, the better one knows Johnson the
more one realizes there is more to learn and say about him.[11] There is,
as it were, other, fundamental scholarly and critical work to be done.
In addition to the completion of the Yale edition of the Works, we still
need full studies of the *Lives of the Poets*, the prayers, the essays as a
genre, and Johnson's position in the line of Renaissance humanist
thought that includes Erasmus, Vives, and More—without confining
Johnson's humanism to Jacobite neo-Latin scholarship, as Jonathan
Clark does.[12] We still need a meticulous and intelligent consideration of
the nature of the Johnson-Boswell collaboration that, as John Radner
has begun to explore,[13] *is* Boswell's *Life of Johnson*—a matrix that is becoming more susceptible of clear discussion by the Yale publication of
the manuscripts of the *Life of Johnson*.[14] And we also need broad and
careful treatments of Johnson's dialogue with *later* critics and theorists
on the materialist and linguistic nature of history and criticism, and on
his historical and political thinking that responds to theoretical currents
of interest in other areas of eighteenth-century cultural studies.

This last point marks a problematic characteristic of the existing
scholarship. While we have now had "postcolonial" discussions of
Rasselas from Srinivas Aravamudan and Clement Hawes,[15] deconstruc-
tive accounts of Johnson's criticism and linguistics from Steven Lynn,
Raman Selden, and Charles Hinnant,[16] new historical treatments of
various aspects of Johnson's social and cultural thought from Thomas
Reinert, Martin Wechselblatt, and Timothy Fulford,[17] and a range of
feminist assessments of Johnson's sexual politics from Felicity
Nussbaum, Toni Bowers, Kathleen Kemmerer, and others,[18] none of
this considerable body of work has done much to change the tone or—
apparently—the future direction of Johnson scholarship. Nor has
it much changed the basic ways in which Johnson is seen—especially
by students and nonspecialists, inside or outside the academy. Significantly, Johnson's writing—or the composite body of Johnson
scholarship that frequently "stands for" Johnson in the academic
mind—apparently seems highly resistant to "theory." Remarkably,
both Johnson's writing and the body of scholarship that is Johnson
studies seem at the end of the century to continue to exhibit the shaping
and identifying marks of its founders in the middle of the century. I
am thinking here of James Clifford, Mary Hyde, Donald Greene, Jean

Hagstrum, William Keast, William Wimsatt, Walter Jackson Bate, Gwin Kolb, John Middendorf, and of their successors (perhaps, in some cases, their students)—Lawrence Lipking, Howard Weinbrot, Paul Korshin, Paul Alkon, Leo Damrosch, Robert Folkenflik, Thomas Kaminski, Thomas Curley, James Engell, and others. Certainly, all of those mentioned here are fine scholars whose joint efforts have contributed not only to establishing the Johnson canon and the texts of most of his works, but also to rescuing Johnson from the obscurities and misunderstandings of nineteenth-century taste, making him into the central canonical eighteenth-century figure, a status that is still widely acknowledged, to the chagrin of many scholars inside and outside the period. By any measure this is an extraordinary collective achievement, which has evolved without the financial or institutional backing enjoyed by the Yale Boswell Papers and other similar large editorial projects, and it is perhaps unmatched by any other similar critical effort of rehabilitation in this or any century.

Nonetheless, it is striking that the work of the great Johnsonians tends to run within the channels of the same liberal-humanist historical understanding of literature and literary history—as John Bender and others in the "new eighteenth century" have observed.[19] The "transformation" that the Modern Language Association registers—in the subtitle to the book in which Bender's essay appears—as the keynote to the recent phase of literary criticism seems not to have occurred in Johnson studies, where there is little *rapprochement* between the "old" and the "new" forms of eighteenth-century scholarship. The mainstream of Johnson scholarship seems thoroughly to have resisted the blandishments and the encroachments of explicitly theoretical ways of reading, unlike the scholarship on the major Renaissance, Romantic, and Modernist figures, as well as that on many canonical and lesser known eighteenth-century figures—some who, like Richardson, Burney, and Burke, were close to Johnson.[20]

This resistance to new ways of reading Johnson is of several kinds. One is rooted in the logic and the politics of academic work: the evolving scholarship has come to identify Johnson with a certain set of priorities and images, which, when supported by the personal and professional investment of some scholars, have come to seem to be essential, and so ethical to uphold in the face of alternative versions of Johnson's interests for us. The extent to which such a stance can harden into uncritical insensitivity can be seen in Donald Greene's relentless attack on the work of Howard Erskine-Hill and Jonathan Clark,[21] and, indeed, on anyone who dared to suggest that Boswell's *Life of Johnson* had anything of interest to say about Johnson.[22]

Another kind of resistance concerns something intrinsic to Johnson's writing. That Johnson was skeptical of all systematizing, and that it is his commitment to discovering and eliciting truth that sustains that skepticism, is, of course, a cliché. Yet, as Christopher Ricks points out, "the deliberate and responsible use of cliché can foster critical self-consciousness";[23] or, as Johnson says *apropos* of Dryden's criticism, it is easy—almost inevitable—to take someone else's wisdom as something we have bestowed on ourselves. Johnson's principled skepticism and commitment to a protocol of reading that almost wilfully registers the appeal from art and literature to nature and life is difficult to grasp or understand fully because—among other reasons—it makes him seem alien to our critical and theoretical preconceptions. Consequently, he may be attractive and compelling to identify with—or to disagree with—yet is never quite within the grasp of the reader seeking manageable answers, intellectual consistency, and doctrinal coherence.

This identifies a third mode of resistance in Johnson's writing in the form of the manifest historical distance between Johnson and ourselves. Until recently eighteenth-century historicism operated as if temporal, conceptual, and experiential difference could be largely overcome by the rigors of research into context, background, and authorial intention. We thought we knew—and could straightforwardly know—what Johnson was about, and we thus had definitive and unapologetic accounts of Johnson-the-neoclassicist, Johnson-the-melancholic, Johnson-the-moralist, and so forth. But the linguistic turn taken by recent historiography, and the widespread and systematic questioning, engineered by poststructuralism, deconstruction, and new historicism, of totalizing and transparent historical truth, has introduced an awareness of the fictional and provisional nature of all forms of historical and critical explanation, even in eighteenth-century studies.[24] Gradually Johnson's writing has become more resistant to our traditional ways of describing it, because our theoretical culture now itself refuses to substitute appropriation for criticism.

What continues to distinguish Johnson's thought, however, is a multiplicity of vision, an ability to stand inside and outside of his historical moment. This stance is characterized by a simultaneous commitment to both the general and the particular in human experience, a combination that has bedeviled critics of the *Lives of the Poets*. His moral thinking manifests a familiarity with a kind of philosophical essentialism *as well as* a cultural materialism; he has an allegiance to political party and church *as well as* an imaginative reach transcending those institutions and their momentary claims; his historical and political thinking displays a participation in the development of cosmopolitan forms of cultural and economic analysis *as well as* in the definition of national identity; and his personal and social politics are expressive of gestures that seem *both* repressive *and* liberal towards the status of women and others on the margins of English culture. All of these different discourses lie within the realm of the historical for Johnson, who, I have argued, recognized the truth of history as residing in the events and facts of the past, *and also* in the fictionally constructed narrative through whose representations the writer conveys historical truth.[25]

Such ambiguities govern Johnson's thought and engagement with a whole range of literary, philosophical, political, social, and moral issues. Johnson's word for these ambiguities, and the kind of intelligent, principled skepticism they enable in his writing, is "comprehensive." Johnson's first definition of the adjective "comprehensive" in the *Dictionary* is "having the power to comprehend or understand many things at once," a definition which moves away from the semantic and asks to be understood imaginatively, as a *form and quality* of knowledge, enforced by the illustrative quotation from Dryden's description of Chaucer's *Canterbury Tales* in the preface to *Fables*: "He must have been a man of a most wonderful *comprehensive* nature, because he has taken into the compass of his Canterbury tales the various manners and humours of the whole English nation in his age; not a single character has escaped him."[26] But comprehensiveness is, by implication, impossible to encompass by any other than imaginative means, whether poetic or critical. In this case, what Johnson says of Shakespeare's mingled drama is applicable to his own manner of writing: "he that tries to recommend him by select quotations, will succeed like the pedant in Hierocles, who, when he offered his house to sale, carried a brick in his pocket as a specimen" (*Shakespeare*, 7:62). Certainly Johnson's comprehensive thinking almost deliberately resists definition, making us pitch our eye either too high or too low to register the discriminations and the largeness of thought that, critic after critic agrees, energizes his argument. For having once established a paradigm within which to identify the interests held out for us by the great neoclassical critic, the common methodologies of the main body of Johnson criticism find themselves unable to step outside of their own parameters and self-authorized methodologies. I should like to give just two brief examples of how the logic of this situation perpetuates errors, or at least lesser critical truths, in our understanding of Johnson's thought.

In *The Ordering of the Arts in Eighteenth-Century England*, published in 1970, and again in *Samuel Johnson: The Life of an Author*, published in 1998, Lawrence Lipking sees the literary history implicit in the *Lives of the Poets* as "summing up" and "authenticating a regular right line of poetry," an evaluation of the literary past borne out in the progressive refinement of versification and correctness in poetics that Johnson traces from Waller and Denham, through Dryden and Addison, and culminating in Pope.[27] In both books the literary history imputed to Johnson takes as part of its evidence a certain chronology of the composition of the individual lives—the "Life of Dryden" was among the first to be written (completed August 1778), and the "Life of Pope" was the last to be written (completed March 1781),[28] thus making possible an analogy between the linear temporal movement in Johnson's process of composition and a linear conception of his literary history, culminating—so the argument goes—in the consummate refinement of the heroic couplet in Pope's writing. However, this notion of the literary history in the *Lives* is actually at odds with Lipking's own more subtle insights into Johnson's biographical form. While the trajectory mapped out by Lipking is indeed one line of thought for Johnson, his overall historical discourse in the *Lives* questions its efficacy as a full account of historical possibilities and actualities. Such questioning is sustained by the *various*, sometimes overlapping literary histories characterizing Johnson's work, one of which argues for the recognition of *Dryden's translations* as a touchstone for all natural poetry, including Pope's.[29] Identifying Johnson's literary history in the *Lives* with the teleological development of the heroic couplet—first articulated by scholars in the 1940s and 1950s—is thus to diminish the nuance and complexity of this great work, and also, erroneously, to situate Johnson as a conventional Augustan, someone like Addison or Pope.[30] The experiential distance between Johnson and Addison and Johnson and Pope represented by the lives of those two writers suggests the extent to which such a conflation overlooks critical distinctions Johnson himself wanted to maintain.

The same kind of synecdochic movement (of making the generalized whole stand for the part), or metaleptic movement (of retrospectively creating the origins your current critical values authorize), weakens Jean Hagstrum's conception of Johnson's criticism. In the first chapter of *Samuel Johnson's Literary Criticism*—still, after fifty years, *the* authoritative treatment of Johnson as a critic—Hagstrum sets out his view of Johnson's notion of experience as the very basis of all of his literary criticism. Experience meant empiricism, and empiricism meant Locke, and although, Hagstrum notes, "I am not prepared to argue for a direct or exclusive philosophical influence, I think it is true to say that Johnson's conception of the mind as necessarily anchored in experience is reminiscent of the main emphasis in Locke's epistemology."[31] By way of exemplifying what this means, Hagstrum quotes Locke (not Johnson), as follows:

All those sublime Thoughts, which towre above the Clouds, and reach as high as Heaven it self, take their Rise and Footing here: In all that great

Extent where the mind wanders, in those remote Speculations, it may seem
to be elevated with, it stirs not one jot beyond those *Ideas*, which *Sense* or
Reflection have offered for its Contemplation.[32]

This quotation, however, occasions neither a deeper inquiry into what
experience might actually *be* for Locke—or, more to the point, for
Johnson; nor is Hagstrum interested in Locke's rhetoric in the passage
quoted, for the discrepancy between such elevated conceptions and language and such an *apparently* limited notion of experience itself contributes to the notion of experience, developed by Locke, and the integral
part of language therein. Furthermore, Locke's passage is expressive,
offering a subtly different but important *experience* in the reading of it
than is conveyed by the summariness with which it is treated. Instead,
by way of determining the critical value of Lockean epistemology as a
basis for criticism, Hagstrum quotes *Coleridge* on the unimaginativeness
of Aristotle (6) and on the godlike powers of the human faculties (7),
and then sums up as follows:

> for Johnson all mental action, whether rational or imaginative, is always
> secondary to the direct experience of reality and is, apart from experience,
> seriously suspect; for Coleridge all mental action, whether rational or imagi-
> native, is primary; it does not depend upon experience but constitutes expe-
> rience.
> The results for literary criticism should be obvious. (7)

The results for this account of Johnson's criticism are also thus obvious,
for by the time we reach page seven of the book, Johnson's criticism
has already been summed up and placed, as being limited by an empirical epistemology and as being less imaginative and less sublime than
Coleridge's. Consequently, it seems, its interest for us is clearly circum-
scribed by its lack of participation in the high truths of romantic tran-
scendentalism. All of this groundwork occurs without Professor
Hagstrum having to build a careful argument on the basis of Johnson's
own writings, and without mentioning or quoting a single word of his
criticism. It is, therefore, no wonder that those relying on this explanation of Johnson's criticism fail to find it very engaging. Other more or
less successful accounts have, of course, appeared since 1952, but the
basic terms of our understanding of the subject seem to have been set
down by Hagstrum's book. We continue to gesture towards the greatness of Johnson as a critic without really being able to demonstrate
what and how that criticism continues to enlighten and challenge us
about poems, poets, and the relations between the two.

Both of these examples—Lipking and Hagstrum—exemplify one of
the general weaknesses in much Johnson scholarship. In writing about

literary history in general, and of the period 1650 to 1800 in particular, R. S. Crane remarks:

> It is impossible . . . to avoid distortion or at least oversimplification of what your critics are saying so long as you have committed yourself to a concern only with their doctrines and to an interpretation of these in the context of a preestablished scheme of dialectical oppositions.[33]

It is precisely as doctrine, however, that so much of Johnson's writing has been taken by our great Johnsonians, the substance of whose ideas lie in their abstractable and summarizable content.[34] But this is to make Johnson into a version of his own Dick Minim, who, to quote Johnson on Soame Jenyns, "imposes words for ideas upon ourselves or others . . . [and] imagine[s] that we are going forward when we are only turning round."[35] Some, of course, have made very grand claims for Johnson's critical works. Leavis found them to be those of a creative and imaginative thinker, to be "living literature as Dryden's . . . are not; they compel, and they repay, a real and disinterested reading, that full attention of the judging mind which is so different from the familiar kind of homage."[36] Yet even this was mere homage of a kind, for to the question—Why do we read Johnson's criticism?—the answer immediately comes back: "Not for enlightenment about the authors with whom it deals . . . , and *not* for direct instruction in critical thinking" (197). And when it came to aspects of Johnson's work on which Leavis had a deep personal and cultural investment —Shakespeare's drama, for example—he could see in Johnson's remarks only a limiting need for novelistic realism and pat moral summary, a "thoroughgoing rejection of all Shakespearian use of language, and, consequently, of all concrete specificity in the rendering of experience" (207).

New scholarship on Johnson—especially that which devotes itself to arguing for the continuing pertinence of Johnson's critical and historical thought in a poststructural and postcolonial academy—will have to find ways of stepping out of the constrictions of the dialectical and the summary modes described by Crane if it is to avoid the rather sterile repetition of the orthodoxies of the immediate past to which even good work on Johnson falls prey. One way of effecting such a change might lie in becoming more intelligent about Johnson's difference, his resistance to us, and by recognizing some compatibility—if no neat coincidence—and dialectical tension between *his* thought and our *own* theoretical resistance to it. The common term governing these different forms of resistance, I would suggest, is "theory." Boswell reported Johnson as saying that "Human experience, which is constantly contradicting theory, is the great test of truth" (*Life*, 1:454). While this remark may be antisystematic, it is not antitheoretical. It is rather about how principled theoretical thinking actually works—by generating a resistance to experience, both residual and newly created, through which existing knowledge is questioned, enlarged, deepened, and reimagined. Many of Johnson's best critical insights—which are, typically, also some of his most notorious judgments—occur through forms of resistance: the critique of the metaphysical poets, the general notes to *King Lear* and *Othello*, the memorable note on Falstaff, the analysis of Pope's artifice, the playing off of Milton's life against his work, to name just a few. Johnson's general critical stance is founded on the supposition that the spectators (or readers) are always in their senses and not imaginatively lost to the work of literature—Mrs. Thrale says that "it is indeed observable in his preface to Shakespeare, that while other critics expatiate on the creative powers and vivid imagination of that matchless poet, Dr. Johnson commends him for giving [a] just . . . representation of human manners" (*Miscellanies*, 1:313)—and from *this* complicated knowledge emerges the cutting edge of his criticism. Yet such a stance is itself a form of resistance. What characterizes each of the instances of critical resistance mentioned above is that Johnson registers a judgment that strikes the modern reader as odd or wrong; but the form of those judgments usually implies a subject position sufficiently separate from and open to the work under consideration to feel and respond to powerful and deep emotion, and it implies likewise a reader sufficiently self-conscious to register the theoretical thrust of the rhetoric.

> Shakespeare has suffered the virtue of Cordelia to perish in a just cause, contrary to the natural ideas of justice, to the hope of the reader, and, what is yet more strange, to the faith of chronicles. . . . I was many years ago so shocked by Cordelia's death, that I know not whether I ever endured to read again the last scenes of the play till I undertook to revise them as an editor. (*Shakespeare*, 8:704)

Of this observation, Frank Kermode—in one of the best pieces of analysis of Johnson's criticism I know—remarks: "This famous sentence convinces me that Johnson had really, so to speak, deeply *scanned* the play. He saw in it not primitive ignorance but a disregard of publicly endorsed and acceptable answers which terrified him because it did *not* arise out of incompetence or carelessness." The very power of *King Lear* is thus a threat to Johnson's fictional yet very real sense of the naturalness of human existence, and his resistance to the reality of the play's horrors is, as Kermode notes, a sign that Johnson "is responding to tragedy more deeply than we, who profess to be more easily persuaded." It is Johnson's complex, multidimensional reading of that which violates one's deepest sense of the natural that prompts Kermode to suggest "that it is in such an understanding that the best criticism consists, since it will work for us regardless of divergencies between our view of the world and that of the critic."[37]

At the same time, it is precisely Johnson's reading *as reading* that constitutes the theoretical nature of his formulations. By "theory" here I do not mean some particular set of ideas against which the empirical is measured, such as the neoclassical doctrine of poetic justice, but rather a rhetorical awareness in Johnson's words of the textuality of Shakespeare's play—an understanding of how powerfully language shapes our vision of the world—and of Johnson's deliberate textual response to it. There is nothing self-evident or empirical for Johnson about *King Lear*, yet its textuality presents a view of life and humankind's powerlessness in it that his text registers as disturbingly true. Johnson's, thus, is a theoretical awareness that is in the vein of Paul de Man's notion of theory *as* resistance, where Shakespeare's text is that which resists Johnson, and Johnson's criticism is that which resists Shakespeare's text, and both uses of language operate within the understanding, as formulated by de Man, that "the resistance to theory is a resistance to the use of language about language. It is therefore a resistance to language itself or the possibility that language contains factors or functions that cannot be reduced to intuition."[38] Somewhere in the confrontation of Johnson's "intuition" and Shakespeare's text—or, in Boswell's words, between "experience" and "theory"—lies the point at which Johnson's writing enters a theoretical discourse that should be of interest to contemporary thinking. This is where it begins to "improve opinion into knowledge" (*Rambler* 92, 4:122). In the *resistance* of the thinking mind to *both* the abstractions of theory (as represented, for example, by the rationalization of Soame Jenyns' *A Free Inquiry*) *and* to the irreducible concreteness of particular, real experiences (as felt by Johnson in his inclination not to reread the play) lies the mechanism by which Johnson's writing generates its truths. "Thus it happens when wrong opinions are entertained, that they mutually destroy each other, and leave the mind open to truth," says Rasselas to his sister Nekayah (104), echoing the structure of the whole tale.

The deliberately performative nature of this manner of thinking and writing uses the mind's resistance to the world and to its own opinions and intuitions so that difference becomes strategic. This performativeness is perhaps different from the kind Johnson saw in Dryden's critical prose when he said that it was "a gay and vigorous dissertation, where delight is mingled with instruction, and where the author proves his right to judgement by his power of performance" (*Lives*, 1:412). For

Johnson's difference might be said to structure his understanding of the inherent discrepancy between the human mind and the natural world, between words and things, and to complicate and deepen the understanding of presence, truth, and history in his writing. This intellectual architecture *does* indeed resemble the relationship among the faculties in Locke's epistemology (as it bears some resemblance to Paul de Man's thinking about language and Richard Rorty's thinking about the human mind), but it has its own focus and its own series of imaginative engagements. Unlike Locke's thought, it is conditioned by the basic understanding that the mind, the world, and human language are all discrepant, and exist in three distinct though continuous dimensions. One does not have to read very far in the *Rambler* or *Rasselas* to recognize Johnson's conviction that it is not within the natural sphere of human desire for these different terms to come together easily, yet it is equally clear that their nexus—their confrontations, and their differences—form the very site of human consciousness and hence the object of his discourse.

Consciousness, and how and with what objects it is to be filled in the course of time, might be said to be Johnson's great subject, not only in the moral essays and the religious writing, but also in his politics and in the biographies and criticism. These complexities will not be tapped by the bland assertions of Harold Bloom, in his attempt to resurrect Johnson as a great writer of the Western tradition.[39] *Some* new work—by James Battersby, Leo Damrosch, Philip Davis, Clement Hawes, Iain McGilchrist, Catherine Parke, Fred Parker, and others[40]—does address that nexus and those complexities with admirable sensitivity. But it remains to be seen whether and in what ways this body of work is able to penetrate the institution that is Johnsonian Studies, from which it stands slightly apart; whether newer theoretical methodologies bear scholarly fruit in the near future; whether more women might turn their attentions to Johnson's considerable interests for women; whether Johnson's cosmopolitan, enlightened thought might be recognized as offering the postcolonial establishment an example of the toughest analysis of Western historiography; and whether genuinely new readers can be found among the undergraduates of our universities and colleges. Certainly each of these constituencies will find Johnson's writing resistant to them just as it is resistant to itself; but perhaps it is in the paradoxes of this encounter—if the requisite flexibility could be summoned—that new Johnson scholarship in the new century might make a start. This resistance might be the place at which to start a process of necessary historicization.

NOTES

1. For the operation of the anecdote as a trope in the *Lives of the Poets*, see Greg Clingham, "Anecdote and Narrative in Johnson's *Lives of the Poets*," in *Johnson's Critical Pertinence and Other Essays* (forthcoming).

2. The Tenth International Congress on the Enlightenment held in Dublin, 24–31 July 1999. A version of this essay was the introduction to the session entitled "Looking Before and After: Johnson at the Millennium."

3. Jack Lynch, "A Bibliography of Johnsonian Studies, 1986–1997," *AJ* 10 (1999): 405–511, online at http://www.english.upenn.edu/~jlynch/Johnson/sjbib.html, and Steven Lynn, "Johnson's Critical Reception" in *The Cambridge Companion to Samuel Johnson*, ed. Greg Clingham (Cambridge: Cambridge University Press, 1997 and 1999), 240–53. See also the section on "Further Reading" in the *Companion*, 254–59.

4. Edward Tomarken, *Samuel Johnson on Shakespeare: The Discipline of Criticism* (Athens: University of Georgia Press, 1991), and G. F. Parker, *Johnson's Shakespeare* (Oxford: Clarendon Press, 1989); Edward Tomarken, *Johnson, "Rasselas," and the Choice of Criticism* (Lexington: University Press of Kentucky, 1989); Gloria Sybil Gross, *The Invisible Riot of the Mind: Samuel Johnson's Psychological Theory* (Philadelphia: University of Pennsylvania Press, 1992); Isobel Grundy, *Samuel Johnson and the Scale of Greatness* (Leicester: Leicester University Press, 1985); John Vance, *Samuel Johnson and the Sense of History* (Athens: University of Georgia Press, 1985); Eithne Henson, *"The Fictions of Romantick Chivalry": Samuel Johnson and Romance* (Rutherford, N.J.: Fairleigh Dickinson University Press); John Wiltshire, *Samuel Johnson in the Medical World: The Doctor and the Patient* (Cambridge: Cambridge University Press, 1991); Philip Davis, *In Mind of Johnson: A Study of Johnson the Rambler* (Athens: University of Georgia Press, 1989), Nicholas Hudson, *Samuel Johnson and Eighteenth-Century Thought* (Oxford: Clarendon Press, 1988), Leo Damrosch, *Fictions of Reality in the Age of Hume and Johnson* (Madison: University of Wisconsin Press, 1989), and Blanford Parker, *The Triumph of Augustan Poetics: English Literary Culture from Butler to Johnson* (Cambridge: Cambridge University Press, 1998); J. C. D. Clark, *Samuel Johnson: Literature, Religion, and English Cultural Politics* (Cambridge: Cambridge University Press, 1994); Martin Wechselblatt, *Bad Behavior: Samuel Johnson and Modern Cultural Authority* (Lewisburg, Pa.: Bucknell University Press, 1998) and Thomas Reinert, *Regulating Confusion: Samuel Johnson and the Crowd* (Durham, N.C.: Duke University Press, 1996); Kathleen Kemmerer, *"A Neutral Being Between the Sexes": Samuel Johnson's Sexual Politics* (Lewisburg, Pa.: Bucknell University Press, 1998); Robert DeMaria, *Johnson's Dictionary and the Language of Learning* (Chapel Hill: University of North Carolina Press, 1986), and Allen Reddick, *The Making of Johnson's "Dictionary," 1746–1773* (Cambridge: Cambridge University Press, 1990); David Venturo, *Johnson the Poet: The Poetic Career of Samuel Johnson* (Newark: University of Delaware Press, 1999); Robert DeMaria, *Samuel Johnson and the Life of Reading* (Baltimore: Johns Hopkins University Press, 1997); and Lawrence Lipking, *Samuel Johnson: The Life of an Author* (Cambridge: Harvard University Press, 1998).

5. Thomas Kaminski, *The Early Career of Samuel Johnson* (Oxford: Oxford University Press, 1987), and Robert DeMaria, *The Life of Samuel Johnson* (Oxford: Blackwell, 1993).

6. Samuel Johnson, *The Latin & Greek Poems of Samuel Johnson*, ed. Barry Baldwin (Duckworth: Newburyport, 1995), *A Journey to the Western Islands of Scotland*, ed. J.D. Fleeman (Oxford: Clarendon Press, 1985), and *Rasselas and Other Tales*, ed. Gwin J. Kolb, vol. 16 of The Yale Edition of the Works of Samuel Johnson (New Haven and London: Yale University Press, 1990).

7. James Basker, "Dancing Dogs, Women Preachers and the Myth of Johnson's

Misogyny," *AJ* 3 (1990): 63–90, and "Radical Affinities: Mary Wollstonecraft and Samuel Johnson," in *Tradition in Transition: Women Writers, Marginal Texts, and the Eighteenth-Century Canon*, ed. Alvaro Ribeiro S.J. and James G. Basker (Oxford: Clarendon Press, 1996), 41–55; and Isobel Grundy, "Samuel Johnson as Patron of Women," *AJ* 1 (1987): 59–77.

8. James Basker, "Samuel Johnson and the African-American Reader," *The New Rambler* 10 (1994–95): 47–57, and "An Eighteenth-Century Critique of Eurocentrism: Samuel Johnson and the Plight of Native Americans," in *La Grand-Bretagne et l'Europe des Lumières*, ed. Serge Soupel (Paris: Sorbonne, 1996), 207–20; Clement Hawes, "Johnson and Imperialism," in *The Cambridge Companion to Samuel Johnson*, 114–26; and John Wiltshire, " 'From China to Peru': Johnson in the Travelled World," in the *Cambridge Companion*, 209–23.

9. Their main publications on this theme are J. C. D. Clark, *Samuel Johnson: Literature, Religion and English Cultural Politics from the Restoration to Romanticism* (Cambridge: Cambridge University Press, 1994); and Howard Erskine-Hill, "The Political Character of Samuel Johnson," in *Samuel Johnson: New Critical Essays*, ed. Isobel Grundy (Totowa, N.J.: Barnes & Noble, 1984), 107–36, "The Poet and the Affairs of State in Johnson's *Lives of the Poets*," *Man and Nature* 6 (1987): 93–113, and "Johnson the Jacobite?" *AJ* 7 (1996): 3–26.

10. Steven Scherwatzky, "Samuel Johnson and Eighteenth-Century Politics," *Eighteenth-Century Life* 15, 3 (1991): 113–24, and "Johnson, *Rasselas*, and the Politics of Empire," *Eighteenth-Century Life* 16 (1992): 103–13; and Thomas Curley, "Johnson and America," *AJ* 6 (1994): 31–74.

11. Frank Kermode, *The Classic* (Cambridge: Harvard University Press, 1975 and 1983), 44, and *Renaissance Essays* (London: Collins, 1973), 164–80; *Samuel Johnson: A Collection of Critical Essays*, ed. Donald J. Greene (Englewood Cliffs, N.J.: Prentice-Hall, 1965), 7.

12. Clark, *Samuel Johnson: Literature, Religion and English Cultural Politics*.

13. John B. Radner, " 'A Very Exact Picture of His Life': Johnson's Role in Writing the *Life of Johnson*," *AJ* 7 (1996): 299–342.

14. *James Boswell's "Life of Johnson": An Edition of the Original Manuscript in Four Volumes*, ed. Marshall Waingrow, 1:1709–65 (New Haven: Yale University Press, 1994).

15. See Srinivas Aravamudan, *Tropicopolitans: Colonialism and Agency, 1688–1804* (Durham, N.C.: Duke University Press, 1999), 202–14, and Clement Hawes, "Johnson and Imperialism," in *The Cambridge Companion to Samuel Johnson*, 114–26.

16. See Steven Lynn, *Samuel Johnson After Deconstruction* (Carbondale: Southern Illinois University Press, 1992), Raman Selden, "Deconstructing the Ramblers," in *Fresh Reflections on Samuel Johnson*, ed. Prem Nath (Troy, NY: Whiston, 1987), 269–82, and Charles H. Hinnant, *"Steel for the Mind": Samuel Johnson and Critical Discourse* (Newark: University of Delaware Press, 1994).

17. See Thomas Reinert, *Regulating Confusion: Johnson and the Crowd* (Durham, N.C.: Duke University Press, 1996), Wechselblatt, *Bad Behavior*, and Timothy Fulford, *Landscape, Liberty, and Authority: Poetry, Criticism and Politics from Thomson to Wordsworth* (Cambridge: Cambridge University Press, 1996), 73–115.

18. See, for example, Felicity Nussbaum, *Torrid Zones: Maternity, Sexuality, and Empire in Eighteenth-Century English Narratives* (Baltimore: Johns Hopkins University Press, 1995), chapter 2; Toni Bowers, "Critical Complicities: Savage Mothers, Johnson's Mother, and the Containment of Maternal Difference," *AJ* 5 (1992): 115–46, and Kemmerer, *Samuel Johnson's Sexual Politics*.

19. See John Bender, "Eighteenth-Century Studies," in *Redrawing the Boundaries: The Transformation of English and American Literary Studies*, ed. Stephen Greenblatt and Giles Gunn (New York: MLA, 1992), 79–99.

20. See the following three articles of reflection on the advent of theory in eighteenth-century studies, all from *The Eighteenth Century: Theory and Interpretation* 28 (1987): G. S. Rousseau, "Old or New Historical Injunctions?: Critical Theory, Referentiality, and Academic Migration," 250–58; Marshall Brown, "Deconstruction and Enlightenment," 259–63; and G. Douglas Atkins, "A Matter of Difference: Deconstruction and Eighteenth-Century Studies," 264–69.

21. See, for example, introduction to the 2nd edition of *The Politics of Samuel Johnson* (Athens: University of Georgia Press, 1990), xix–lxv, and "The Double Tradition of Samuel Johnson's Politics," *HLQ* 59 (1997): 105–23.

22. See, for example, Greene's review of *New Light on Boswell: Critical and Historical Essays on the Occasion of the Bicentenary of Boswell's "Life of Johnson,"* ed. Greg Clingham (Cambridge: Cambridge University Press, 1991), in *The Eighteenth-Century: A Current Bibliography*, n.s. 17 (1991) [pub. 1998], 338–39.

23. Christopher Ricks, "Clichés," in *The Force of Poetry* (New York: Oxford University Press, 1987), 364.

24. See Greg Clingham, "The Question of History and Eighteenth-Century Studies," in *Questioning History: The Postmodern Turn to the Eighteenth Century*, ed. Greg Clingham (London: Associated University Presses, 1998), 11–20.

25. See my "Johnson and the Past," *Essays in Criticism* 36 (1988): 255–63.

26. The quotation from the 1st and 4th editions of the *Dictionary* (1755, 1773) is slightly (but not substantively) different from Dryden's actual words in the preface; see George Watson, ed., *Of Dramatic Poesy and Other Essays*, 2 vols. (London: Dent, 1968), 2:284.

27. Lawrence Lipking, *The Ordering of the Arts in Eighteenth-Century England* (Princeton: Princeton University Press, 1970), 454–62, esp. 459, and his *Samuel Johnson: The Life of an Author* (Cambridge: Harvard University Press, 1998), 285.

28. See *Letters*, 3:124, and *Diaries*, 1:303–4. In neither the *Prefaces* (1779–81) nor the 1781 or 1783 edition of the *Lives* was the "Life of Pope" placed last in the text.

29. See, for example, Greg Clingham, "Another and the Same: Johnson's Dryden," in *Literary Transmission and Authority: Dryden and Other Writers*, ed. Earl Miner and Jennifer Brady (Cambridge: Cambridge University Press, 1993), 121–59.

30. See, for example, Howard Erskine-Hill, "Augustans on Augustanism," *Renaissance and Modern Studies* 11 (1967): 55–83.

31. Jean Hagstrum, *Samuel Johnson's Literary Criticism* (Minneapolis: University of Minnesota Press, 1952; Chicago: University of Chicago Press, 1967), 6.

32. Ibid., 6. The punctuation is given as it is in Locke and not Hagstrum. John Locke, *An Essay Concerning Human Understanding*, ed. Peter H. Nidditch (Oxford: Clarendon Press, 1975), 2.1.118.

33. R. S. Crane, "On Writing the History of Criticism in England, 1650–1800," in *The Idea of the Humanities and Other Essays Critical and Historical*, 2 vols. (Chicago: University of Chicago Press, 1967), 2:160–61.

34. Philip Smallwood has found *The Eighteenth Century* (1997), vol. 4 of the new *Cambridge History of Literary Criticism*, to appropriate Johnson's criticism in a similar vein, "by taking statements by Johnson out of the context of Johnson's works to re-align them in the generalized fabric of eighteenth-century literary theory." See the review in *AJ* 10 (1999): 392–99, esp. 394.

35. Quoted from *Samuel Johnson: The Oxford Authors*, ed. Donald J. Greene (London: Oxford University Press, 1984), 534.

36. F. R. Leavis, "Johnson as Critic" (1944), in *"Anna Karenina" and Other Essays* (London: Chatto and Windus, 1973), 197.

37. Kermode, *Renaissance Essays*, 171.

38. Paul de Man, *The Resistance to Theory* (Minneapolis: University of Minnesota Press, 1986), 12–13 quoted; see 3–20.

39. Harold Bloom, *The Western Canon: The Books and School of the Ages* (New York: Harcourt, Brace, 1994), chapter 8.

40. See James L. Battersby, "Life, Art, and the Lives of the Poets," in *Domestick Privacies: Samuel Johnson and the Art of Biography*, ed. David Wheeler (Lexington: University Press of Kentucky, 1987), 26–56; Leo Damrosch, "Samuel Johnson and Reader-Response Criticism," *The Eighteenth Century: Theory and Interpretation* 21 (1980): 91–108, and his "Johnson's *Rasselas*: Limits of Wisdom, Limits of Art," in *Augustan Studies: Essays in Honor of Irvin Ehrenpreis*, ed. Douglas Lane Patey and Timothy Keegan (London: Associated University Presses, 1985), 205–14; Philip Davis, *In Mind of Johnson: A Study of Johnson the Rambler* (Athens: University of Georgia Press, 1989); Clement Hawes, "Johnson and Imperialism," in *The Cambridge Companion to Samuel Johnson*, 114–26; Iain McGilchrist, *Against Criticism* (London: Faber and Faber, 1982), chapter 3; Catherine N. Parke, *Samuel Johnson and Biographical Thinking* (Columbia: University Press of Missouri, 1991); and G. F. Parker, *Johnson's Shakespeare* (Oxford: Clarendon Press, 1989).

BIBLIOGRAPHY

AJ 7 (1996) and 8 (1997). Edited by Paul Korshin. Special issues on Johnson and Jacobitism.

Bender, John. "Eighteenth-Century Studies." In *Redrawing the Boundaries: The Transformation of English and American Literary Studies*. Edited by Stephen Greenblatt and Giles Gunn. New York: MLA, 1992, 79–99.

Bloom, Harold. *The Western Canon: The Books and School of the Ages*. New York: Harcourt, Brace, 1994.

Boswell, James. *Boswell's Life of Johnson*. 6 vols. Edited by George Birkbeck Hill. Revised by L. F. Powell. Oxford: Clarendon Press, 1934–64.

———. *Life of Johnson: An Edition of the Original Manuscript in Four Volumes*. Edited by Marshall Waingrow. 1:1709–65. New Haven: Yale University Press, 1994.

Clingham, Greg, ed. *The Cambridge Companion to Samuel Johnson*. Cambridge: Cambridge University Press, 1997 and 1999.

Crane, R. S. *The Idea of the Humanities and Other Essays Critical and Historical*. 2 vols. Chicago: Chicago University Press, 1967.

Damrosch, Leo. "Johnson's *Rasselas*: Limits of Wisdom, Limits of Art," in *Augustan Studies: Essays in Honor of Irvin Ehrenpreis*. Edited by Douglas Lane Patey and Timothy Keegan. Newark: University of Delaware Press, 1985, 205–14.

———. "Samuel Johnson and Reader-Response Criticism." *The Eighteenth Century: Theory and Interpretation* 21 (1980): 91–108.

de Man, Paul. *The Resistance to Theory*. Minneapolis: University of Minnesota Press, 1986.

Greene, Donald J. "The Double Tradition of Samuel Johnson's Politics." *Huntington Library Quarterly* 59 (1997): 105–23.

———. *The Politics of Samuel Johnson*. 2nd ed. Athens: University of Georgia Press, 1990.

———, ed. *Samuel Johnson: A Collection of Critical Essays*. Englewood Cliffs, N.J.: Prentice-Hall, 1965.

Hagstrum, Jean H. *Samuel Johnson's Literary Criticism*. Minneapolis: University of Minnesota Press, 1952; Chicago: University of Chicago Press, 1967.

Hill, George Birkbeck, ed. *Johnsonian Miscellanies*. 2 vols. Oxford: Clarendon Press, 1897.

Jacobitism and Eighteenth-Century English Literature. Special Number of *ELH* 64, no. 4 (winter 1997), 843–1100.

Johnson, Samuel. *A Dictionary of the English Language*. 1st and 4th eds. Edited by Anne McDermott. CD-ROM. Cambridge: Cambridge University Press, 1996.

―――. *The Idler and the Adventurer*. Edited by W. J. Bate, J. M. Bullitt, and L. F. Powell. Vol. 14 of The Yale Edition of the Works of Samuel Johnson. New Haven and London: Yale University Press, 1963.

―――. *Lives of the Poets*. 3 vols. Edited by George Birkbeck Hill. Oxford: Clarendon Press, 1905.

―――. *The Rambler*. Edited by W. J. Bate and Albrecht B. Strauss. Vols. 3–5 of The Yale Edition of the Works of Samuel Johnson. New Haven and London: Yale University Press, 1969.

―――. *Rasselas and Other Tales*. Edited by Gwin J. Kolb. Vol. 16 of The Yale Edition of the Works of Samuel Johnson. New Haven and London: Yale University Press, 1990.

―――. Review of *A Free Enquiry into the Nature and Origin of Evil*. In *Samuel Johnson: The Oxford Authors*. Edited by Donald J. Greene. London: Oxford University Press, 1984.

Kemmerer, Kathleen Nulton. *"A Neutral Being Between the Sexes": Samuel Johnson's Sexual Politics*. Lewisburg, Pa.: Bucknell University Press, 1998.

Kermode, Frank. *The Classic*. Cambridge: Harvard University Press, 1975 and 1983.

―――. *Renaissance Essays* (London: Collins, 1973).

Leavis, F. R. "Johnson as Critic." In *"Anna Karenina" and Other Essays*. London: Chatto and Windus, 1973.

Lipking, Lawrence. *The Ordering of the Arts in Eighteenth-Century England*. Princeton: Princeton University Press, 1970.

―――. *Samuel Johnson: The Life of an Author*. Cambridge: Harvard University Press, 1998.

Lynch, Jack. "A Bibliography of Johnson Studies, 1986–1997." *AJ* 10 (1999): 405–511.

Lynn, Steven. "Johnson's Critical Reception." In *The Cambridge Companion to Samuel Johnson*. Cambridge: Cambridge University Press, 1997, 240–53.

Radner, John B. " 'A Very Exact Picture of His Life': Johnson's Role in Writing the *Life of Johnson*." *AJ* 7 (1996): 299–342.

Ricks, Christopher. "Clichés." In *The Force of Poetry*. Oxford: Oxford University Press, 1987, 356–68.

South Central Review 9, no. 4 (1992). Edited by Charles H. Hinnant. Special issue on *Johnson and Gender*.

Johnson's Cosmopolitan Nationalism

CLEMENT HAWES

> There is no permanent national character; it varies according to circumstances. Alexander the Great swept India: now the Turks sweep Greece.
>
> —Samuel Johnson, as quoted in Boswell's *Life*

THE OXYMORON IN MY TITLE IS OFFERED AS A PREEMPTIVE RECOGNItion that any invocation of belonging to a larger world must nevertheless be locally situated. Hence, as Bruce Robbins notes, the currency of such terms as "rooted" or "vernacular" cosmopolitanism. And hence a new emphasis as well on what Robbins terms "actually existing cosmopolitanisms": solidarities, that is, which—if inevitably less than perfectly universal—do trouble or jump across national boundaries in productively enlarging ways.[1] Given current interest in theorizing the cosmopolitan anew,[2] it should be productive to revisit the Enlightenment: the great moment, that is, of both nationalism on the one hand and widespread cosmopolitan aspirations on the other. We need to look with clearer eyes at the options available to the nimblest thinkers of the time. The idea of cosmopolitan nationalism, moreover, provides a new focus for comprehending Samuel Johnson's fraught relationship to English and, especially, to British nationalism.

The paradox of Johnson's simultaneous investment in nationalism and in cosmopolitanism has given rise to contradictory explanations. Johnson's critical attack on Thomas Gray's "The Bard," for example, has raised questions about the nature of his national loyalties. Howard Weinbrot is alert to this when he writes as follows:

> Johnson's attack on Gray seemed an attack on an energetic and brilliant example of British history and values expressed in the Pindaric mode. To suggest otherwise was implicitly to obstruct a major path in the lyric's development. . . . In this obstructive sense, the great nationalist Samuel Johnson was a traitor to Britain.[3]

This is perhaps the most sophisticated form of the judgment that Johnson was essentially a "Little Englander," a bulky stumbling-block in the

37

eighteenth-century cultural transition from England to Great Britain. For Katie Trumpener, for whom this same making of Britishness is symptomatic of English hegemony, the target for criticism is Johnson's *Journey to the Western Islands of Scotland* (1773). She sees the *Journey* as an Anglocentric attempt "to establish the primacy of a cosmopolitan and imperial vision of Enlightenment activity over what it sees as Scotland's nationalist Enlightenment. . . ."[4] Here Johnson figures as a quintessential voice of the Enlightenment whose excessively modern cosmopolitanism is merely a disguised form of imperialism. Our perplexities increase further when we turn to J. C. D. Clark. While Clark's claims about Johnson's Jacobitism seem overstated, he does marshal important evidence about a broader range of Johnson's non-Hanoverian affiliations: above all, his residual attachment to a continent-wide and Latin-based Christian humanism.[5] Here Anglo-Latinity—the dynastic high culture inherited from what E. R. Curtius terms "the Latin Middle Ages"—is used to frame Johnson as a poster boy for the wholesale rejection of the modernizing project of building vernacular national cultures. None of these explanations, however, seems adequate to the task of mapping Johnson's sophisticated balancing acts.

The concept of cosmopolitan nationalism offers a productive way of rethinking the paradoxes that surround Johnson's relation to Englishness, to Britishness, and to a cosmopolitan impulse common to many Enlightenment thinkers. It is a relation that can be explained neither as parochial insularity nor as Anglo imperialism. Nor can it be fully understood as the residue of Johnson's investment, in opposition to vernacular culture, in a classical Latinity oriented to a continental elite. It is instead a hard-earned and sometimes paradoxical effect of Johnson's cosmopolitan engagement with the various nationalisms of his moment.

"SOFT" NATIONALISM: MAKING VERNACULAR ENGLISHNESS

The dual commitment both to a rooted or vernacular culture and to the challenge of going beyond national cultures—the hallmark of a cosmopolitan nationalism—is evident in the way that Johnson conceives of English national culture. When he refers in his biography of Jonathan Swift to England's current status as a "nation of readers" (*Lives*, 3:19), Johnson locates himself squarely within the eighteenth-century making of a print-based public culture. This was a process of imagining community, as Benedict Anderson has shown, that was intimately connected to the cultivation of new identities on the print-mediated scale of the nation. In his preface to the 1740 volume of the *Gentleman's Magazine*, Johnson writes as follows of the imagined community of readers:

Every-body must allow that our News-Papers (and the other Collections of Intelligence periodically published) by the Materials they afford for Discourse and Speculation, contribute very much to the Emolument of Society; their Cheapness brings them into universal Use; their Variety adapts them to everyone's Taste: The Scholar instructs himself with Advice from the literary World; the Soldier makes a Campaign in safety, and censures the Conduct of Generals without fear of being punished for Mutiny; the Politician, inspired by the Fumes of the Coffee-pot, unravels the knotty Intrigues of Ministers; the industrious Merchant observes the Course of Trade and Navigation; and the honest Shop-keeper nods over the Account of a Robbery and the Prices of Goods, till his Pipe is out.[6]

Johnson wrote pamphlets on public affairs; he wrote hundreds of periodical essays for a reading public engaged in working through such problems as the tyranny of parents, the social plight of prostitutes, and the ethics of capital punishment. Surveying the Harleian collection of pamphlets generated a century earlier by the English Civil War, Johnson highlights the Habermasian significance of the public sphere that England had developed as inhering in "the form of our government, which gives every man that has leisure, or curiosity, or vanity the right of inquiring into the propriety of public measures, and, by consequence, obliges those who are intrusted with the administration of national affairs to give an account of their conduct. . . ."[7] And it is precisely to serve the function of public accountability that Johnson reported on parliamentary debates for the *Gentleman's Magazine,* circumventing the laws against such reporting through the transparent fiction that his reports concerned the public affairs of "Magna Lilliputia."

Above all, perhaps, Johnson made such landmark contributions to a vernacular literary culture as his *Dictionary,* his Shakespeare edition, and his *Lives of the English Poets.* Through these achievements, in the words of Nicholas Hudson, "Johnson made a signal contribution to the very concept of 'England' by promoting a general recognition of a common linguistic and literary heritage of English people."[8] Johnson's *Dictionary* was widely seen as single-handedly rivaling the achievement of the entire French Academy; his Shakespeare edition helped to consolidate the reputation of Shakespeare; and his *Lives of the English Poets* gave intellectual substance to his remark in the preface to the *Dictionary* that authors are the "chief glory" of every people. Johnson was, as Alvin Kernan, Robert DeMaria, Jr., and Lawrence Lipking have variously shown, a quintessential creature of print culture, a figure effectively engaged in the vernacular production of Englishness.[9]

Yet Johnson's affirmation of Englishness also insistently troubles the ideological closure often represented by national boundaries. In conceding a peculiar bravery to the English common soldier, for example, he refuses to make the occasion of the Seven Years' War with France an excuse for glossing over internal social divisions within England. One could easily imagine how the sentimental treatment of "bravery amongst the low" might be used to overstress national unity in the face of an external adversary. That "nationalization" of English society Johnson flatly declines. Thus he demystifies the much-vaunted "liberty" of England in the following terms: "Liberty is, to the lowest rank of every nation, little more than the choice of working or starving; and this choice is, I suppose, equally allowed in every country." He goes on to attribute the bravery of the English common soldier precisely to a contingent social circumstance: his relative insubordination vis-à-vis his more feudalized French counterpart within the social hierarchy. This class-based analysis of uppity plebs then engenders a wry mode of patriotism that allows Johnson to tweak the English elite with the thought that "good and evil will grow up together; and they who complain, in peace, of insolence of the populace, must remember that their insolence in peace is bravery in war" ("The Bravery of the English Common Soldiers," *Politics*, 283–84). The community constituted by "Englishness," in short, remains a polity imagined as sharing very unevenly in its most celebrated benefit, and so potentially fissured by its own internal alienation.

The project of writing English literary history, moreover, does not tempt Johnson to naturalize the national community and its boundaries. Consider the following passage on Samuel Butler's *Hudibras*, which finds and celebrates mixture in its historical analysis:

> The poem of *Hudibras* is one of those compositions of which a nation may justly boast, as the images which it exhibits are domestick, the sentiments unborrowed and unexpected, and the strain of diction original and peculiar. We must not, however, suffer the pride, which we assume as the countrymen of Butler, to make any encroachment upon justice, nor appropriate those honours which others have a right to share. The poem of *Hudibras* is not wholly English; the original is to be found in the *History of Don Quixote*, a book to which a mind of the greatest powers may be indebted without disgrace. (*Lives*, 1:209)

Merely having English subject-matter, as Johnson knows very well, does not license an overweening claim to cultural autonomy. What may appear to be immanent, or "inside" the national horizon, often requires defamiliarization with reference to external history and influences: to a process of construction, that is, that partly works from the outside in. Purely indigenous genius, moreover, is not necessarily the highest good: Butler's engagement with Cervantes, though given due emphasis, is not used to detract from his accomplishment.

It is in the same spirit that Johnson is willing to use French critical formulations wherever he finds them useful. He refers, indeed, to almost thirty French authors in the *Lives of the Poets*, including Boileau, Fénelon, Montesquieu, Racine, Rousseau, and Voltaire. Boileau was a special favorite, and Johnson absorbed from him, as G. F. Parker demonstrates, a refined skepticism linked to sheer mental agility.[10] At the crucial moment when he requires a framework to approach the epic achievement of *Paradise Lost*, moreover, he turns to René Le Bossu's *Traité du poëme épique* (*Lives*, 1:171). At the same time, Johnson is also an equal opportunity debunker: he grandly dismisses Voltaire's strictures against Shakespeare, along with those of John Dennis and Thomas Rymer, as "the petty cavils of petty minds" (*Shakespeare*, 7:66). He thus refuses, on the one hand, to bask in the aristocratic aura surrounding all things French in Georgian England: such merely snobbish Francophilia threatened to give cosmopolitanism a bad name. On the other hand, however, Johnson largely declines the populist rhetoric of Gallophobic nativism.[11] During the Seven Years' War, indeed, Johnson argued specifically against an "Englishmen First" rationale for excluding French prisoners of war from charity: a refusal to equate national boundaries with the horizons of moral concern.[12] To be sure, he does briefly entertain the worry that the English language is becoming overly Frenchified, "deviating toward a Gallic structure and phraseology," as he puts it in the preface to his *Dictionary*.[13] However, Johnson more often treats the sort of collective identities that can be built through language as inevitably impure, and perhaps as productively porous. The polyglot extravaganza of Sir Thomas Browne's diction, for example—"a tissue of many languages" as Johnson says—does not tempt him into a policing of linguistic boundaries. He finds both usefulness, and even a certain sublimity, in Browne's daring linguistic importations.[14]

We come close to the heart of Johnson's wariness toward patriotic excess in his warning during a skirmish with Jonas Hanway, that "The love of our country, when it rises to enthusiasm, is an ambiguous and uncertain virtue; when a man is enthusiastic he ceases to be reasonable. . . ."[15] Indeed, it is precisely by refusing to invest a specifically sacred awe in any secular national icon that Johnson positions himself outside the mainstream of cultural nationalism. By withholding "superstitious veneration" for Shakespeare, for instance, and thus enumerating his faults in a sobering disquisition some found shocking, Johnson goes against the grain of a growing bardolatry that Michael Dobson describes as, in the full anthropological sense, a national religion.[16] By the same token, only a scant handful of Johnson's literary biographies affirm the greatness of the poets described therein. Not all of Johnson's contemporaries were pleased by such astringency. Robert

Potter complained in 1783 as follows: "It is not without some degree of honest indignation that a person of candor observes this spirit of detraction diffused so universally through these volumes: of more than fifty of our poets, how few have passed free from very severe censures?"[17] Those few of Johnson's biographies that do celebrate greatness, moreover, aside from registering the uneven performances of even this handful of stellar figures, decline the opportunity that a cult of home-grown genius would afford for national aggrandizement. His "soft" nationalism precludes so chauvinistic an approach to critical judgments.

Resisting National Teleologies

Johnson's cosmopolitanism can also be seen in his negative response to the way that cultural nationalism, obsessed with articulating historical time in the mythic terms of national destiny, involves a violent appropriation of religious awe. Noting the quasi-religious fervor often inspired by cultural nationalism, Benedict Anderson suggests that the key to this sacralization of national culture is, precisely, a sense of destiny: in his words, "a secular transformation of fatality into continuity, contingency into meaning."[18] Nation-based mythmaking is the recuperation, in short, of history's randomness. There is no more central icon for the cultural making of later eighteenth-century Britishness, moreover, than that of the bard, supposedly the "indigenous historian of a nation."[19] To quote Trumpener again: "Even while the bard signifies collective and tribal memory, functioning as the repository and transmitter of cultural memory, he becomes the representative of poetic art as a compensatory, secular religion."[20]

Johnson's biography of Gray illustrates his reservations about sacralizing national icons. This life is, along with the "Life of Milton," among the most controversial of the critical biographies precisely because it expresses his distaste for "The Bard." An anonymous contemporary of Johnson was provoked to offer the following trope to encapsulate Johnson's manifest lack of receptivity to Gray's poem: "But the Doctor is *determined* not to be pleased; he *will not* be interested at all in the affair: like the *ruthless Edward*, he turns a deaf ear to all the poor *Bard*'s threats and exclamations. . . ."[21] Cleverly absorbed into the world of Gray's poem, Johnson figures in this trope as a tyrannical dictator who attempts — but, of course, implicitly fails — to silence the bard's prophetic voice. Because such a critique will certainly resonate with current critical themes of voicelessness and marginality, it is worth looking more closely at some of Johnson's objections to the poem's prophetic mode:

The Bard appears to be, as Algarotti and others have remarked, an imitation of the prophecy of Nereus. Algarotti thinks it superior to its original, and, if preference depends only on the imagery and animation of the two poems, his judgement is right. There is in *The Bard* more force, more thought, and more variety. But to copy is less than to invent, and the copy has been unhappily produced at the wrong time. The fiction of Horace was to the Romans credible; but its revival disgusts us with apparent and unconquerable falsehood. 'Incredulus odi.' (*Lives*, 3:438)

The invocation here of an Italian critic, Francesco Algarotti, is perhaps itself another stubborn reminder that even vernacular print culture has an international dimension.

It is by the indirect route of Algarotti's favorable commentary that Johnson raises the issue of Gray's debt to Horace. It is in his fifteenth ode, Book 1, that Horace represents Nereus as prophesying to Paris, disrupting the latter's journey at sea with the kidnapped Helen. Nereus grimly predicts both the eventual fall of Troy and the violent death of Paris himself. In this elaboration on the matter of Troy, Horace indulges in the luxury of "prophesying after the fact." He achieves, in effect, a heavy sense of fatality by retrospectively assigning the known outcome to a prophecy supposedly uttered before the events occurred. Johnson then quotes Horace the critic against Horace the prophecy-monger. Horace professes disgust, in the *Ars Poetica*, at the clumsiness of attempting to *stage*, as opposed to merely narrating, especially improbable events such as the miraculous transformation of Cadmus into a snake: *Incredulus odi* ("disbelieving, I hate"). The point, then, is not merely that Gray has borrowed from a classic author in order to feed the desire for supposedly homegrown poetic materials. The further and more complex point is that the Horatian original was itself unworthy of revival: an analysis that entirely belies the commonplace notion that Johnson, as an adherent to Anglo-Latinate culture, was merely resistant to literary innovation.

What provokes Johnson's ire is, above all, the use of prophecy in "The Bard" to sanctify national icons. Gray's Welsh bard prophesies ex post facto, as it were, for the one simple reason that nothing could so cheaply convey a sense of destiny as regards "Britannia's issue" as the prediction, with the dramatic immediacy of declaimed speech, of events already known.[22] As Gray wrote wryly to a friend, "I annex a piece of the Prophecy; which must be true at least, as it was wrote so many hundred years after the events."[23] It is against the stilted hokeyness of such rhetoric that Johnson directs his deflationary jabs: "To select a singular event, and swell it to a giant's bulk by fabulous appendages of spectres and predictions, has little difficulty," Johnson writes, "for he that for-

sakes the probable may always find the marvellous" (*Lives*, 3:438).
Johnson's enunciated standard is "the probable": verisimilitude, rather
than truth per se, a standard that he insists is historically relative. What
he dislikes in Gray's Nostradamus-like prophecy is the author's pretense of naïveté: the sentimentality, in short, of writing like that, now,
"at the wrong time."

RESISTING NATIONAL GENEALOGIES

Johnson's problem with the fashionable primitivism of his own moment had many levels and dimensions. One such involves the modal
distinction between truth and fiction. He saw that the project of cultural
nationalism tended toward mythmaking gestures that appropriate—or
simply invent—a heroic past suitable to the aspirations of the present.
For the nationalist compulsion to recuperate history through myth also
takes the form of questing for so-called roots—the eighteenth century
being, as Ian Haywood points out, "a great age of origin-seeking."[24]
Such nationalist claims about "original genius," as Nick Groom observes, were articulated in terms of competing antiquarian strategies—
ancient manuscripts versus oral tradition, and so on—for re-presenting
the literary source.[25] To the mythmaking aspect of this eighteenth-century project of "forging" Britishness, in Linda Colley's phrase, Johnson
manifests a studied aloofness.

The obfuscation bound up with antiquarian claims to recover lost
roots served in general to mask precisely the historical break represented by the changing social relations, new divisions of labor, and
more secular politics associated with the structure of the modern na-
tion-state. Writing about "the ruptures of the later eighteenth century,"
Anderson describes how they created a "new consciousness" afflicted
by "amnesias and estrangements parallel to the forgetting of childhood
brought on by puberty." "At just this juncture," he continues, "emerged
the narrative of the nation. . . ."[26] This description dovetails seamlessly
with the historiographical notion of "invented traditions": the pattern,
definitively encapsulated by Eric Hobsbawm and Terence Ranger, by
which nationalist intellectuals programmatically create a properly monumental past that they then pretend to "discover."[27] Johnson himself is
the great precursor of such insights into the retrospective inventions of
nation-based history. "If we know little of the ancient Highlands," he
urges in response to the most notorious of such inventions, "let us not
fill the vacuity with *Ossian*" (*Journey*, 119).

The particular appropriation of Celtic antiquities associated with the
making of "Ossian" was to inspire some of Johnson's most trenchant

critiques of such claims about natural authenticity and ancient folkish "roots." One dimension of his critique focused on the fakery involved in this episode. The "Ossian" controversy, indeed, galvanized by fraudulence on several levels, was an especially egregious example of the power of a committed cultural nationalism to brush aside considerations of truth or aesthetic standards. The single-minded desire for a home-grown "British" counterpart to Homer, by which the achievements of classical civilization could be trumped, thus spawned a central episode in historiographical fabrication. The undeniable importance of "Ossian" as an event in literary history, especially on the continent, makes it all the more worthwhile to scrutinize its curious production.[28]

Here is how James Macpherson, whose sheer creativity and ingenuity cannot be gainsaid, set out to satisfy the perceived need for a homegrown Homer. At least for his first epic, *Fingal* (1761), he cobbled together some shards from some fourteen or fifteen extant ballads, perhaps a few centuries old, belonging to an almost entirely oral Highland tradition.[29] With cavalier freedom, he rearranged the themes and plots in these late-medieval materials for his own epic purposes.[30] He further massaged the relatively recent fragments so as to harmonize with scattered references to the *Caledonii* by ancient Roman historians, also interpolating invented Gaelic cognates (such as "Caracul") for historical personages mentioned therein (such as Caracalla, son of the Roman emperor Severus). Casting about for resonant heroes, he coolly appropriated such Irish figures as Fionn Mac Cumhal and Oisín, well-established in written Irish sources dating back as far as the twelfth century. These sources he scrupulously cleansed of any telltale traces of Irish roots, such as St. Patrick: for Fingal and Ossian would now be shown orbiting around the mythical Scottish kingdom of "Morven" rather than Ulster or Connacht. Even this tenuous degree of dependence on Highland sources disappears, moreover, from the subsequent epic *Temora* (1763), a simple fact that convincingly explains, far better than excuses about the orthographic idiosyncrasies of his sources, why Macpherson so obstinately refused to allow contemporary scholars access to his supposed sources.

Macpherson went on to depict his "Caledonian Homer," Ossian, in accordance with certain notions about ancient Greek rhapsodes set forth in Thomas Blackwell's *Enquiry into the Life and Writings of Homer* (1735). He fleshed out the rest of his epic in the rhythmic cadences of the King James Bible, shrewdly leavening the bloodthirsty and misogynist ethos of tribal warfare with a heavy dose of moistly tender "sensibility" themes.[31] The resulting lachrymose fabrication he then passed off as his "extremely literal translation" of a quasi-Homeric cycle of ancient Caledonian bardic poetry: a translation supposedly based partly on manuscript sources and partly on oral tradition.[32] Indeed, he allowed the public to understand the Ossianic poems as nothing less than his translation of an oral epic tradition preserved, and supposedly transmitted "with great purity," through some sixty generations of turbulent Highland history. As for the crowning touch of Ossian's blindness, one cannot top Malcolm Laing's dry conclusion of 1800: "We know that Homer and Milton were blind, but a third blind bard, like them the author of two epic poems, must be ascribed to imitation, not to chance."[33]

What raised the stakes of the controversy for Johnson, however, was the collective nature of the Ossianic enterprise: for "Ossian" was by no means the work of a single perverse individual. Richard Sher demonstrates that "Ossian" was indeed to a large extent the product of an Edinburgh cabal also concerned with such current political issues as the parliamentary debate about a Scottish militia. This cabal—John Home, Hugh Blair, Adam Ferguson, William Robertson, and Alexander Carlyle—in effect commissioned Macpherson, providing him "inspiration, incentive, financial support, letters of introduction, editorial assistance, publishing connections, and emotional support."[34] Many of the leading intellectuals of the Scottish Enlightenment, in other words, collaborated to some extent with what Johnson went so far in a letter to James Boswell as to term a "conspiracy in national falsehood" (*Letters*, 2:178). Hugh Blair, whom Johnson chose to regard as innocently duped, ventured far out on the proverbial limb for Macpherson. Blair, while dwelling in his monograph *A Critical Dissertation on the Poems of Ossian* (1763) on Ossian's quasi-Homeric sublimity, claims that the Caledonian bard out-Virgils Virgil: "The tenderness of Virgil softens," according to Blair, but "that of Ossian dissolves and overcomes the heart."[35] This effort to canonize "Ossian," as John Valdimir Price demonstrates, was part of a concerted Scottish campaign that also came to include boosterism from the pens of Henry Home (Lord Kames), John Smith, William Duff, Alexander Gerard, and John Gardiner. The critical framework these critics generally deployed, derived from the Scottish Enlightenment's evolutionary theories of social development, was, in Price's words, a "half-baked" anthropology that equated literary sublimity with primitive times.[36]

The insidious nature of this collective "Ossian industry" begins to appear more fully, however, only when we consider that the poems anthologized in Macpherson's various redactions of Ossian in the 1760s appeared before the public through the medium of a self-described editor, and surrounded by, as Ian Haywood puts it, an "apparatus of authentication."[37] Authenticating scholarly devices included introductions, learned dissertations, footnotes, and so on, all of which tended to "verify" the authenticity of their source materials by reference to a past inferred from those same sources. Eventually Macpherson was driven to the extreme of fabricating, through a reverse translation, a Gaelic pseudo-original of *Fingal*: an act, as Gauti Kristmannson puts it, "which finally condemned him to the forger's bench."[38] However sophisticated we may become in recognizing that the concept of "fraud" is embedded within a particular forensic and economic system of property relations;[39] however much we insist on "Macpherson's peculiar situation at the confluence of two very different cultures";[40] however much we attempt to discern a discrete trickle of "authentic Gaelic materials" in the muddy torrents of "Ossian," we cannot afford to overlook Macpherson's bad faith, his abusive intent to make personal and political capital out of public deception. As Price points out, Macpherson simply refused the candid option of offering "Ossian" to the public as, say, epic poems based on his acquaintance with Gaelic tradition, or even as a historical novel.[41] The issue raised by material framed thus—as *translated antiquities*—is neither the license of imaginative literature nor the vicissitudes of cultural difference: it is the integrity of historical scholarship.

Another objectionable layer in Macpherson's palimpsest, as Johnson recognized, was its obfuscation of the internal politics of Scotland. Such re-creations of an "unmediated" past often serve to impose a false unity on collectivities otherwise divided in the present, and "Ossian" was no exception. Eighteenth-century Lowland Scots had in fact often actively crusaded to extirpate the Highland's Gaelic culture. Indeed, the Society in Scotland for Propagating Christian Knowledge—founded two years after the 1707 Act of Union—quickly began to displace the Highlands' traditional parish schools. The evangelical society was begun, as Paul J. Degategno points out, with the express intention of "eliminating the Gaelic language."[42] Johnson registers in his *Journey* the alienating impact of this situation as follows: "Here [in the Hebrides] the children are taught to read; but by the rule of their institution, they teach only *English*, so that the natives read a language which they may never use or understand" (103). And indeed, as in his piece on the "English Common Soldiers," Johnson refuses in the case of Scotland to paper over internal divisions in the name of a supposedly shared national culture. He observes early on in the *Journey* that Highlanders disdain to learn English from their Lowland neighbors (36). Near the end of the *Journey* he reflects again on the gulf between the Lowlands and the Highlands, remarking as follows:

> To the southern inhabitants of Scotland, the state of the mountains and the islands is equally unknown with that of Borneo or Sumatra: Of both they have only heard a little, and guess the rest.

"They are strangers to the language and the people," he concludes, "whose life they would model, and whose evils they would remedy" (88).

That Macpherson's bogus translation nevertheless had so many distinguished Lowland illuminati closing ranks behind it provoked from Johnson the following pitiless apothegm: "A Scotchman must be a very sturdy moralist who does not love Scotland better than truth: he will always love it better than inquiry; and if falsehood flatters his vanity, will not be very diligent to detect it" (119). This finely calibrated skepticism, as Karen O'Brien has argued, is aimed specifically at the Lowland intelligentsia and their opportunistic literary and ethnographic appropriation of Highland culture. The literary myth of the Highlands, O'Brien points out—based on the suddenly convenient apotheosis of a society otherwise despised as primitive and kept at a great distance— "underpins the Lowland construction of its own identity." With the appearance of *Fingal* in 1761, Lowland Scotland gained what she describes as "a compensatory myth of origins, an outlet for repressed national narcissism in an age of anglicization."[43] Or, to quote Johnson's *Journey* again: "The Scots have something to plead for their easy reception of an improbable fiction: they are seduced by their fondness for their supposed ancestors" (119). The deadly word *supposed* in this comment glances again at the lack of organic connection in such a genealogy.

It is crucial, moreover, that Johnson is not insensitive to what Michael Hechter described a generation ago as the "internal colonialism" of England toward the "Celtic fringe" (Scotland, Wales, and Ireland).[44] The current celebration of Macpherson is often elaborated along these "anti-colonial" lines, and usually at Johnson's expense. It must thus be emphasized that it is Johnson himself, rather than Macpherson, who gives an unflinching contemporary description of the post-Culloden demoralization of Highland culture by English oppression. Of the Highlanders he writes in the *Journey*, "Their pride has been crushed by the heavy hand of a vindictive conqueror, whose severities have been followed by laws, which, though they cannot be called cruel, have produced much discontent, because they operate on the surface of life, and make every eye bear witness to subjection" (89). It is again Johnson who directly attacks the Disarming Act of 1746, a law by which, as he writes, "every house was despoiled of its defense" (90). Pointing out that the British sovereign affords the Highlanders no real protection, whether from robbers or armed invaders, he concludes as follows: "Laws that place the subjects in such a state, contravene the first principles of the compact of authority: they exact obedience, and yield no protection" (91). And it is Johnson who recommends, as an antidote to mass emigration out from the Highlands, government concessions both on the arms issue and on the question of traditional plaid, also banned by law in 1746:

> To allure them [Highlanders] into the [British] army, it was thought proper to indulge them in the continuance of their national dress. If this concession could have any effect, it might easily be made. That dissimilitude of appearance, which was supposed to keep them distinct from the rest of the [British] nation, might disincline them from coalescing with the Pensylvanians [*sic*] or people of Connecticut. If the restitution of their arms will reconcile them to their country, let them have again those weapons, which will not be more mischievous at home than in the Colonies. . . .
>
> To hinder insurrection, by driving away the people, and to govern peaceably, by having no subjects, is an expedient that argues no great profundity of politicks. . . . [I]t affords a legislator little self-applause to consider, that where there was formerly an insurrection, there is now a wilderness. (97)

This last phrase is more resonant still for those who catch the echo of a phrase from Tacitus: *ubi solitudinem faciunt, pacem appellant.* This famous phrase comes from the history of a previous encounter between the Highlands and an aggressive empire: the Scottish campaign, during the time of Boudicca's rebellion, that in AD 84 pitted the Roman general Agricola against the still-unconquered Caledonians. Tacitus quotes a rousing speech by the Caledonian leader Calgacus to his troops that concludes as follows: "To robbery, butchery, and rapine, they [the Romans] give the lying name of 'government'; they create a desolation and call it peace."[45] Here Johnson mobilizes classical learning precisely to indict the "modern Romans" of 1746.

Some may still be tempted to argue that Macpherson-the-Trickster was a necessary stimulant to the decolonization of the Celtic peripheries. And there are indeed signs, despite Macpherson's daunting baggage, that Howard Gaskill's campaign to rehabilitate "Ossian" is finding a bit of traction.[46] Macpherson figures, for example, amongst the "peripheral visions" recently heralded by Janet Sorenson in her review of Trumpener's *Bardic Nationalism.*[47] In a similar vein, Fiona J. Stafford has recently suggested that new critical approaches—"the great interest in colonialism, cultural imperialism, and post-colonial theory"—are likely to consolidate the rehabilitation of Macpherson and deliver *The Poems of Ossian* from the category of "quaint hoax."[48] However, even if one were to concede that cultural nationalisms based on some sort of "necessary myth" may sometimes be justified, the specific case of "Ossian" involves imperial contradictions that can scarcely be recuperated. "Ossian" represents a case where an obdurate cultural nationalism intersects with a broader imperial agenda, much as Highland regiments were permitted to assert their "traditional dress" while mobilizing at Ticonderoga and elsewhere on behalf of empire.

As Johnson understood, Macpherson's historiographical project is tainted by agendas that go well beyond the simple issue of forgery. In his prefaces to *Fingal* and *Temora*, as Clare O'Halloran points out, Macpherson launches a preemptive strike against well-attested Irish antiquities, attempting thereby "to undermine the potential of Irish literary and historical sources to demonstrate that his Ossian was fraudulent."[49] "The bards of Ireland," in the words of Macpherson, "by ascribing to Ossian compositions which are evidently their own, have occasioned a general belief in that country, that Fingal was of Irish extraction, and not of the ancient Caledonians, as is said in the genuine poems of Ossian." Moreover, Macpherson introduces *Fragments of Ancient Poetry* with an assertion of the special ethnic purity of the Highlands, a country notably "free," in his words, of "intermixture with foreigners."[50] This emphasis on the purity of the "ancient Caledonians" is backed up in the text through physiognomic details: the emphatically blue eyes of warriors, the snowy white bosoms of maidens, and so on. The context for Macpherson's purity complex is, in the first degree, rivalries within the British Isles. Turning the historical record upside down, Macpherson attempts to reposition the Highlands as the original Celtic motherland. Johnson hints at this problem of highjacked antiquities in the *Journey*, noting that a putatively Earse translation of the Bible proved to be "nothing else than the Irish Bible" (117). He reports in the same vein that he and James Boswell "had heard of manuscripts that were, or had been in the hands of somebody's father, or grandfather; but at last . . . had no reason to believe they were other than Irish" (118).

Macpherson's emphasis on pure roots in the Ossianic controversy, as Kristmannson demonstrates, can indeed be read in part as "a battle of Celtic antiquaries" and as "a tribal tug of war between the Scots and the Irish" also involving Charles O'Conor.[51] O'Conor, an Irish Catholic and, in Clare O'Halloran's phrase, "one of the few Gaelic scholars of the time," had published in 1753 his *Dissertations on the Antient History of Ireland*, a book depicting pre-Christian Gaelic Ireland as "a sophisticated, aristocratic, and, above all, literate society." As O'Halloran points out, this antiprimitivist portrayal—a direct challenge to British stereotypes about the "wild Irish"—was especially important at a juncture when Catholics were beginning their campaign to end the odious Penal Laws.[52] The anti-Irish dimension of Macpherson's "translating" project comes into greater focus, moreover, when juxtaposed with his judgments about that country's history in his subsequent opus, *The History of Great Britain* (1771). As regards William III's "pacification" of Ireland in 1689–90, for example, he writes as follows: "The Irish ought to have been considered as enemies, rather than rebels. If, therefore, the pacification was expedient, it was certainly just." Such sentiments are very different from his description of the massacre of Glencoe in 1692 as "barbarous, impolitic, and inhuman," a difference that reflects Macpherson's position as a Highlander operating within the unionist—antipapist and imperial—framework of Hanoverian Britain.[53]

In this dispute, Johnson tilted toward O'Conor. In 1757, having received a copy of O'Conor's book, Johnson wrote to the Irish scholar praising his work and expressing a desire "to be further informed of a people so ancient, and once so illustrious" (*Letters*, 1:152). In the preface to his subsequent edition of *Dissertations on the Antient History of Ireland* (1766), O'Conor praises Johnson for his receptivity to research in Celtic antiquities: "Far from joining in the current Prejudice versus the present Subject, or oppressing the writer who undertook it with Censure . . . he approved of an Endeavor to revive . . . the antient Language and Literature of a Sister Isle" (*Letters*, 1:151 n). Johnson wrote again to O'Conor in 1777, expressing a particular desire to know more about the period prior to the English conquest when Ireland was, in his words, "the school of the West, the quiet habitation of Sanctity and literature" (*Letters*, 3:24). He lent support as well to a maverick Scottish researcher in Celtic antiquities, William Shaw, author of a rudimentary Gaelic grammar and dictionary, who refused to rally around Macpherson's attempts to make Scotland, rather than Ireland, the original Celtic motherland. Shaw was a Highland Scot who was sensitive not only to the telling anachronisms in *Fingal*, but, perhaps above all, to Macpherson's attempt to aggrandize Scottish "roots" precisely by marginalizing the heavily Irish dimension of extant Celtic antiquities. In Shaw's words, Macpherson, "in order to serve his purpose, wrests facts as they may serve his end, and, apprehensive of a future detection, labours with great zeal to destroy the credit of all Irish history, and with a few bold strokes of his pen, obliterates all the Celtic learning ever known any where, in order to make way for a new system of Celtic emigration and Hebridean and Fingalian history. . . ."[54]

Johnson's stance in the "Ossian" affair, entirely consistent with his lifelong loathing for the pastoral genre, finally serves to disrupt the touristic pleasure afforded to consumers sighing from Virginia to Weimar over the melancholy fate of weepy warrior-bards. Here is the deflating dish he serves up in the *Journey* to a public hungry for underdeveloped forms of life conveniently preserved in the poverty of the Highlands:

We came thither too late to see what we expected, a people of peculiar appearance, and a system of antiquated life. . . . Of what they had before the late conquest of their country, there remain only their language and their poverty. . . . Such is the effect of the late regulations, that a longer journey than to the Highlands must be taken by him whose curiosity pants for savage virtues and barbarous grandeur. (57)

And though Johnson resolutely refuses to glamorize the Highlands, he does not thereby merely lapse back into an unsympathetic essentialism. He insists instead, with a salutary emphasis on present conditions, that the "primitive manners" of the Highlanders are "produced by their situation rather than derived from their ancestors" (44). And just as he appreciates Ireland's historical role as "the school of the West," Johnson responds with equivalent warmth to the Scottish site of an ancient monastery, Iona, which he terms "that illustrious island, which was once the luminary of the Caledonian regions, whence savage clans and roving barbarians derived the benefits of knowledge, and the blessings of religion" (148).

Macpherson, however, wrote precisely to satisfy readers panting "for savage virtues and barbarous grandeur." He pandered to an eighteenth-century sentimental ethos defined, as Adam Potkay points out, by a perceived conflict between the ruggedly "masculine" civic virtue of classical antiquity and the more "effeminate" manners of the refined present.[55] In this sense it is finally not just a supposedly indigenous Scottish tradition, but also a certain construction of "Britishness," that is ultimately at stake in the controversy over "Ossian." The "voice" of Ossian, published in the wake of the '45, conjured up a past that is meant to be Scottish and British simultaneously. The voice of Ossian, as Martin Wechselblatt points out:

> names clan losses as national losses, retrospectively inaugurating the historical moment of a Scottish national culture at the same point its impossibility is acknowledged. . . . 'Ossian' recovers the past in the image of a present loss, as the simultaneous immanence and impossibility of nationhood. In short, *the nation as forgery*, and not just the Scottish nation. For the proper name 'Ossian' marks the translation of Gaelic culture into England's national myth of Britain.[56]

A literary history that unquestioningly celebrates the contribution of "Ossian," then, also risks loving Great Britain "more than truth." And Johnson must surely be the great precursor of Peter T. Murphy's insight that Macpherson's "crime" in the whole affair ought to be defined as the "crime of Pastoral," a betrayal defined by the way in which "the virtues of the primitive are depicted as translatable, and the way this translation pretends that the resulting mixture is not unstable or exploitative." The resulting concoction, Murphy concludes, is "an imperial elixir."[57] Johnson's interventions, then, serve to check a British appetite for romanticized backwardness no less than the excesses of Scottish nationalism. And it is not an imperial perspective that determines his perspective so much as a more generalized suspicion of national genealogies as such.

RESISTING ETHNIC ABSOLUTISM

It is significant that Johnson maintains a cool distance from any "roots-finding" projects that seek to inflate a supposed national essence by magnifying its glorious origins in antiquity. He thus turns a skeptical gaze as well on Anglocentric antiquarianism, with its parallel program of Saxon revivalism. *Rambler* 177 (1751), in portraying the elderly antiquarian Hirsutus, depicts him as introducing his favorite studies "by a severe censure of those who want due regard for their native country" (5:170). Whereas Hirsutus collects only books printed in Roman or Gothic letters, his ballad-mongering associate Cantilenus "turned all his thoughts upon old ballads, for he considered them as the genuine records of the national taste" (171). Both Hirsutus and Cantilenus seem to prefigure impending developments. By 1764, Thomas Percy's *Reliques of Ancient English Poetry* had generated the figure of the medieval minstrel, of pointedly Saxon ancestry, as an English mirror-image of Macpherson's ancient Caledonian bard. Percy's *Reliques*, a collection of English (and Scottish) ballads geographically centered in the northern border country, claimed that most of the ballads therein came from a seventeenth-century folio manuscript, though the majority were in fact from printed sources. Percy's transcriptions, moreover, in a process highly typical of "fakelore," were in fact not faithful to the originals in the manuscript.[58] Encouraged by William Shenstone to "let the Liberties taken by the translator of the Erse-fragments [that is, Macpherson] be a Precedent for you," Percy sanitized and amended his originals.[59] He succumbed to the temptation, as Gwendolyn A. Morgan explains, to "eliminate what he considered as imperfect grammar, to exaggerate heroic effects, to emphasize medievalism, and to soften what may have been considered vulgarity by his readers' delicate tastes."[60] Percy also interpolated freely, adding more than 150 lines, for example, to the fragmentary "Child of Elle."[61] Joseph Ritson, Percy's rival antiquarian, delivered in 1792 a definitive judgment on the latter's failures to specify exactly where he had "improved": "no confidence can be placed in any of the 'old Minstrel ballads' inserted in that collection, and not to be found elsewhere."[62] Nick Groom, though he ultimately exculpates Percy from charges of bad editing or deliberate forgery, demonstrates in great detail how the *Reliques*, in his words, "evolved so dramatically that any similarities between the seventeenth-century *manuscrit trouvé* and what emerged from Dodsley's shop under the sign of Tully's Head in 1765 are more likely to be coincidental than symptomatic of any consistent editorial theory."[63]

Though Johnson shared membership with Percy in the celebrated literary society of the Club, such fraternization, in the words of Bertram H. Davis, "was not such a fellowship . . . that it resolved differences of taste between Johnson and Percy or prompted Johnson to repress his disagreement with his younger clubmate."[64] Indeed, despite his lengthy acquaintance with Percy, which also led him into ghostwriting the dedication of *Ancient Reliques* to the Countess of Northumberland, Johnson indulged throughout his life in "sportive anathemas" on ballads and their revivalists.[65] His doubts about their literary merits—and especially about the merits of *modern* ballad imitations—were expressed in a number of amusing parodies, the improvisational genius and "merry malice" of which are extensively recorded by Hester Lynch Piozzi (*Miscellanies*, 1:192–95). One of the best of Johnson's impromptu parodies directly targeted a poem that did much to stimulate the ballad revival, Percy's anemic *Hermit of Warkworth*. Here is a sample stanza from Percy:

> And soon he saw his love descend
> Wrapt in a tartan plaid;
> Assisted by a sturdy youth
> In highland garb y-clad.

It would be hard to match the deliberate flatness of Johnson's lampoon, its cheerily bovine banality:

> I put my hat upon my head
> And walked into the Strand,
> And there I met another man
> Who's hat was in his hand.
>   (*Poems*, 6:269)

This stupefying quatrain was delivered in public, at a 1771 Oxford coffeehouse, in response to fashionable cant by some present about the "Classical Simplicity" of the *Hermit of Warkworth*. Johnson prefaced his improvisation with the outrageous claim that—given sufficiently dull listeners—he could go on for seven years speaking extemporaneous verse in such a vein.[66]

Johnson was in fact not entirely complacent about the value of supposedly ancient ballads as documents of social history, suspecting, indeed, that Percy's *Reliques* might be placed in the same category as

Ossian.[67] Given his attacks on the eager credulity of Scots as regards the antiquity of "Ossian," moreover, it is salutary to register his claim, during his tour of Scotland, that he could produce a ballad-based English equivalent to Macpherson's chorus of true-believers. According to Boswell's *Tour of the Hebrides*, Johnson told Lord Elibank he would undertake "to write an epick poem on the story of *Robin Hood*, and half England, to whom the names and places he should mention in it are familiar, would believe and declare they had heard it from their earliest years."[68] His particular target, then, is neither old poetry nor popular poetry per se, but rather, as Clark puts it, "the creation of a mythic vernacular literature."[69]

Johnson had little patience with that literary primitivism, cultivated during the Walpole era by Whiggish "Patriot poets," that glorified the Gothic past for national agendas.[70] Indeed, he rejected the "studied barbarity" of even Edmund Spenser's literary archaisms, never mind the faux medieval diction of a Thomas Warton, or a William Shenstone, or a Thomas Percy.[71] About such contemporary imitators of Spenser, he makes the following comment on their stylistic anachronisms: "It would indeed be difficult to exclude from a long poem all modern phrases, though it is easy to sprinkle it with gleanings of antiquity." He closes this disquisition with a Nietzschean disdain for the merely antiquarian: "Perhaps, however, the style of Spenser might by long labour be justly copied; but life is surely given us for higher purposes than to gather what our ancestors have wisely thrown away, and to learn what is of no value but because it has been forgotten" (*Rambler* 121, 4:286). It is a salutary warning about reifying the "marginal" as such: life requires some forgetfulness.

CONCLUSION: REFRAMING NATIONAL HISTORIES

In deflating the ethos of Percy's *Reliques*, Johnson enacts something well beyond the aesthetic or political conservatism that is often ascribed to him. While this gesture is of a piece with his general reluctance to mummify national characteristics—"there is no permanent national character"—it is connected as well to his opposition to imperial expansion. As I have argued elsewhere, Johnson's universalism, which includes a sustained and pointed critique of European expansion, simply cannot be dismissed as mere Eurocentrism in disguise.[72] Johnson articulates a universalism that is explicitly opposed to the imperial construction of hierarchies based on "racial difference." Laura Doyle has recently argued that *Reliques of Ancient English Poetry*, a ballad collection framed by the agenda of aggrandizing a people named as *Anglo-Saxons*,

constitutes "a new narrative for English culture: a racial narrative."[73]
To be sure, Percy could scarcely have foreseen the future deployments
of "Anglo-Saxon" identity. Johnson's so-called obstructionism, however, is at least as prescient in its wary forebodings as is Percy's antici-
pation of the literary achievements of the next age. Knowing in advance
how the plots of literary and cultural history "come out," as it were, we
have chosen to misunderstand—and indeed bury—the striking alternative to nation-based and race-based historiography represented by
Johnson.

It is far from accidental that Johnson distances himself decisively
from emerging forms of ethnic absolutism. It is worthwhile in this connection to recall how, in the crucial introduction to his serial coverage
of the parliamentary debates for the *Gentleman's Magazine*—part of his
vibrant participation in the national public sphere—Johnson under-
stands his ethical and political obligations as a journalist. Though inter-
vening in a national discussion, he insists on extending the boundaries
of moral concern to humanity as whole. Thus in 1738 he frames the
affairs of Magna Lilliputia, or Great Britain, within the context of a
macro-historical global conflict that is both immoral and unlawful:

> The people of Degulia, or the Lilliputian Europe . . . are, above those of
> the other parts of the world, famous for arts, arms, and navigation, and, in
> consequence of their superiority, have made conquests and settled colonies
> in very distant regions, the inhabitants of which they look upon as barba-
> rous, though in simplicity of manners, probity, and temperance superior to
> themselves; and seem to think that they have a right to treat them as passion,
> interest, or caprice shall direct, without much regard to the rules of justice
> or humanity; they have carried this imaginary sovereignty so far that they
> have sometimes proceeded to rapine, bloodshed, and desolation. If you en-
> deavour to examine the foundation of this authority, they neither produce
> any grant from a superior jurisdiction, nor plead the consent of the people
> whom they govern in this tyrannical manner; but either threaten you with
> punishment for threatening the Emperor's sovereignty, or pity your stupid-
> ity, or tell you in positive terms that *Power is right.*[74]

It is precisely through such framing strategies that Johnson maintains
a dual allegiance both to a modernizing national project and to a world
polity increasingly blighted by the imperial dynamics of European
expansion. Indeed, he repeats exactly this globalizing strategy in 1759,
when he reframes the contents of *The World Displayed*—a twenty-volume
collection of European voyage-and-discovery literature—with an introduction instructing readers in the anticolonial analysis of historical
sources. To concede that Johnson was right would entail a significant
rethinking of literary and cultural history.

Johnson's cosmopolitanism disrupts the trajectory by which, in Howard Weinbrot's useful summary, "powerful quasi-European England becomes more powerful and imperial Britain."[75] Johnson's voice, however, belongs neither to a quasi-European ancien régime nor to a new imperial Britain. His "soft" nationalism is pointedly secular and civic precisely because the mystical and folkloric brands of nationalism are so easily hijacked for racial and expansionist myths, myths, in Doyle's words, "of an ancient soil-rooted folk fit to become modern, global conquerors. . . ."[76] Perhaps Johnson's most striking achievement, however, is to have demonstrated that "national" and "cosmopolitan" are not necessarily antinomies. His cosmopolitan nationalism challenges us, in a moment that has already made "global" into an annoying buzzword, to write cultural histories that balance attention to global dynamics with the density of analysis available only in local and vernacular frameworks.

NOTES

I am very grateful to Mrinalini Sinha, Philip Smallwood, Greg Clingham, Jim Thorson, Anne Chandler, and Martha Navarro for many useful comments about earlier versions of this essay.

1. See Pheng Cheah and Bruce Robbins, eds., *Cosmopolitics: Thinking and Feeling beyond the Nation* (Minneapolis: University of Minnesota Press, 1998), 2–3.

2. See also Martha Nussbaum, *For Love of Country: Debating the Limits of Patriotism*, ed. Joshua Cohen (Boston: Beacon Press, 1996); Timothy Brennan, *At Home in the World: Cosmopolitanism Now* (Cambridge: Harvard University Press, 1997); and Karen O'Brien, *Narratives of Enlightenment: Cosmopolitan History from Voltaire to Gibbon* (Cambridge: Cambridge University Press, 1997).

3. Howard Weinbrot, *Britannia's Issue: The Rise of British Literature from Dryden to Ossian* (Cambridge: Cambridge University Press, 1993), 389.

4. Katie Trumpener, *Bardic Nationalism: The Romantic Novel and the British Empire* (Princeton: Princeton University Press, 1997), 70.

5. See J. C. D. Clark, *Samuel Johnson: Literature, Religion and English Cultural Politics from the Restoration to Romanticism* (Cambridge: Cambridge University Press, 1994); and "The Cultural Identity of Samuel Johnson," in *AJ* 8 (1997): 15–70.

6. Preface, *Gentleman's Magazine* 10 (1740): iii–iv.

7. "Introduction to the Harleian Miscellany: An Essay on the Importance of Small Tracts and Fugitive Pieces," in Donald J. Greene, ed., *The Oxford Authors: Samuel Johnson* (Oxford: Oxford University Press, 1984), 123.

8. Nicholas Hudson, review of John Cannon's *Samuel Johnson and the Politics of Hanoverian England* (Oxford: Clarendon Press, 1994), in *AJ* 9 (1998): 342.

9. Alvin Kernan, *Printing Technology, Letters, and Samuel Johnson* (Princeton: Princeton University Press, 1987); Robert DeMaria, Jr., *Samuel Johnson and the Life of Reading* (Baltimore: Johns Hopkins University Press, 1997); and Lawrence Lipking, *Samuel Johnson: The Life of an Author* (Cambridge: Harvard University Press, 1998).

10. See G. F. Parker, *Johnson's Shakespeare* (Oxford: Clarendon Press, 1989), 31; also James Gray, "Arras/Hélas! A Fresh Look at Samuel Johnson's French," in *Johnson*

after Two Hundred Years, ed. Paul J. Korshin (Philadelphia: University of Pennsylvania Press, 1986), 88.

11. For a study of social class in the shaping of English attitudes toward French culture, see Gerald Newman, *The Rise of English Nationalism: A Cultural History, 1740–1830* (New York: St. Martin's Press, 1997).

12. Samuel Johnson, "Introduction to the Proceedings of the Committee on French Prisoners," in *The Works of Samuel Johnson, LL.D.*, 11 vols. (1825; New York: AMS Press, 1970), 10: 287–89.

13. Samuel Johnson, preface to *A Dictionary of the English Language*, in *The Oxford Authors: Samuel Johnson*, 319.

14. "Browne," in *The Works of Samuel Johnson, LL.D.*, 10:500.

15. "Reply to a Paper in the Gazetteer," in *The Works of Samuel Johnson, LL.D.*, 10:35.

16. Michael Dobson, *The Making of a National Poet: Shakespeare, Adaptation, and Authorship, 1660–1769* (Oxford: Clarendon Press, 1992), 6.

17. Robert Potter, *An Inquiry into Some Passages in Dr. Johnson's Lives of the Poets: Particularly His Observations on Lyric Poetry and the Odes of Gray* (London, 1783), 9.

18. Benedict Anderson, *Imagined Communities: Reflections on the Origin and Spread of Nationalism* (London: Verso, 1983), 19.

19. Ian Haywood, *A Study of the Literary Forgeries of James Macpherson and Thomas Chatterton in Relation to Eighteenth-Century Ideas of History and Fiction* (London: Associated University Presses, 1986), 36.

20. Trumpener, *Bardic Nationalism*, 294–95, n. 14.

21. *A Cursory Examination of Dr. Johnson's Strictures on the Lyric Performances of Gray* (London, 1781), 15.

22. For views of "The Bard" that highlight Gray's self-reflexivity, see Suvir Kaul's *Thomas Gray and Literary Authority: A Study in Ideology and Poetics* (Stanford: Stanford University Press, 1992); and Paul Odney's "Thomas Gray's 'Daring Spirit': Forging the Poetics of an Alternative Nationalism," in *Clio* 28, no. 3 (1999): 245–60.

23. Thomas Gray to Stonhewer, 21 August 1755. *Correspondence of Thomas Gray*, ed. Paget Toynbee and Leonard Toynbee, 3 vols. (Oxford: Clarendon Press, 1935), 1:432–33.

24. Haywood, *Literary Forgeries*, 35.

25. Nick Groom, "Celts, Goths, and the Nature of the Literary Source," in *Tradition in Transition: Women Writers, Marginal texts, and the Eighteenth-Century Canon*, ed. Alvaro Ribeiro S.J. and James G. Basker (Oxford: Clarendon Press, 1996), 275–96.

26. Benedict Anderson, *The Spectre of Comparisons: Nationalism, Southeast Asia, and the World* (London: Verso, 1998), 57.

27. See Terence O. Ranger and Eric Hobsbawm, eds., *The Invention of Tradition* (Cambridge: Cambridge University Press, 1983).

28. See Hugh Trevor-Roper, "The Invention of Tradition: The Highland Tradition of Scotland," in *The Invention of Tradition*, 15–42; also, *From Gaelic to Romantic: Ossianic Translations*, ed. Fiona J. Stafford and Howard Gaskill (Amsterdam: Rodopi, 1998).

29. See Howard Gaskill, introduction, *Ossian Revisited*, ed. Howard Gaskill (Edinburgh: Edinburgh University Press, 1991), 1–18; and Donald E. Meek, "The Gaelic Ballads of Scotland: Creativity and Adaptation," in the same volume, 9–48. The phrase "mainly oral" is intended to cover whatever use Macpherson made of "The Book of the Dean of Lismore," an early-sixteenth-century compilation, in Roman characters, of Highland ballads.

30. See Derick Thomson, " 'Ossian' Macpherson and the Gaelic World of the Eighteenth Century," *Aberdeen University Review* 40 (1963): 7–20.

31. See John Dwyer, "The Melancholy Savage: Text and Context in the *Poems of Ossian*," in Gaskill, *Ossian Revisited*, 164–206.

32. James Macpherson, preface to *Fragments of Ancient Poetry* in *The Poems of Ossian and Related Works*, ed. Howard Gaskill (Edinburgh University Press, 1996), 6.

33. Malcolm Laing, *The History of Scotland* (London and Edinburgh, 1800), 2:399. Cited in John Valdimir Price, "Ossian and the Canon in the Scottish Enlightenment," in Gaskill, *Ossian Revisited*, 120.

34. Richard B. Sher, " 'Those Scotch Imposters and Their Cabal': Ossian and the Scottish Enlightenment," in *Man and Nature: Proceedings of the Canadian Society for Eighteenth-Century Studies* (1982): 1:55.

35. Hugh Blair, A *Critical Dissertation on the Poems of Ossian, the Son of Fingal*, 2nd ed. (London, 1765), 112.

36. John Valdimir Price, "Ossian and the Canon in the Scottish Enlightenment," in Gaskill, *Ossian Revisited*, 118–19.

37. Haywood, *Literary Forgeries*, 21.

38. Gauti Kristmannson, "Ossian: A Case of Celtic Tribalism or a Translation without an Original," in *Transfer: Übersetzen-Dolmetschen-Interkulturalität* (Sonderdruck: Peter Lang, 1997), 460.

39. See Paul Baines, " 'Our Annius': Antiquaries and Fraud in the Eighteenth Century," *BJECS* 20 (1997): 33–51, and the same author's *The House of Forgery in Eighteenth-Century Britain* (Aldershot: Ashgate, 1999).

40. See Fiona J. Stafford, "Introduction: The Ossianic Poems of James Macpherson," in *The Poems of Ossian and Related Works*, ed. Howard Gaskill (Edinburgh: Edinburgh University Press, 1996), xv.

41. Gaskill, *Ossian Revisited*, 125.

42. Paul J. Degategno, " 'The Source of Daily and Exalted Pleasure': Jefferson Reads the Poems of Ossian," in Gaskill, *Ossian Revisited*, 103.

43. Karen O'Brien, "Johnson's View of the Scottish Enlightenment in *A Journey to the Western Islands of Scotland*," in *AJ* 4 (1991): 64; 63.

44. See Michael Hechter, *Internal Colonialism: The Celtic Fringe in British National Development, 1536–1966* (Berkeley: University of California Press, 1975).

45. See Tacitus, *The Agricola and the Germanica*, trans. H. Mattingly, revised S. A. Handford (London: Penguin, 1970), 81.

46. Howard Gaskill, " 'Ossian' Macpherson: Towards a Rehabilitation," in *Comparative Criticism* 8 (1986): 113–46.

47. Janet Sorenson, "Peripheral Visions: Remaking the Map of British Cultural History," in *The Eighteenth Century* 40, 1 (1999): 68–79.

48. Fiona J. Stafford, "Introduction: The Ossianic Poems of James Macpherson," in Gaskill, *The Poems of Ossian and Related Works*, xvii.

49. Clare O'Halloran, "Irish Re-Creation of the Gaelic Past: The Challenge of Macpherson's Ossian," in *Past and Present* 124 (1989): 74.

50. James Macpherson, preface (to 1st ed. of *Fingal*, 1761–62), and preface (to *Fragments of Ancient Poetry*), in Gaskill, *The Poems of Ossian and Related Works*, 37; 5.

51. Kristmannson, "Ossian: A Case of Celtic Tribalism," 449; 452.

52. O'Halloran, "Irish Re-Creation," 75; 77; 75.

53. James Macpherson, *The History of Great Britain from the Restoration to the Accession of the House of Hanover*, 2 vols. (London, 1775), 2:697; 705.

54. William Shaw, *An Enquiry into the Authenticity of the Poems Ascribed to Ossian* (London, 1781), 35–36.

55. See Adam Potkay, *The Fate of Eloquence in the Age of Hume* (Ithaca: Cornell University Press, 1994), 193–207.

56. Martin Wechselblatt, "The Canonical Ossian," in *Making History: Textuality and the Forms of Eighteenth-Century Culture*, ed. Greg Clingham (London: Associated University Presses, 1998), 31.

57. Peter T. Murphy, "Fool's Gold: The Highland Treasures of Macpherson's Ossian," *ELH* 53, no. 3 (1986): 588.

58. See Richard M. Dorson, *Folklore and Fakelore: Essays toward a Discipline of Folk Studies* (Cambridge: Harvard University Press, 1976).

59. See Arthur Johnston, *Enchanted Ground: The Study of Medieval Romance in the Eighteenth Century* (London: Athlone Press, 1964), 79.

60. Gwendolyn A. Morgan, "Percy, the Antiquarians, the Ballad, and the Middle Ages," in *Studies in Medievalism* 7 (1995): 26.

61. G. Malcolm Laws, Jr., *The British Literary Ballad: A Study in Poetic Imitation* (Carbondale: Southern Illinois University Press, 1972), 5.

62. Joseph Ritson, introduction to *Ancient Songs from the Time of King Henry the Third to the Revolution* (London, 1792), xxi.

63. Nick Groom, *The Making of Percy's "Reliques"* (Oxford: Clarendon Press, 1999), 121.

64. Bertram H. Davis, *Thomas Percy* (Boston: Twayne, 1981), 117.

65. Sigurd Bernhard Hustvedt, *Ballad Criticism in Scandanavia and Great Britain during the Eighteenth Century* (London: Humphrey Milford, 1916), 218.

66. Bertram H. Davis, *Thomas Percy: A Scholar-Cleric in the Age of Johnson* (Philadelphia: University of Pennsylvania Press, 1989), 183; 182.

67. Alice C. C. Gaussen, *Percy: Prelate and Poet* (London: Smith, Elder, 1908), 46–47.

68. See James Boswell, *The Journal of a Tour to the Hebrides with Samuel Johnson,* ed. L. F. Powell (London: Dent, 1958), 271; and Hustvedt, *Ballad Criticism,* 216.

69. Clark, *Samuel Johnson: Literature, Religion and English Cultural Politics,* 82.

70. See Christine Gerrard, *The Patriot Opposition to Walpole: Politics, Poetry and National Myth, 1725–1742* (Oxford: Clarendon Press, 1994).

71. See Jack Lynch, "Studied Barbarity: Johnson, Spenser, and the Idea of Progress," in *AJ* 9 (1998): 81–108.

72. See Clement Hawes, "Johnson and Imperialism," in *The Cambridge Companion to Samuel Johnson,* ed. Greg Clingham (Cambridge: Cambridge University Press, 1997 and 1999), 114–26.

73. Laura Doyle, "The Racial Sublime," in *Romanticism, Race, and Imperial Culture, 1780–1834,* ed. Alan Richardson and Sonia Hofkosh (Bloomington: Indiana University Press, 1996). It can scarcely be a coincidence, moreover, that Percy's American contemporary, Thomas Jefferson—a staunch white supremacist—was likewise the instigator of Anglo-Saxon Studies as an academic subject both at William and Mary and the University of Virginia. I am grateful to Jim Basker for pointing out this connection to me.

74. Samuel Johnson, "The State of Affairs in *Lilliput,*" in *The Gentleman's Magazine* 8 (June 1738; reprinted London: Pickering and Chatto, 1998), 285.

75. Weinbrot, *Britannia's Issue,* 2.

76. Doyle, "The Racial Sublime," 22.

BIBLIOGRAPHY

Anderson, Benedict. *Imagined Communities: Reflections on the Origin and Spread of Nationalism.* London: Verso, 1983.

———. *The Spectre of Comparisons: Nationalism, Southeast Asia, and the World.* London: Verso, 1998.

Anon. *A Cursory Examination of Dr. Johnson's Strictures on the Lyric Performances of Gray.* London: 1781.

Blair, Hugh. A *Critical Dissertation on the Poems of Ossian, the Son of Fingal.* 2nd ed. London: 1765.

Boswell, James. *The Journal of a Tour to the Hebrides.* Edited by L. F. Powell. London: Dent, 1958.

Clark, J. C. D. "The Cultural Identity of Samuel Johnson." *AJ* 8 (1997): 15–70.

———. *Samuel Johnson: Literature, Religion and English Cultural Politics from the Restoration to Romanticism.* Cambridge: Cambridge University Press, 1994.

Davis, Bertram H. *Thomas Percy.* Boston: Twayne, 1981.

———. *Thomas Percy: A Scholar-Cleric in the Age of Johnson.* Philadelphia: University of Pennsylvania Press, 1989.

Dobson, Michael. *The Making of a National Poet: Shakespeare, Adaptation, and Authorship, 1660–1769.* Oxford: Clarendon Press, 1992.

Doyle, Laura. "The Racial Sublime." In *Romanticism, Race, and Imperial Culture, 1780–1834.* Edited by Alan Richardson and Sonia Hofkosh. Bloomington: Indiana University Press, 1996, 15–39.

Gaskill, Howard. " 'Ossian' Macpherson: Towards a Rehabilitation." *Comparative Criticism* 8 (1986): 113–46.

———, ed. *Ossian Revisited.* Edinburgh: Edinburgh University Press, 1991.

———, ed. *The Poems of Ossian and Related Works.* Edinburgh: Edinburgh University Press, 1996.

Gerrard, Christine. *The Patriot Opposition to Walpole: Politics, Poetry, and National Myth, 1725–1742.* Oxford: Clarendon Press, 1994.

Gray, Thomas. *Correspondence of Thomas Gray.* 3 vols. Edited by Paget Toynbee and Leonard Toynbee. Oxford: Clarendon Press, 1935.

Groom, Nick. "Celts, Goths, and the Nature of the Literary Source." In *Tradition in Transition: Women Writers, Marginal Texts, and the Eighteenth-Century Canon.* Edited by Alvaro Ribeiro S.J. and James G. Basker. Oxford: Clarendon Press, 1996, 275–96.

———. *The Making of Percy's "Reliques."* Oxford: Clarendon Press, 1999.

Hawes, Clement. "Johnson and Imperialism." In *The Cambridge Companion to Samuel Johnson.* Edited by Greg Clingham. Cambridge: Cambridge University Press, 1997 and 1999, 114–26.

Hechter, Michael. *Internal Colonialism: The Celtic Fringe in British National Development, 1536–1966.* Berkeley: University of California Press, 1975.

Hill, George Birkbeck, ed. *Johnsonian Miscellanies.* 2 vols. Oxford: Clarendon Press, 1897.

Hobsbawm, Eric, and Terence O. Ranger, eds. *The Invention of Tradition.* Cambridge: Cambridge University Press, 1983.

Hudson, Nicholas. Review of John Cannon's *Samuel Johnson and the Politics of Hanoverian England. AJ* 9 (1998): 337–47.

Hustvedt, Sigurd Bernhard. *Ballad Criticism in Scandanavia and Great Britain during the Eighteenth Century.* London: Humphrey Milford, 1916.

Johnson, Samuel. *Johnson on Shakespeare.* Edited by Arthur Sherbo. Vol. 7 of The Yale Edition of the Works of Samuel Johnson. New Haven and London: Yale University Press, 1968.

———. *A Journey to the Western Islands of Scotland.* Edited by Mary Lascelles. Vol. 9 of

The Yale Edition of the Works of Samuel Johnson. New Haven and London: Yale University Press, 1971.

------. *Letters of Samuel Johnson.* 5 vols. Edited by Bruce Redford. Princeton: Princeton University Press, 1992.

------. *Lives of the English Poets.* 3 vols. Edited by George Birkbeck Hill. Oxford: Clarendon Press, 1905.

------. *The Oxford Authors: Samuel Johnson.* Edited by Donald J. Greene. Oxford: Oxford University Press, 1984.

------. *Poems.* Edited by E. L. McAdam, Jr. and George Milne. Vol. 6 of The Yale Edition of the Works of Samuel Johnson. New Haven and London: Yale University Press, 1964.

------. *The Political Writings.* Edited by Donald J. Greene. Vol. 10 of The Yale Edition of the Works of Samuel Johnson. New Haven and London: Yale University Press, 1977.

------. Preface to *A Dictionary of the English Language.* In *The Oxford Authors: Samuel Johnson.* Edited by Donald J. Greene. Oxford: Oxford University Press, 1984.

------. Preface, *Gentleman's Magazine* 10 (1740): iii–iv.

------. *Rambler.* Edited by W. J. Bate and Albrecht B. Strauss. Vols. 3–5 of The Yale Edition of the Works of Samuel Johnson. New Haven and London: Yale University Press, 1969.

------. "The State of Affairs in *Lilliput*." *The Gentleman's Magazine* 8 (June 1738). Reprinted, London: Pickering and Chatto, 1998.

------. *The Works of Samuel Johnson, LL.D.* 11 vols. 1825; New York: AMS Press, 1970.

Kristmannson, Gauti. "Ossian: A Case of Celtic Tribalism or a Translation without an Original." In *Transfer: Übersetzen-Dolmetschen-Interkulturalität.* Sonderdruck: Peter Lang, 1997, 449–62.

Laing, Malcolm. *The History of Scotland.* London: 1800.

Macpherson, James. *The History of Great Britain from the Restoration to the Accession of the House of Hanover.* 2 vols. London: 1775.

Morgan, Gwendolyn A. "Percy, the Antiquarians, the Ballad, and the Middle Ages." *Studies in Medievalism* 7 (1995): 22–32.

Murphy, Peter T. "Fool's Gold: The Highland Treasures of Macpherson's Ossian." *ELH* 53, no. 3 (1986): 567–91.

O'Brien, Karen. "Johnson's View of the Scottish Enlightenment in *A Journey to the Western Islands of Scotland.*" *AJ* 4 (1991): 59–82.

O'Halloran, Clare. "Irish Re-Creation of the Gaelic Past: The Challenge of Macpherson's Ossian." *Past and Present* 124 (1989): 69–95.

Parker, G. F. *Johnson's Shakespeare.* Oxford: Clarendon Press, 1989.

Percy, Thomas. *The Hermit of Warkworth: A Northumberland Ballad in Three Fits or Cantos.* London: 1771.

Potkay, Adam. *The Fate of Eloquence in the Age of Hume.* Ithaca: Cornell University Press, 1994.

------. "Virtue and Manners in Macpherson's Poems of Ossian." *PMLA* 107, no. 1 (1992): 120–30.

Potter, Robert. *An Inquiry into Some Passages in Dr. Johnson's Lives of the Poets: Particularly His Observations on Lyric Poetry and the Odes of Gray.* London: 1783.

Ritson, Joseph. *Ancient Songs from the Time of King Henry the Third to the Revolution.* London: 1792.

Robbins, Bruce, and Pheng Cheah, eds. *Cosmopolitics: Thinking and Feeling beyond the Nation.* Minneapolis: University of Minnesota Press, 1998.

Shaw, William. *An Inquiry into the Authenticity of the Poems Ascribed to Ossian.* London: 1781.

Sher, Richard B." 'Those Scotch Imposters and Their Cabal': Ossian and the Scottish Enlightenment." *Man and Nature: Proceedings of the Canadian Society for Eighteenth-Century Studies* 1 (1982): 55–63.

Sorensen, Janet. "Peripheral Visions: Remaking the Map of British Cultural History." *The Eighteenth Century* 40, no. 1 (1999): 68–79.

Stafford, Fiona J., and Howard Gaskill, eds. *From Gaelic to Romantic: Ossianic Translations.* Amsterdam: Rodopi, 1998.

Tacitus, Publius Cornelius. *The Agricola and the Germanica.* Translated by H. Mattingly. Revised by S. A. Handford. London: Penguin, 1970.

Trumpener, Katie. *Bardic Nationalism: The Romantic Novel and the British Empire.* Princeton: Princeton University Press, 1997.

Weinbrot, Howard. *Britannia's Issue: The Rise of British Literature from Dryden to Ossian.* Cambridge: Cambridge University Press, 1993.

Multicultural Perspectives:
Johnson, Race, and Gender

JAMES G. BASKER

THERE IS A PASSAGE IN A LETTER OF HESTER THRALE PIOZZI THAT serves as a useful starting point for my topic. Writing from Bath in December 1789, five years after Johnson's death and five years into her marriage to the Italian singer Gabriel Piozzi, Mrs. Piozzi regales a friend in London with the latest gossip. Her tone is excited. She reports feeling "impatient to write upon a Subject which engrosses the Attention of everybody here":

> Bridge Tower the African Negro is that Subject, whose son plays so enchantingly upon the Violin as to extort Applause from the first Professors — while his Father amazes me a hundred Times more by the showy Elegance of his Address — the polished Brilliancy of his Language, the Accumulation and Variety of his Knowledge, and the interesting Situation in which he stands towards an Absent Wife; who born a Polish Woman of high Rank in her own Country, has been forcibly separated from him, who seems to run round the Globe with an Arrow in his Heart, and this astonishing Son by his Side. Was he sent hither by Providence to prove the Equality of Blacks to Whites I wonder, he would make a beautiful Figure at the Bar of the House of Commons; and charming Miss Williams will make such sweet Verses about him when they meet. . . . I want her to see what a Man may come to, tho' born a Slave, and educated for no higher Purpose. When She hears him talk of his Wife, She will be really quite melted: The Ladies here wept when he presented his Son so gracefully in the Orchestra at a Benefit — for the Comforts and Profits of which he yesterday returned publick Thanks in our Abbey Church, and afterwards received the Sacrament.

She proceeds to rattle off other celebrity news: applause for her husband's public concerts, the improved health of the actress Mrs. Siddons, the presence of the Cavalier Pindemonte from Europe and "a world of Foreigners beside." "But," she notes emphatically in closing, "the African carries off all the Applause — he is so very flashy a Talker, and has a Manner so distinguished for lofty Gayety, and universality of

64

Conversation I can but think all Day how Dr. Johnson would have adored that Man!"[1]

"*I can but think all Day how Dr. Johnson would have adored that Man*": Why would she suddenly connect this extraordinary black man with her memories of Samuel Johnson? Why, according to her account, such a persistent association, recurring again and again, of which she "can but think all Day"? Why would she imagine such an *intense* response from Johnson to this accomplished black man—Johnson "would have *adored* that man"? This intriguing little passage from Mrs. Piozzi's letter combines three qualities that converge in the topic of my essay. First, it approaches Johnson through the perspective of a woman, an intelligent and independent woman, and in this case a woman who, with the exception of his wife Tetty, probably knew Johnson better than any other. Second, it connects Johnson with black people, here an African man and his son whom he never actually met, who serve to remind us of Johnson's important relationships with blacks, from Frank Barber to Ignatius Sancho, as well as the anonymous millions he had in mind when he attacked slavery repeatedly over the course of his life. Third, as contemporary testimony, Mrs. Piozzi's letter suggests ways that documentary historical evidence may prove at least as valuable—in approaching the topic of Johnson, race, and gender—as modern critical theory, particularly in correcting some of the misconceptions and inherited prejudices about Johnson that still linger at the turn of the twenty-first century.

Images of Johnson the "Great Cham ["Khan"] of Literature" and Johnson the "Literary Dictator" still dominate not only the popular but, too often, the academic reputation of Johnson. At the turn of the millennium, Johnson continues to be conjured up as a symbol of misogyny, insensitivity to people of color, and other sins of patriarchal white male Eurocentrism. The new edition of *The Norton Anthology of Literature by Women*, for example, concludes its account of misogyny among eighteenth-century male writers this way: "Toward the end of the century, when Dr. Johnson compared a woman preacher to a dancing dog, or when he condemned portrait-painting as improper in women . . . he was assuming that creativity and femininity were contradictory terms."[2] The award-winning *Dictionary of British and American Women Writers, 1660–1800* sets Johnson up (on the first page of its introduction) as the spokesman for eighteenth-century antifeminists who, it is claimed, saw the emergence of women writers "as a threat to male hegemony."[3] Scholarship over the past two decades by Isobel Grundy, the late Donald Greene, Charmaine Wellington, Gae Annette Brack, Katharine Rogers, Marlene C. Hansen, Martine Watson Brownley, Claudia Thomas, Bonnie Hain, Carole McAllister, and Catherine Parke, among others, has worked to redress Johnson's undeserved reputation as a misogynist, but with only limited success, and that primarily in the small community of eighteenth-century scholars.[4] Knee-jerk invocations of Johnson the misogynist continue to appear in such influential literary publications as *The Women's Review of Books*, where a 1993 review of a book about women and nineteenth-century religion opened by citing yet again Johnson's remark about women preachers and dancing dogs.[5]

Similar myths and misconceptions persist about Johnson and race. It was one thing that a twentieth-century edition of the *Encyclopedia Britannica* (11th ed., 1910) could matter-of-factly state that Johnson was "opposed to the anti-slavery movement."[6] At least that error was eliminated in subsequent editions. It is another when the editors of *The New York Review of Books* allow a major author to make a comparable mistake in the 1990s. In reviewing a book called *The Earth Shall Weep: A History of Native America*, the accomplished writer Larry McMurtry gratuitously mentions "Dr. Johnson" as the paradigmatic enemy of Native American rights ("Dr. Johnson . . . wouldn't have been on [the Cherokee] Corn Tassel's side"), which, unfortunately, is exactly the opposite of Johnson's actual views on the European conquest of indigenous peoples in the Americas and elsewhere.[7] Some corrective letters to the editor followed, but even when McMurtry partially admitted his mistake a few weeks later, he seemed to dismiss Johnson's recorded moments of sympathy for people of color as minor exceptions to the "true" Johnson, derived from what "is still," in McMurtry's words, the "only . . . *great* book about him, Boswell's, in which the Tory Johnson is seen in all his glorious crankiness and complex greatness."[8] Such are the boilerplate images of Johnson, clung to even when challenged with concrete evidence in a public forum. Comparably misinformed and stereotypical views of Johnson on race and gender have appeared in various contexts, from scholarly books to poems and essays over the past few years.[9]

My central argument is that our understanding of Johnson on race and gender is hampered by not one, but *two* kinds of cultural forgetfulness (or is it selective memory?). We have forgotten or ignored the very ones of Johnson's own writings that would show him sympathetic to the condition of women, of African slaves, of Native Americans, of other groups of the poor and powerless. (Mr. McMurtry would be surprised and pleased to read *Idler* 81, in the voice of an American Indian, listed below.) We have also forgotten, or ceased to care about, the ways other people have read Johnson and responded to him in the past, many of them people whose views—as women, as feminists, as minorities, as abolitionists, as members of marginal or excluded groups—we are at pains to protect and promote in so many other contexts. This neglect, it could be argued, not only contributes to our distorted image of Johnson, but also amounts to a kind of double or compound suppression of these historically marginalized groups—an inadvertent tyranny of present-day voices and perspectives over those of nonelite readers in the past.

The balance of my essay therefore is devoted to two simple purposes. First, to look at a sampling of historic responses to Johnson that help us to "see" him through these historic perspectives, to get past our own modern or postmodern limitations and recover what he seemed to mean to earlier peoples whose views (in other contexts) we value. Second, to propose a short list of readings from Johnson—a mini-canon of "The Other Johnson"—that could best serve the interests and needs of the multicultural student bodies and readerships of the new millennium.

Let's start with women readers whom, as I have argued elsewhere, Johnson consciously regarded as part of his readership and who responded positively to Johnson from his own time down to the twentieth century.[10] What are we to make of an array of major women writers who found Johnson not intimidating or repulsive but supportive and encouraging—to the point that an almost cloying tradition emerged of referring to Johnson in terms of endearment. In various places in their private writings, Fanny Burney called him "my dear, dear Johnson"; Hannah More referred to him as "poor dear Johnson"; Jane Austen called him "my dear Johnson"; and George Eliot "dear old Johnson."[11] Writing of Boswell's *Life of Johnson*, Mary Shelley said: "it is the most amusing book in the world, beside that I do love the kind hearted[,] wise[,] and Gentle Bear [Johnson]—& think him as loveable a (Man) friend as a profound philosopher."[12] This, from Mary Shelley?—a radical, transgressive, even avant-garde writer whom many would regard as the very antithesis of Johnson. What efforts have we made to interpret, or even to remember, such a response from such a figure? Why is it generally Boswell's sound bite about women preachers and dancing dogs that we hear, that we allow to dominate the popular memory and the academic conversation? That *The Letters of Mrs. Piozzi* from which I quoted at the beginning of this essay only appeared within the past decade is a reminder that other writings and observations about Johnson by women remain un- or under-explored, among them materials by Elizabeth Carter, Letitia Hawkins, Lady Cornelia Knight, Hannah More, and Frances Reynolds that still lie buried in the collection assembled by Birkbeck Hill more than one hundred years ago (*Miscellanies*, 2).

The history of Johnson's women readers raises other questions. Do we remember that such a pillar of the feminist movement as Mary Wollstonecraft read Johnson with admiration? Indeed, quoted him approvingly in *A Vindication of the Rights of Woman* and elsewhere *defended* him from what she regarded as Boswell's lack of appreciation and respect?[13] Or that she included five pieces by Johnson in her book *The Female Reader* (1789), which has been called the first feminist anthology and which was widely used in female academies in the 1790s both in Britain and America? This in turn raises more questions, perhaps ultimately unanswerable but interesting nonetheless, about how ordinary female adolescents and young women read Johnson. What of another female anthology, *The Lady's Preceptor* (London, 1792), that included Johnson's letter to young "Susy" Thrale encouraging her to pursue her education diligently, a book that enjoyed a transatlantic readership as it was also republished in America in at least three further editions during the 1790s?[14] What of the many women who were reading Johnson in schools, in subscription libraries, in reading societies, in anthologies and magazines as the machinery and reach of print culture burgeoned in the eighteenth and nineteenth centuries? The multitude of these women's experiences as common readers is so hard to recover that one must settle for vivid examples: Boswell's fiancée Margaret Montgomerie reading the *Rambler* in 1769 while Boswell is away; Charlotte Forten, an American free black woman who in 1858 responded to what she called "Johnson's Boswell" as one of the "finest pen-and-ink portraits that I have ever known"; a nineteen-year-old Virginia belle who, according to her private journal, in 1863 tried to distract herself from the horrors of the Civil War by reading Johnson's *Rambler*; Louisa May Alcott's seventy-six-year-old mother reading Johnson while sewing in the 1870s; the writer Katherine Anne Porter in the 1930s in Paris turning, in her depression, to "Dr. Johnson, whom," she confesses, "I read for consolation as other painful souls read their Bible, or Homer, or Nietzsche, or Karl Marx."[15]

What, finally, of a feminist reader like Virginia Woolf, who expressed her admiration for Johnson in so many places, as a critic, as an enemy to social pretense, and as a kind of oracle from whom (she wrote in *Orlando*) "rolled out the most magnificent phrases that have ever left human lips."[16] Most striking of all is Woolf's presentation of Johnson as the spokesman for an enlightened view of the intellectual capabilities of women. "Are [women] capable of education or incapable?" she asked rhetorically in one of her most influential works: "Napoleon thought them incapable. Dr. Johnson thought the opposite."[17] Why is it we so seldom hear this passage from *A Room of One's Own*, rather than the tired old bit about dancing dogs? From Wollstonecraft in the eighteenth century to Woolf in the twentieth, we have a lot to do to recover and explain such readings of Johnson, and to integrate them into our understanding of gender and literature.

One could point to comparable examples of historic readings of Johnson in the context of race. Eighteenth-century apologists for slavery clearly read Johnson as their enemy, especially after he published *Taxation No Tyranny* (1775) with its call for the emancipation of American slaves. Their private records show that Jefferson, Washington, Adams, and other revolutionary Americans read Johnson's pamphlet with varying degrees of alarm and anger; several newspapers and pro-American pamphleteers attacked Johnson's emancipation proposal as a bloody strategy to induce the slaves to rise up and murder their masters in their beds.[18] Even the phlegmatic Benjamin Franklin, normally unsympathetic to slaveholders, reacted violently to Johnson's call for emancipation. Franklin denounced Johnson for recommending a measure that would lead to "an Insurrection among the Blacks" and "excite the Domestic Slaves . . . to cut their Masters' Throats."[19] Similarly, few of us seem to have noticed the fervor with which James Boswell read and reacted to Johnson's antislavery ideas. Boswell, who published a pamphlet in defense of the slave trade before he finished the *Life of Johnson*, felt compelled to editorialize at length against Johnson's fierce opposition (what Boswell calls "zeal without knowledge") to slavery.[20] Having dutifully presented a summary of Johnson's views, Boswell tries to rebut them, entering what he calls a "most solemn protest against his general doctrine with respect to the *Slave Trade*" and dismissing Johnson's "unfavourable opinion of it [as] owing to prejudice, and imperfect or false information" (*Life*, 3:200–204). Significantly, this passage marks Boswell's boldest disagreement with Johnson anywhere in the *Life*.

Conversely, the abolitionists read Johnson as their ally. In the dedication to his monumental treatise against racism, *On the Cultural Achievements of Negroes* (1808), the Abbé Henri Gregoire lists Samuel Johnson among the dedicatees, "those men who have had the courage to plead the cause of the unhappy blacks . . . in order to relieve the sufferings of the slaves and to free them."[21] Thus Johnson's name is included in a group that also includes the more familiar abolitionist heroes Anthony Benezet, Granville Sharp, Thomas Clarkson, and William Wilberforce. In the 1820s, British abolitionists quoted Johnson as they campaigned to end slavery in the colonies; in the 1840s the American abolitionist Lydia Maria Child noted Johnson's antislavery views and Boswell's defensive response in an article for *The National Anti-Slavery Standard*; and in the late 1850s a Philadelphia abolitionist pamphlet was quoting Johnson among those whose works leant moral authority to the antislavery cause.[22] Most dramatically, on 4 June 1860, in a speech in the U.S. Senate about free states versus slave states, the abolitionist Charles Sumner invoked "the great English moralist, Dr. Johnson" to quote his scathing opinion of "Slave-Masters." (The speech was also published, under the title "The Barbarism of Slavery.") Five years later, Sumner would again quote Johnson on slavery in a speech he made in the U.S. Senate, this time to denounce the legacy of the Dred Scott decision.[23]

Among blacks themselves, Johnson has had admirers from Francis Barber (who named a son after Johnson) and Joseph Knight (the former slave who gained his freedom in Scotland partly with Johnson's help) and Ignatius Sancho (of whom Johnson was once rumored to be writing a biography) in the eighteenth century, to William Wells Brown in the nineteenth, and Stanley Braithwaite and Henry Louis Gates, Jr. in the twentieth.[24] Most interesting are the young African-American and Afro-Caribbean novelists in the 1990s such as Darryl Pinckney (*High Cotton*, 1992) and Caryl Phillips (unpublished talk, Barnard College, March 1997) who are rediscovering Johnson's enlightened ideas about race through his relationship with Francis Barber. Others such as Gretchen Gerzina and S. I. Martin are bringing Johnsonian London under close scrutiny from a black perspective. Gerzina's breakthrough book, *Black London* (1995), provides the most coherent and insightful account yet of Johnson's relationship with Frank Barber, while also setting the antislavery ideas of Johnson and other whites against the reality of black experience.[25] In his recent novel *Incomparable World*, Martin explores the underworld of blacks in 1780s London, devoting a full episode to Francis Barber, who is rather despised by other blacks, in part for living ostentatiously off his inheritance from Johnson.[26]

Readings of Johnson as an advocate for people of color turn up in surprising places, as my own classroom experience has shown me. Several Navajo Indian high school students (from the Tuba City, Arizona, reservation school) read Johnson with me in a summer school at Oxford University in 1991 and 1992. Understandably, they reacted with great enthusiasm to *Idler* 81, written in the voice of an Indian chief who systematically denounces the European conquest of America. By the end of his speech, Johnson's Chief is condoning violent resistance: "remember that the death of every European delivers the country from a tyrant and a robber." As one of the Navajo students said, "I never knew there were any Anglos [people of European descent] back then who thought this way at all."[27] Given the dearth of awareness both in the academy and among the general public, he could hardly have been expected to.

His response brings me to the final section of my essay: a modest proposal for some dozen or so readings that might make up "The Other Johnson." The pieces I list below are not among the more familiar of Johnson's writings, which is quite understandable, given how infrequently they appear. They are rarely anthologized. The current edition of *The Norton Anthology of English Literature* (5th ed., 1986) prints one; the more recent *Longman Anthology of British Literature* (1999) includes only two.[28] More specialized collections are no better. The period anthology *British Literature 1640–1789* (Blackwell, 1996) includes none of the selected Johnson pieces on race and gender, and the long-running Penguin paperback *Samuel Johnson: Selected Writings* (in print since 1968) contains only one.[29] In no anthology or selected edition of Johnson can one find as many as six of these writings printed together, and three of the listed works are not even included in the definitive Yale Edition of the Works of Samuel Johnson (begun in 1958) as published thus far.[30]

Yet the need for them was never greater. Teachers, students, and general readers alike are making new demands of canonical writers, framed by such issues as race and gender. Precisely because Johnson's reputation has such a powerful aura of white male Eurocentric authority, his writings, more than those of long-familiar radical writers such as Blake and Wollstonecraft, or those of the many recently recovered eighteenth-century women and minority writers, hold sharp surprises and serious challenges for twenty-first-century readers. How many would expect Johnson, as early as 1740, to pause to describe a community of Caribbean maroons ("Symerons, or fugitive Negroes, who, having escaped from the tyranny of their masters in great numbers, had settled themselves under two kings, or leaders"), and to applaud them for having "not only asserted their natural rights to liberty and independence, but endeavoured to revenge the cruelties they had suffered" by attacking the slaveholding Spanish colonies from which they had escaped?[31] How many would have any inkling that in 1759, Johnson systematically denounced the Portuguese not only for conquering Africa and starting the slave trade, but for holding such racist views of Africans that "they scarcely considered them as distinct from beasts." Or that Johnson linked their attitude to that evident in his own time among his fellow Englishmen: "The practice of all the European nations, and among others of the English barbarians that cultivate the southern islands of America proves, that this opinion, however absurd and foolish, however wicked and injurious, still continues to prevail." Or that Johnson would broaden his indictment to attack the whole thrust of European imperialism: "The Europeans have scarcely visited any coast, but to gratify avarice, and extend corruption; to arrogate dominion without right, and practise cruelty without incentive."[32] Or that in drafting an abolitionist legal brief in 1777 on behalf of the slave Joseph Knight (ten years before the Abolition Society was founded), Johnson could expound such radical views as: "no man is by nature the property of another," "men in their original condition were equal," and "it is to be lamented that moral right should ever give way to political convenience" (*Life*, 3:202–3). Yet this is the Johnson to be found in these writings.

Johnson on gender can be equally startling. His female character Generosa complains of sexist male attitudes in terms that might touch a chord with women in some settings today: "The world seems to have formed an universal conspiracy against our understandings; our questions are supposed not to expect answers, our arguments are confuted with a jest, and we are treated like beings who transgress the limits of our nature whenever we aspire to seriousness or improvement" (*Rambler* 126, 4:310). His depiction of Victoria, the beauty who is ruined by smallpox, dramatizes a timeless feminist truth, what Johnson terms the "calamitous" vulnerability "of a young woman who has never thought or heard of any other excellence than beauty" (*Rambler* 133, 4:342). (Mary Wollstonecraft recognized the force of the story and included it in her feminist anthology *The Female Reader* in 1789.) Elsewhere his sympathy for the condition of women is coupled with a raging anger at males who exploit and abuse them, as in the story of Misella, who is entrapped, raped, and discarded not by a street criminal but by a prosperous middle-class family man. Johnson is at pains to condemn even such powerful and socially protected male predators as "Reptiles whom their own servants would have despised" (*Rambler* 170, 5:139). In another essay, Johnson deploys the language of prostitution—daughters who feel "tricked out for sale"—to expose the excesses of the marriage market to which society subjects young women (*Idler* 42, 2:133). As these quotations suggest, the Johnson to be found in these writings is much more the proto-feminist friend of Wollstonecraft and Woolf than the misogynist bogeyman trotted out by *The Norton Anthology of Literature by Women*.

In a few instances these texts also generate moments of intriguing cross-connection between questions of race and gender. For all the vehemence of his language in denouncing the conquest of Africa and the rise of the slave trade, for example, Johnson clearly did not see the subject as inappropriate for women readers: he is known to have presented a copy of *The World Displayed* as a gift to Joshua Reynolds's niece Mary Palmer.[33] Did Johnson sense that slavery was a subject of particular interest to women? In the case of Joseph Knight, which Johnson followed so closely, he undoubtedly knew (as the newspapers reported) that women flocked to the courtroom to hear the lawyers' arguments and wept publicly when the slave was freed. Was Johnson's interest in that case deepened in some way by his awareness that Joseph Knight, like his own beloved Frank Barber, was married to a white woman and had mixed-race children, with all the further trouble that might bring? (Late in life Johnson took Barber and his wife, when they were struggling, back into his house to live, and he defended them from the racist jibes their interracial marriage attracted.) And after all, how were Johnson's views on race informed or elaborated over time through his friendship with Hester Thrale, whose diaries reveal both her abiding hatred of slavery and, as I noted at the beginning of this essay, her sense of Johnson's deep investment in the subject of race?

The "Other Johnson" writings listed below do not pretend to offer a comprehensive view of Johnson, nor do they exhaust by any means the relevant material in his life and writings. But they do give us a useful starting point to pursue such questions. More fundamentally, they offer a necessary elaboration and enrichment of our understanding of Johnson, and some inviting avenues of connection for the increasingly diverse readerships of the twenty-first century.

APPENDIX
"Johnson, Race, and Gender":
Readings for "The Other Johnson"

On Race:

1. "The Life of Francis Drake" (1740) [excerpts]—particularly those passages in which Johnson describes the maroons of sixteenth-century Central America and the Caribbean, defends their attacks on Europeans and comments on their natural rights.
2. *Idler* 81 (3 November 1759)—a fictionalized monologue in the voice of a Native American chief, condemning the European conquest and atrocities, and calling for violent resistance.
3. Introduction to *The World Displayed* (1759)—essay condemning the fifteenth-century European conquest of Africa, the beginnings of the slave trade, and subsequent progress of European imperialism.
4. Letter to Francis Barber at boarding school (25 September 1770)—in which Johnson unconsciously reveals his assumptions about black intellectual capabilities in his expectations of Frank: "Let me know what English books you read for your entertainment. You can never be wise unless you love reading."
5. *Taxation No Tyranny* (1775) (excerpts)—the passages in which Johnson calls for the emancipation of the slaves and indicts the hypocrisy of American "drivers of Negroes" clamoring for liberty.
6. Legal brief for the Joseph Knight case in Scotland (1777)—printed in Boswell's *Life of Johnson*; Johnson's short but potent argument on

behalf of a slave seeking manumission before the Court of Session in Edinburgh.

On Gender:

1. *Rambler* 126 — Johnson creates three female voices, including "Generosa" who offers a sharp critique of male condescension toward female intelligence.
2. *Rambler* 130 and 133 — "Victoria" tells her story, of a beauty whose ruin reveals the sexist nature of society and the vulnerability of women conditioned to value only physical beauty, a story Wollstonecraft included in her feminist anthology *The Female Reader* (1789).
3. *Rambler* 170 and 171 — "Misella's" story of rape and betrayal by her guardian exposes the ugliness of male codes of sexual predation, compounded by inequalities of age and class.
4. *Rambler* 191 — fifteen-year-old "Bellaria" reveals, in her adolescent silliness, the emptiness and danger of middle-class social conventions for females.
5. *Idler* 42 — "Perdita" protests her boorish father's control of her in the marriage market, exposing her to the drunkenness and lechery of his friends, making her feel "tricked out for sale" as if she were a prostitute.

NOTES

1. Hester Lynch Piozzi to the Reverend Leonard Chappelow, 7 December 1789, *The Piozzi Letters: Correspondence of Hester Lynch Piozzi, 1784–1821*, ed. Edward A. Bloom and Lillian D. Bloom, 6 vols. (Newark: University of Delaware Press, 1989), 1:330–31.

2. Sandra M. Gilbert and Susan Gubar, *The Norton Anthology of Literature by Women: The Traditions in English*, 2nd ed. (New York: Norton, 1996), 75. The passage is unchanged from the first edition (1985).

3. Introduction, *A Dictionary of British and American Women Writers, 1660–1800*, ed. Janet Todd (Totowa, N.J., Rowman and Allanheld, 1985; revised ed., Rowman and Littlefield, 1987), 1.

4. For bibliographical details of these studies, see *Johnson and Gender*, ed. Charles Hinnant, a special issue of *South Central Review*, 9, no. 4 (winter 1992) and Basker, "Dancing Dogs, Women Preachers and the Myth of Johnson's Misogyny," *AJ* 3 (1990): 90 n. 47.

5. See Elizabeth Langland, "Sin and Sensibility" (a review of Christine L. Krueger, *The Reader's Repentance: Women Preachers, Women Writers, and Nineteenth-Century Discourse*), *The Women's Review of Books* 10 (September 1993): 23.

6. In "Edward Gibbon," vol. 11 of the *The Encyclopedia Britannica*, 11th ed., 32 vols. (New York, 1910).

7. Larry McMurtry, review of *The Earth Shall Weep: A History of Native America* by James Wilson, *The New York Review of Books* 46, no. 7 (22 April, 1999): 24–27.

8. Larry McMurtry, reply to Lawrence Ladin, "What Would Dr. Johnson Think?" in *The New York Review of Books* 46, no. 11 (24 June 1999): 81–82.

9. See John Mullan, *Sentiment and Sociability: The Language of Feeling in the Eighteenth Century* (Oxford: Clarendon Press, 1988), 97–98, where he argues that Johnson is among those who make "the female a metaphor of the misreader"; Adrienne Rich, "Snapshots of a Daughter-in-Law," *The Fact of a Doorframe: Poems Selected and New, 1950–1984* (New York: Norton, 1984), 38; Cynthia Ozick, "Women and Creativity: The Demise of the Dancing Dog," in *Women in Sexist Society: Studies in Power and Powerlessness*, ed. Vivian Gornick and Barbara K. Moran (New York: Basic Books, 1971); and, for a discussion of these and other examples, Basker, "Myth Upon Myth: Johnson, Gender, and the Misogyny Question," *AJ* 8 (1997): 175–87. McMurtry's clinging to a certain "Tory" image of Johnson even in the face of contrary evidence is not unusual. The first response to a paper I presented on "Samuel Johnson as Abolitionist" to the Johnsonian Society of Southern California in Los Angeles on 7 December 1997, was from a distinguished senior scholar of the eighteenth century who remarked—without offering a single bit of evidence—"You have made an interesting case for Johnson as an abolitionist, but still isn't it widely known that he held racist views about the inferiority of non-whites?"

10. See Basker, "Dancing Dogs, Women Preachers and the Myth of Johnson's Misogyny."

11. See *Dr. Johnson and Fanny Burney*, ed. Chauncey Brewster Tinker (New York: Moffat, Yard, 1911), 113; "Anecdotes by Hannah More," in *Miscellanies*, 2:203, 207; *Jane Austen's Letters to Her Sister Cassandra and Others*, ed. R. W. Chapman (Oxford: Oxford University Press, 1932; reprinted 1979), 181; George Eliot, *Selections from George Eliot's Letters*, ed. Gordon S. Haight (New Haven: Yale University Press, 1958), 416.

12. *The Letters of Mary Wollstonecraft Shelley*, ed. Betty T. Bennett, 3 vols. (Baltimore: Johns Hopkins University Press, 1983), 2:223.

13. For a detailed treatment of Wollstonecraft's lifelong admiration for Johnson, see Basker, "Radical Affinities: Mary Wollstonecraft and Samuel Johnson," *Tradition in Transition: Women Writers, Marginal Texts, and the Eighteenth-Century Canon*, ed. Alvaro Ribeiro S.J. and James G. Basker (Oxford: Clarendon Press, 1996), 41–55.

14. *The Lady's Preceptor* (London, 1792) had at least three American editions: Philadelphia 1794, New York 1794, and Boston 1798.

15. Margaret Montgomerie to James Boswell, 17 October 1769, *Boswell in Search of a Wife: 1766–1769*, ed. Frank Brady and Frederick Pottle (New York: McGraw-Hill, 1956), 334–37; *The Journal of Charlotte Forten, A Free Negro in the Slave Era*, ed. Ray Allen Billington (London: Collier Books, 1969), 115; *Lucy Breckinridge of Grove Hill: The Journal of a Virginia Girl, 1862–1864*, ed. Mary D. Robertson (Kent, Ohio: Kent State University Press, 1979), 153 and passim; entry for "January-February 1877," *The Journals of Louisa May Alcott (1832–1888)*, ed. Joel Myerson et al. (Boston: Little Brown, 1989), 204; *Letters of Katherine Anne Porter*, ed. Isabel Bayley (New York: Atlantic Monthly, 1990), 99.

16. See Woolf's comments in "Coleridge as Critic," *TLS*, 7 February 1918, reprinted in *Books and Portraits* (London: Triad/Granada, 1979), 31–34; "Dr. Burney's Dinner Party," *The Common Reader: Second Series* (London: Hogarth Press, 1932); and *Orlando* (London, 1928; reprinted Harcourt Brace Jovanovich, n.d.), 223.

17. Virginia Woolf, *A Room of One's Own* (London: Hogarth Press, 1929), 30.

18. See *An Answer to . . . Taxation No Tyranny* (London, 1775), quoted in the *Gentleman's Magazine* for April 1775, and *Letters . . . in Reply to "Taxation No Tyranny"* (London, 1775), quoted in *The [London] Gazette* (19 September 1776).

19. Benjamin Franklin to Jonathan Shipley, 7 July 1775, *The Papers of Benjamin Franklin*, ed. William B. Willcox et al. (New Haven: Yale University Press, 1982), 22:97.

20. James Boswell, *No Abolition of Slavery; or the Universal Empire of Love* (London, 1791).

21. See Henri Gregoire, *On the Cultural Achievements of Negroes*, trans. Thomas Cassirer and Jean-François Brière (Amherst: University of Massachusetts Press, 1996), 1–2. Interestingly, Gregoire's credit to Johnson as an antislavery writer seems to have been deliberately suppressed from the first edition in English, perhaps in accordance with the translator's politics. Johnson's is among the names omitted from the dedication as printed in *An Enquiry concerning the Intellectual and Moral Faculties, and Literature of Negroes* (Brooklyn, N.Y., 1810), translated by the Irish-American David Bailie Warden. Warden participated in the failed Irish Revolution of 1798, was banished forever from British territory, emigrated to America, and by 1810 was serving as American consul in Paris.

22. Lydia Maria Child, "Letters from New York — No. 30," *The National Anti-Slavery Standard* 3, no. 5 (7 July 1842): 19, reprinted as Letter 23 in *Letters from New York* (New York, 1843; reprinted, Athens: University of Georgia Press, 1998), 101; *Views of American Slavery, Taken a Century Ago* (Philadelphia: Association of Friends for the Diffusion of Religious and Useful Knowledge, 1858), 118.

23. "The Barbarism of Slavery," *The Works of Charles Sumner*, 15 vols. (Boston: Lee and Shepard, 1875–83), 5:53; "No Bust for Author of Dred Scott Decision" (23 February 1865 speech on a bill to erect a bust in honor of the late Chief Justice Taney), 9:291.

24. For an account of Johnson's involvement on behalf of Joseph Knight, see Basker, "Samuel Johnson and the African-American Reader," *The New Rambler* (1994–95): 52–55; *Letters of the Late Ignatius Sancho, An African*, ed. Vincent Carretta (New York: Penguin, 1998), 119 and 248 n. 1; William Wells Brown to William Lloyd Garrison, 12 November 1857, printed in *The Mind of the Negro As Reflected in Letters Written During the Crisis 1800–1860*, ed. Carter G. Woodson (Washington, D.C.: The Association for the Study of Negro Life and History, Inc., n.d.), 383; William Stanley Braithwaite, *The Book of Georgian Verse* (London: Grant Richards, 1909), 1270–71; Henry Louis Gates, Jr., "Let Them Talk," *The New Republic* (27 September, 1993): 38.

25. Gretchen Gerzina, *Black London: Life before Emancipation* (New Brunswick, N.J.: Rutgers University Press, 1995), 43–54 and passim.

26. S. I. Martin, *Incomparable World* (London: Quartet Books, 1996; republished New York: George Braziller, 1998), 154–63.

27. For details see Basker, "An Eighteenth-Century Critique of Eurocentrism: Samuel Johnson and the Plight of Native Americans," *La Grande-Bretagne et l'Europe des Lumières*, ed. Serge Soupel (Paris: Sorbonne, 1996), 207–8, 220.

28. M. H. Abrams et al., eds., *The Norton Anthology of English Literature*, 5th ed. (New York: Norton, 1986). The piece included is Johnson's "Brief to Free a Slave" (1:2391–92). That it was included in this edition after not having appeared in the preceding four, dating back to 1962, perhaps signals a new editorial direction. See also David Damrosch, Stuart Sherman, et al., eds., *The Longman Anthology of British Literature* (New York: Longman, 1999), which includes two, the pair of *Rambler* essays about Misella (1:2711–16).

29. Robert DeMaria, Jr., ed., *British Literature, 1640–1789: An Anthology* (Oxford: Blackwell, 1996); *Samuel Johnson: Selected Writings*, ed. Patrick Cruttwell (London: Penguin English Library, 1968; reprinted Penguin Classics, 1986). The Oxford one-volume *Samuel Johnson*, ed. Donald J. Greene (Oxford: Oxford University Press, 1984) is more helpful, but even it includes only four of these writings on race and gender (*Ramblers* 170, 171, and 191, and *Idler* 81).

30. The three are the "Life of Drake," the introduction to *The World Displayed*, and the legal brief on behalf of the slave Joseph Knight, all apparently intended for inclusion in the several volumes still in preparation for the Yale edition.

31. Johnson, "Life of Sir Francis Drake," *Gentleman's Magazine* (1740), quoted here from *The Works of Johnson*, 12 vols. (London, 1823), 6:313–14.

32. Introduction to *The World Displayed* (1759), reprinted in *Samuel Johnson's Prefaces and Dedications*, ed. Allen T. Hazen (New Haven: Yale University Press, 1937), 227–28.

33. Hazen, *Johnson's Prefaces and Dedications*, 219.

BIBLIOGRAPHY

Alcott, Louisa May. *The Journals of Louisa May Alcott (1832–1888)*. Edited by Joel Myerson et al. Boston: Little Brown, 1989.

M. H. Abrams et al., eds. *Norton Anthology of English Literature*. 5th ed. New York: Norton, 1986.

Austen, Jane. *Jane Austen's Letters to her Sister Cassandra and Others*. Edited by R. W. Chapman. Oxford: Oxford University Press, 1932. Reprinted 1979.

Basker, James G. "Dancing Dogs, Women Preachers and the Myth of Johnson's Misogyny." *AJ* 3 (1990): 63–90.

Boswell, James. *Boswell's Life of Johnson*. 6 vols. Edited by George Birkbeck Hill. Revised by L. F. Powell. Oxford: Clarendon Press, 1934–64.

———. *No Abolition of Slavery; or the Universal Empire of Love*. London: 1791.

Brady, Frank, and Frederick Pottle, eds. *Boswell in Search of a Wife: 1766–1769*. New York: McGraw Hill, 1956.

Braithwaite, Stanley. *The Book of Georgian Verse*. London: Grant Richards, 1909.

Breckinridge, Lucy. *Lucy Breckinridge of Grove Hill: The Journal of a Virginia Girl, 1862–1864*. Edited by Mary D. Robertson. Kent, Ohio: Kent State University Press, 1979.

Brown, William Wells. Letters to William Lloyd Garrison. In *The Mind of the Negro As Reflected in Letters Written During the Crisis, 1800–1860*.

Child, Lydia Maria. "Letters from New York—No. 30." *The National Anti-Slavery Standard* 3, no. 5 (7 July 1842): 19.

David Damrosch, Stuart Sherman, et al., eds. *Longman Anthology of British Literature*. New York: Longman, 1999.

DeMaria, Jr., Robert, ed. *British Literature 1640–1789*. Oxford: Blackwell, 1996.

Encyclopedia Britannica. 11th ed. 32 vols. New York: 1910.

Forten, Charlotte. *The Journal of Charlotte Forten, A Free Negro in the Slave Era*. Edited by Ray Allen Billington. London: Collier Books, 1969.

Franklin, Benjamin. *The Papers of Benjamin Franklin*. Edited by William B. Willcox et al. New Haven: Yale University Press, 1959–.

Gates, Jr., Henry Louis, "Let Them Talk." In *The New Republic* (27 September 1993): 38.

Gerzina, Gretchen. *Black London: Life before Emancipation*. New Brunswick, N.J.: Rutgers University Press, 1995.

Gilbert, Sandra M., and Susan Gubar, eds. *The Norton Anthology of Literature by Women: The Traditions in English*. 2nd ed. New York: Norton, 1996.

Gregoire, Henri. *On the Cultural Achievements of Negroes*. Translated by Thomas Cassirer and Jean-François Brière. Amherst: University of Massachusetts Press, 1996.

Hazen, Allen T., ed. *Samuel Johnson's Prefaces and Dedications*. New Haven: Yale University Press, 1937.

Hill, George Birkbeck, ed. *Johnsonian Miscellanies*. 2 vols. Oxford: Clarendon Press, 1897.

Johnson, Samuel. *The Idler and the Adventurer*. Edited by W. J. Bate, J. M. Bullitt, and L. F. Powell. Vol. 14 of The Yale Edition of the Works of Samuel Johnson. New Haven and London: Yale University Press, 1963.

———. *Political Writings*. Edited by Donald J. Greene. Vol. 10 of The Yale Edition of the Works of Samuel Johnson. New Haven and London: Yale University Press, 1977.

———. *Rambler*. Edited by W. J. Bate and Albrecht B. Strauss. Vols. 3–5 of The Yale Edition of the Works of Samuel Johnson. New Haven: Yale University Press, 1969.

———. *Samuel Johnson: Selected Writings*. Edited by Patrick Cruttwell. London: Penguin English Library, 1968; reprinted, Penguin Classics, 1986.

———. *The Works of Johnson*. 12 vols. Edited by Alexander Chalmers. London: 1823.

Lady's Preceptor, The. London: 1792.

Langland, Elizabeth. "Sin and Sensibility." In *The Women's Review of Books* 10 (September 1993): 23.

Martin, S. I. *Incomparable World*. London: Quartet Books, 1996; New York: George Braziller, 1998.

McMurtry, Larry. Review of James Wilson, *The Earth Shall Weep: A History of Native America*. *The New York Review of Books* 46, no. 7 (22 April 1999): 24–27.

———. "What Would Dr. Johnson Think?" *The New York Review of Books* 46, no. 11 (24 June 1999): 81–82.

Phillips, Caryl. Unpublished talk. Barnard College, Columbia University, March 1997.

Pinckney, Darryl. *High Cotton*. New York: Penguin, 1992.

Piozzi, Hester Lynch. *The Piozzi Letters: Correspondence of Hester Lynch Piozzi, 1784–1821*. 6 vols. Edited by Edward A. Bloom and Lillian D. Bloom. Newark: University of Delaware Press, 1989.

Porter, Katherine Anne. *Letters of Katherine Anne Porter*. Edited by Isabel Bayley. New York: Atlantic Monthly, 1990.

Sancho, Ignatius. *Letters of the Late Ignatius Sancho*. Edited by Vincent Carretta. New York: Penguin, 1998.

Sumner, Charles. *The Works of Charles Sumner*. 15 vols. Boston: Lee and Shepard, 1875–83.

Todd, Janet, ed. *A Dictionary of British and American Women Writers, 1600–1800*. Totowa, N.J.: Rowman and Littlefield, 1987.

Views of American Slavery, Taken a Century Ago. Philadelphia: Association of Friends for the Diffusion of Religious and Useful Knowledge, 1858.

Wollstonecraft (Shelley), Mary. *The Female Reader*. London: 1789.

———. *The Letters of Mary Wollstonecraft Shelley*. 3 vols. Edited by Betty T. Bennett. Baltimore: Johns Hopkins University Press, 1983.

————. *A Vindication of the Rights of Woman*. London: 1792.

Woolf, Virginia. *Books and Portraits*. London: Triad/Granada, 1979.

————. *The Common Reader: Second Series*. London: Hogarth Press, 1932.

————. *Orlando*. London: Hogarth Press, 1928.

————. *A Room of One's Own*. London: Hogarth Press, 1929.

The Unnarrated Life: Samuel Johnson, Female Friendship, and the Rise of the Novel Revisited

JACLYN GELLER

DISCUSSIONS OF SAMUEL JOHNSON'S RELATIONSHIP TO THE EIGH-
teenth-century novel often entail an anecdote from Boswell's *Life of
Johnson*. In 1768, Johnson reportedly distinguished between Fielding's
broad, satirical style and Richardson's pious realism with the image of
a clock, stating that there was as great a difference between the two
authors "as between a man who knew how a watch was made, and a
man who could tell the hour by looking on the dial plate" (*Life*, 2:49).
For many historians of the novel, this image has come to neatly represent the Fielding/Richardson binary. A relatively little known fact reported by Richardson himself is that the original compliment was not
to him or his rival but to another novelist altogether, Henry Fielding's
sister Sarah. Years earlier Johnson had used the metaphor of a watch
to symbolize the human heart, praising Sarah Fielding's prose as that
of an author who understood "the finer springs and movements of the
inside."[1] In later dialogue with Boswell, and/or in Boswell's subsequent
account, the focus of Johnson's praise shifted to the eighteenth-century
novel's most celebrated practitioner, Samuel Richardson.

This minute incident—the burial of Johnson's praise of Sarah Fielding—demonstrates a few larger tendencies that seem worth noting in a
discussion of Johnson at the millennium. It exemplifies the process of
canon formation which has resulted in misrepresentative histories of the
novel that omit female authorship and have until fairly recently dominated critical discussions of eighteenth-century fiction. It reminds us of
the scholarly tendency to rely on Boswell's totemic account at the expense of the rich biographical material generated by Johnson's female
associates, and sometimes at the expense of Johnson's own corpus.
Boswell's alteration of the original compliment also suggests the obfuscation of Johnson's relationship to the community of eighteenth-century female practitioners of the novel in England. Johnson's active
promotion of these authors—Isobel Grundy calls it "patronage"—has
only recently received critical attention. Its long-standing omission

probably has multiple causes, but the myth of Johnson the intractable patriarch seems to begin in 1791 with Boswell's memorialization of his mentor as a late Augustan, a coterie man, a misogynistic figure of conversational omnipotence. It continues to the present day with angry feminist responses to Boswell's masculinist history rather than Johnson's work itself.[2] Boswell's stylized portrait of a clubbish male world continues to fuel our image of a gender-stratified eighteenth-century writing culture whose social conditions produced a schism in literary consciousness. A brief glance at Johnson's unnarrated life complicates the picture considerably, demonstrating a far more integrated, mutually supportive, and cooperative community of male and female authors than many contemporary scholars have imagined. As this world comes into focus and we observe male-female friendship, coauthorship, study, sponsorship, mutual influence, and male mentorship of nascent female writers in the eighteenth century, our notion of a canon that separates neatly along lines of genre or gender—what Blanford Parker has called the "too rigorous distinction between the prose and poetic genres of the period"[3]—begins to break down. And the novel, always a popular genre, recently claimed as a female genre, appears to intertwine deeply with the more established genres produced by male authors like Johnson: formal satire, essays, and history.[4]

It is in some ways difficult to disabuse ourselves of the notion of gender segregation and utter female subordination in the eighteenth century. To do so entails relinquishing our view of an inexorably progressive feminist history, a perspective that highlights the enlightened tendencies of our own ages. Boswell's *Life of Johnson* has proven most useful in the imposition of such a teleological history upon the period. That this text is skewed against women and dismissive of Johnson's female acquaintances is not news. In explaining Boswell's antifemale bias, critics have tended to psychologize the text, citing Boswell's personal sexism,[5] his sexual excesses,[6] and his hostility toward Hester Thrale Piozzi. Various biographers throughout the twentieth century have understood Boswell's animosity toward Piozzi as the product of a feud between competing friends who were also competing memoirists.[7] (Annette Wheeler Cafarelli, however, has discussed Boswell's animus as part of a larger pattern of sexist behavior that entailed discrediting the more high-powered, intellectual woman of Johnson's circle.)[8]

More important than Boswell's psychosexual makeup, I believe, are the literary designs of the *Life of Johnson*. Boswell's sexism, which has over time fueled popular notions of Johnsonian misogyny, is related to the former's satirical bent.[9] Boswell's project goes well beyond the general masculinizing of Johnson that Wheeler Cafarelli discusses at length. Boswell's protagonist is not merely, in Cafarelli's words, "a man's man."[10] He is a verbal combatant who deploys satiric energy with laser-like precision, exposing the motives of those around him or curbing their excesses with his own common sense. Boswell's dedication memorializes Johnson as "that great man," "the grand composition," "the literary Colossus," and, "the most invulnerable man he [Joshua Reynolds] knew" (*Life*, 1:2). One of the chief pleasures of the *Life of Johnson* is its shaping of this larger-than-life Augustan and its emphasis on the exquisite tone of Johnson's superiority as he deftly uncovers the self interest and misprisions of his contemporaries. Never the dupe of fancy, Boswell's Johnson stands apart from the crowd, distinguished from his peers by the quality of judgment. Whether the symptom is deference to random authority ("Men will submit to any rule, by which they may be exempted from the tyranny of caprice and of chance" [1:365]), chronic mental imprecision which conflates opinion and fact ("Some men relate what they think, as what they know" [3:229]), or inflated self-esteem ("There is nothing more likely to betray a man into absurdity than *condescension*" [4:3]), Johnson is quick to isolate and diagnose the pathology.[11] He is especially adept at deflating the creations of overarching system builders, as in his famed rejection of Bishop Berkeley's empirical philosophy: "I observed, that though we are satisfied his doctrine is not true, it is impossible to refute it. I never shall forget the alacrity with which Johnson answered, striking his foot with mighty force against a large stone, till he rebounded from it, 'I refute it *thus*' " (1:471).

It would be difficult to integrate these qualities of elevated observation and satiric acerbity with an account of earnest patronage of female authors and a lifelong dependence on women friends, and Boswell does not attempt to do so. But when we note the omissions and distortions of the *Life*, a different Johnson begins to emerge. When we turn away from Boswell to the scattered but copious body of Johnsonian memoir and biography, we consistently encounter an individual who has a talent for intimate, Platonic friendship with women—a demanding mentor, collaborator, and editor, whose rigor was a form of respect and who encouraged women to stake their claim in eighteenth-century literary society. And we find in Johnson's social life with the intellectual women of his day, many of whom wrote fiction, an important and overlooked part of the eighteenth-century novel's development.

Boswell tells us that Johnson began writing for the *Gentleman's Magazine* in 1738 (*Life*, 1:111–12), but omits the names of the female authors who wrote for the periodical, many of whom, as Grundy notes (64), entered Johnson's circle: Mary Barber, Elizabeth Carter, Mary Masters, Elizabeth Rowe, and Catharine Trotter. Boswell mentions Johnson's unwitting participation in William Lauder's attempt to defame

Milton in 1751—a minor incident in Johnson's literary career (1:229–31). But Boswell fails to mention the all-night party Johnson threw that year to celebrate the publication of Charlotte Lennox's first novel, *Harriet Stuart*. At this gala Johnson paid public tribute to Lennox, crowning her with a laurel of bay leaves.[12] (And Johnson of course continued to work on Lennox's behalf; he wrote five dedications for her including the dedication to *The Female Quixote*, a novel to which he may or may not have contributed directly as a coauthor. When her financial situation deteriorated, he endeavored to raise subscriptions for a collection of her work.)[13] Boswell claims that Johnson elevated English and created a "national taste," "too masculine for the delicate gentleness of female writing" (1:222–23). The *Life* presents this new standard in terms of a male cultural elite, reproducing Courtenay's couplets on Johnson's titanic leadership of the cadre that included Goldsmith, Reynolds, and Burney:

> By nature's gifts ordain'd mankind to rule,
> He, like a Titian, form'd his brilliant school;
> And taught congenial spirits to excel,
> While from his lips impressive wisdom fell.
> Our boasted GOLDSMITH felt the sovereign sway;
> From him deriv'd the sweet, yet nervous lay.
> To Fame's proud cliff he bade our Raphael rise;
> Hence REYNOLDS' pen with REYNOLDS' pencil vies.
> With Johnson's flame melodious BURNEY glows,
> While the grand strain in smoother cadence flows.
>
> (*Life*, 1:222)

But it was Joshua Reynolds' sister Frances whom Johnson visited with frequently, for whom he sat, who may have painted the final portrait of Johnson generally attributed to Sir Joshua, and whose mind Johnson praised as being "near to purity itself" (*Miscellanies*, 1:207).[14] While Boswell does mention Charles Burney's daughter Frances as a Johnson imitator (4:389), he omits significantly the details of Johnson's mentorship of Burney, tutelage that acknowledged no gender difference. Johnson effusively praised Burney's 1778 novel *Evelina*, and he also encouraged her to learn Latin, write drama, publish under her own name, and assert herself publicly in conversation.[15] When daunted by the prospect of dinner with the formidable salonière Mrs. Montagu, Frances Burney was coached by Johnson, who cried out: "*Down* with her, Burney!—*down* with her!—spare her not! attack her, fight her, & *down* with her at once! *You* are a *rising* Wit,—*she* is at the *Top*,—& when *I* was beginning the World, & was nothing & nobody, the Joy of my Life was to fire at all the established Wits!—& then, every body loved to hallow me on. . . . So at her, Burney!—at her, & *down* with her!"[16] As Wheeler Cafarelli points out, Boswell does not mention Johnson's invitation to Burney to survey the ruins of the Gordon Riots on Grub Street: "you and I, Burney, will go together; we have a very good right to go, so we'll visit the mansions of our progenitors, and take up our freedom together."[17] And Boswell omits Johnson's attempt to fuel ambition in Frances Burney's sister Susan, as well as Burney's private moments with Johnson at the closing stages of his life when she distracted him from his deteriorating health with discussions of Shakespeare.[18]

Boswell condemns Johnson's lodger and friend Anna Williams as being "of a peevish temper" (*Life*, 2:99), and throughout the *Life* she appears as a rather cranky dependent whose presence illustrates Johnson's magnanimity. Boswell concedes that Williams is well read and articulate, but extols as her paramount quality her proximity to Johnson: "but her peculiar value was the intimacy in which she had long lived with Johnson, by which she was well acquainted with his habits, and knew how to lead him on to talk" (1:463). Isobel Grundy has pointed out that Williams was not merely a lucky vagabond who received Johnson's charity, nor was she, as early sources claimed, his housekeeper.[19] She was a valued companion who, prior to her blindness and her career as a poet, had been a working scientist. Johnson records Williams as being the first scientist to note the emission of an electrical spark from a human body, and his activities on her behalf included promoting a *Dictionary of Science* that she might author and obtaining a pension for her.

Boswell famously memorializes Hester Thrale Piozzi as a vain parvenu whose narcissistic impulses were kept in check by marital constraint, but who turned on Johnson after her husband's death (*Life*, 1:494; 4:158; 339–40). Piozzi herself anticipates Boswell's hegemony over Johnsonian biography with her offhand remark in her *Diary* that Boswell possessed ten times the number of anecdotes that she did despite the fact that she had spent infinitely more time in Johnson's company.[20] And Boswell's text, geared as it is toward epigram and quip, of course omits the details of Johnson's and Thrale Piozzi's long-standing intellectual camaraderie: their joint translations of Boethius, their amateur experiments in chemistry conducted in a makeshift laboratory in Streatham, Johnson's encouragement of the epistolary writing that has ensured her place in literary history, his badgering her daughters to learn mathematics, his admonitions to his favorite, Queeney, to better her mind: "You, my Love, are now in the time of flood, your powers are hourly encreasing, do not lose the time. When you are alone read diligently, they who do not read can have nothing to think, and little to say" (*Letters*, 3:288). Thrale Piozzi remembered Johnson prior to their

separation as a person intolerant of ignorance in his interlocutors regardless of their gender: "He was indeed often pained by the ignorance
or causeless wonder of those who knew less than himself, though he
seldom drove them away with apparent scorn, unless he thought they
added presumption to stupidity" (*Miscellanies*, 1:308).[21] Johnson's letters to Piozzi are not just candid; they are philosophical reflections on
the place of writing within Platonic friendship. In 1777, Johnson wrote
to her from Lichfield that "In a Man's Letters, you know, Madam, his
soul lies naked, his letters are only the mirrour of his breast; whatever
passes within him is shown undisguised in its natural process. . . ." This
epistle closes with the affirmation, "I have indeed concealed nothing
from you, nor do I expect ever to repent of having opened my heart"
(*Letters*, 3:89–90).[22]

Gerda Lerner has written that the seventeenth and eighteenth centuries are a watershed period in European history in that they saw the
first rumblings of feminism in the form of "affinity clusters" of intellectual women; gatherings in private homes and salons to discuss literature
and philosophy led female intellectuals to an awareness of their own
legal and educational disenfranchisement, analysis which paved the
way for later, organized demands for reform.[23] A historian and nonspe-
cialist in literary studies, Lerner lists among notable eighteenth-century
English bluestockings Elizabeth Carter, Elizabeth Montagu, Catherine
Talbot, Hester Chapone, and Samuel Johnson.[24] The *Life of Johnson*
does make mention of Johnson's female circle, but with little feeling for
the seriousness that seems to have characterized these associations, and
with no sense of the unique opportunities that this social sphere afforded its female members: a forum for debate, a discrete space in which
thinking women could test their ideas in the presence of a simultaneously challenging and supportive audience, and the opportunity for dialogue with mentors whose presence lent credence to their inquiry and
whose academic training could sharpen their thinking (1:312). It is
these conditions which enable women of every period to perceive themselves not merely as individuals with personal grievances but as members of an aggrieved collectivity, and it is within this context that we
should view Johnson's literary collaborations with his female friends:
Catherine Talbot's and Hester Chapone's contributions to the *Rambler*
(1:203), and Johnson's and Hannah More's 1776 "Sir Eldred of the
Bower" (*Poems*, 6:356–59). In this context Johnson's literary discussions with More on the merits of Richardson's prose (*Miscellanies*,
2:190) take on a peculiar luster, and the anecdote of More sitting in his
chair so that his genius might rub off on her seems less absurd (*Miscellanies*, 2:180). Significantly, the *Life of Johnson* trivializes Johnson's female
circle as his *"Seraglio"* (3:368). It presents Johnson with women as an

amusingly outrageous bully, as in his reluctant 1781 visit to a London bluestocking's salon, when Johnson dismisses his hostess's sentimental interpretation of Laurence Sterne, exclaiming, "dearest, you're a dunce" (4:109). And the *Life* contains a stunning omission. The year 1784 is filled with correspondence documenting personal distress over Johnson's deteriorating health. It features a vintage moment of Boswellian double entendre when Johnson returns from dinner with Mrs. Carter, Hannah More, and Fanny Burney: "What! had you them all to yourself, Sir?" (4:275). But it does not mention the meeting that took place that year between Johnson and Mary Wollstonecraft, an incident documented by Wollstonecraft's husband William Godwin:

> she was introduced to the acquaintance of Dr. Johnson, who was at that time considered as some sort of father of English literature. The doctor treated her with particular kindness and attention, had a long conversation with her, desired her to repeat her visit often. This she firmly purposed to do; but the news of his last illness, and then of his death, intervened.[25]

Nineteenth-century biographies often took their cue from Boswell, sometimes softening Johnson's hard-edged, eighteenth-century skepticism. Toward this end the body of anecdote regarding Johnson and women proved useful. W. H. Craig for instance dichotomizes his subject, distinguishing sharply between Johnson the intellectual and Johnson the companion of women:

> For this ordinarily uncouth and quarrelsome old man; this rampaging, brow-beating controversialist—who, at other times, betrayed a savage pleasure in flouting the amenities of social intercourse—could change himself into a vastly different monster when in the company of women,—could sheathe his claws, smooth his bristles, and moderate his roar, when they patted and fondled him. What is stranger, he was always ready to forsake his predatory pursuits for the patting and fondling in question. All through his life, from early boyhood to extreme old age, he exhibited this curious preference. Impelled by it, he would desert his accustomed haunts at club or tavern, where he domineered over lesser monsters with the unchallenged supremacy beloved by masterful natures, for those brilliant scenes where beauty and fashion were ruling powers, and where his ungainly presence seemed an incongruity. He would hurry from his natural diet on books and papers to spend a quiet evening in copious tea-drinking with a few female friends. He would throw over Burke and Reynolds, Langton and Beauclerk, Goldsmith and Warton, to have a cosy chat behind the scenes with Mrs. Abington or sweet Kitty Clive. He would forego classics, criticism, philosophy, *belles-lettres*, to talk of caps and manteaux and other female gear with the gentle creatures to whom they were the main business of life.[26]

In this evocation Johnson is an uncouth social dissident soothed into complacency by doting Victorian ladies who pat, fondle, caress, and de-claw him, smoothing his brow and medicating him with cups of tea. This absurdly anachronistic image of an eccentrically domestic John-son, a man who forsakes mental combat for fireside gossip, a critic who eschews his volumes of Juvenal for discussions of female headgear, bears mentioning, as it flows directly from Boswell's *Life*. Craig in fact begins his discussion of Johnson and women with the quotation from Boswell: "If I had no duties, and no reference to futurity, I would spend my life driving briskly in a post-chaise with a pretty woman."[27] In ob-fuscating the highly charged, intellectual quality of Johnson's female friendships, the *Life of Johnson* paved the way for a purely gendered reading of Johnson's career which pits masculine, intellectual rigor against feminine nicety. In imposing its own gender ideals upon the eighteenth-century such a reading obscures the reality of Johnson's so-cial world and the genres to which this world gave birth.

Scholars have only recently completely disentangled themselves from this Boswell-influenced, Victorian creation, devoting energy to the Johnson who composed somber couplets with Frances Reynolds ("As late disconsolate in pensive mood, / I sat revolving Life's vicissitude / Oft sigh'd to think how Youth had pass'd away, / And saw with sorrow Hopes diminish'd ray"), and *ironized* the fetish for women's fashion, as in his "On Hearing Miss Thrale deliberate about her Hat":

> Wear the gown, and wear the hat,
>   Snatch your pleasures while they last;
> Hadst thou nine lives like a cat,
>   Soon those nine lives would be past.
>
> (*Poems*, 6:306)

It has required some digging to locate this more intimate Johnsonian patron of women, because, unlike Boswell's domineering celebrity, he operated in private. But the nonpublic nature of Johnson's relation-ships with women appears to have provided a space for him to relin-quish his role as performer and openly express his loneliness and his religious sentiments. A letter written to Hester Thrale Piozzi on 19 June 1783 just prior to her second marriage closes with an unself-con-scious prayer: "O God, give me comfort and confidence in Thee, forgive my sins, and if it be thy good pleasure, relieve my diseases for Jesus Christs sake. Amen" (*Letters*, 4:153). Anna Seward reports that she vis-ited Johnson regularly at the end of his life because of his frequent, fervent requests for her company, and Frances Burney provides similar accounts.[28] Hannah More in her "Anecdotes" described Johnson's last year with intimate knowledge of his state of mind: "I am grieved to find that his mind is still a prey to melancholy, and that the fear of death operates on him to the destruction of his peace. It is grievous—it is unaccountable! He who has the Christian hope upon the best foundation; whose faith is strong, whose morals are irreproachable! But I am willing to ascribe it to bad nerves, and bodily disease" (*Miscellanies*, 2:202).

Boswell wrote that there is in everything of consequence a "secret history which it would be amusing to know" (*Life*, 1:183). Thanks to recent scholarly efforts, Johnson's meaningful relationships with women are no longer secret, but Boswell's text still determines perceptions of Johnson, particularly among non-Johnsonian scholars of literature. And it is still fairly commonplace for the most careful researchers to quote Johnson directly from Boswell's *Life*, conflating the identities of the two authors. Perhaps more important, among scholars of eighteenth-century literature, the context that Johnson's female network provides for interpreting his work has been neglected. When we shift our attention from Johnson the literary lion presiding over his weekly club to Johnson the friend and patron of female novelists who worked within a mixed sex literary community, his oeuvre looks quite different, and the thematic concerns that Johnson shared with his female contemporaries and his influence on the domestic novel become clear.

Recovery work done recently on the history of the eighteenth-century novel has demonstrated how far conventional accounts of the genre focusing on the triangular configuration of Defoe, Richardson, and Fielding are incorrect.[29] It is clear that most novelists in the eighteenth century were women and that female contributions to English language fiction were obscured in the process of canon formation that occurred in the early twentieth century. Where does Johnson fit into this picture as a patron of women writers and a seminal author? One answer to this question—and it is only one—is that Johnson was a voice in the eighteenth century's ongoing cultural debate about marriage, a debate that informed the novel. Two important and I believe related themes in Johnson's writing are the destructive capacities of the human imagination and the frivolous and deluded world of marriage-oriented courtship, and these are two of the primary concerns of the eighteenth-century domestic novel. Both Johnson's work and that of his female colleagues explore the pressures that wedlock and courtship place on the imagination. I would argue that the novelists of the later century adapt Johnson's treatment of the subject to their female protagonists. A brief reading of Johnson's *Rasselas* demonstrates the extent to which Johnson's writing provides a thematic framework for authors of domestic fiction.

Johnson's *Dictionary* defines "imagination" as "Fancy; the power of forming ideal pictures; the power of representing things absent to one's self or others."[30] The entry continues to include the nouns "contrivance," and "scheme," and the word "imaginary" is denoted as "Fancied; visionary; existing only in the imagination." *Rambler* 125 refers to the imagination as a "licentious and vagrant faculty, unsusceptible of limitations, and impatient of restraint" (4:300), and *Rambler* 89 portrays a permanently isolated, dreaming recluse who "retires to his own apartments, shuts out the cares and interruptions of mankind, and abandons himself to his own fancy" (4:104). This figure reappears in *Rasselas* in both the opaque philosopher and the paranoid astronomer who is convinced that he controls the seasons.[31] In this text as in so many eighteenth-century novels, imagination is the wellspring of vice. As Imlac explains to Rasselas, "No man will be found in whose mind airy notions do not sometimes tyrannize, and force him to hope or fear beyond the limits of sober probability. All power of fancy over reason is a degree of insanity" (150). Imlac further explains that latent imaginative impulses are not considered harmful as long as they go undetected. Once they make themselves manifest they are seen as symptoms of madness, but the initial deleterious impulses of self-gratification through fantasy—Imlac calls it "luscious falsehood" (152)—contain the seeds of human self-destruction.

We see the results of imaginative self-delusion in the marriage debate of chapters 26–29, when Nekayah dislodges her brother's amorous fantasies. The debate is marked by unusual gender reversals. Like the idealized domestic woman of the period, the prince has lived in a state of enforced leisure and material comfort in which entertainment has been his sole occupation and in which his misery has been offset by reminders of his own privilege. Monotonous, oppressive, and safe, life in the Happy Valley seems to contain a subtle indictment of the middle-class domestic ideal of bourgeois marital isolation, in which the household is, in Nancy Armstrong's words, a "self-enclosed world whose means of support were elsewhere, invisible, removed from the scene."[32] Rasselas's defense of marriage mimics the cultural propaganda to which eighteenth-century women were treated; he expresses the companionate marriage ideal, arguing that each conjugal unit serves the larger good, that the married couple reflects a stable, tightly knit, social world, and that there is a natural principle of heterosexual doubling based on mutual affection.[33] Johnson uses a male character to vocalize these beliefs and expose their naïveté. Rasselas's notions of connubial life are, in the words of Johnson's *Dictionary*, "ideal pictures," and they are the kind of sentimental images that one would expect from a young girl saturated with conduct books and romantic novels.

Nekayah's response is informed by her observations of private life in the preceding chapter. She has seen young women bred for courtship inhabiting a narrow domestic sphere dominated by whim and erotic fancy. Such women are socialized as vain, envious, shallow coquettes with no sense of social duty. Their world is that of *Rambler* 191, in which the fictional Bellaria boasts of her prestige on the marriage market, celebrating her own beauty (5:233–38). It is also the world of amorous game-playing envisioned in Pope's *The Rape of the Lock* and in Johnson's and Hester Chapone's *Rambler* 10, in which the gay Flirtilla cracks her fan (3:86). It is repeatedly the mise-en-scène of the domestic novel, in which "delicious falsehoods" lure women into conjugal commitment. We should not be surprised that these genres overlap, as their authors were so closely involved. We should likewise not be surprised to find a subversive, antiwedlock argument within Johnson's apologue. Scholars of the period who assume Johnson's traditional stance in regard to wedlock may do so because of Lawrence Stone's claim that Johnson was a proponent of arranged marriages,[34] but Stone's source seems to be the infamous quotation in Boswell's *Life*: "I believe marriages would in general be as happy, and often more so, if they were all made by the Lord Chancellor, upon a due consideration of characters and circumstances, without the parties having any choice in the matter" (2:461) rather than any published opinion by Johnson himself. This is a distinctly Boswellian epigram. In fact, when we recall Johnson's well-known abolitionist tendencies (*Life*, 3:202–3), and the fact that married, eighteenth-century Englishwomen were property under Blackstone's laws of coverture, we might well imagine Johnson as a skeptic of matrimony rather than a crusty, backward-looking Tory.[35] It should therefore not surprise us to find a strand of antimarriage critique in Johnson's literary productions.

Nekayah challenges her brother's idealization of wedlock with three arguments. She claims that the basis of conjugal life is power rather than affection, that marriage is not necessary for the propagation of the species, and that maturity does not improve domestic relationships. While she concedes that celibacy offers few pleasures, Nekayah's own final goal—the establishment of a college for learned women—seems to entail celibacy and personal privacy.[36] Nekayah's plot implies recognition of the fact that eighteenth-century women's gender indoctrination focused relentlessly on the family, so that liberation from gender constraints could only take place in a sphere outside of the family's domain. She is one of the only young, female protagonists of eighteenth-century fiction whose life is not plotted along the trajectory of wedlock and who intrudes upon and alters what has at first appeared to be a Quixotic or Hudibrastic quest narrative of a male protagonist and his squire. (Rasselas and Imlac had at first planned to leave the Happy Valley alone.)

Both the content of Nekayah's antimarriage polemic and the plot that she enacts, in which a male quest narrative is transformed into a gender-neutral series of Platonic dialogues, sympathetically anticipate later feminist arguments about women's social role.

Like every dialogue in *Rasselas*, the marriage debate is unresolved. But it is taken up in the work of Johnson's contemporaries and successors, female authors who deepen and extend his critique. The eighteenth-century novel's marriage plot, in which action moves toward the wedding day and then abruptly ceases, is often said to codify companionate wedlock.[37] But with its incorporation of Johnsonian material, the genre more often explores conjugal paradoxes, painfully illustrating the shortcomings of bourgeois wedlock in the plights of those punished by the institution of marriage. Burney's 1778 *Evelina*, for instance, demonstrates the point made in *Rasselas* that wedlock is power-based social drama rather than a spontaneous effusion of love between two fated partners. The novel sympathetically depicts a woman of ambiguous social standing disadvantaged on a marriage market that values superficialities and encourages mutual deception, an arena described by Rasselas himself as one in which men and women are "brought together by artifice" (107). Burney's narrative echoes the concerns of her mentor, Samuel Johnson, for disenfranchised women: spinsters, elderly women, and prostitutes.[38] The protagonist's random exclusion from marital privilege throughout the novel ironizes her final betrothal to an aristocrat, as does her disorientation, when, having finally discovered her biological origins and become engaged, she moves rapidly from male guardian to father to husband, exclaiming, "I hardly know, my Lord, I hardly know myself to whom I most belong!"[39]

Nekayah's claim that wedlock is not essential to human survival is demonstrated in the eighteenth-century novel's myriad illegitimate characters whose precarious legal status and social dishonor amplify the Johnsonian marriage critique.[40] We need only reflect on the work of Charlotte Lennox, Jane Austen, and others deeply influenced by Johnson to see vivid illustrations of Nekayah's point; in an early chapter of Lennox's 1752 *The Female Quixote*, a minor figure, the impetuous Miss Groves, gives birth to two illegitimate children, earning but also rebuffing the heroine's sympathy.[41] Her mind corrupted by French romances, Lennox's heroine Arabella is herself a Johnsonian caricature who demonstrates the thin partition between amorous daydreaming, ritualized courtship, and madness. Her mind a swirl of romantic clichés, Arabella believes herself to be the central object of pursuit in every social situation until her conversion to common sense by a Johnsonian clergyman. When the clergyman intones, "Love, Madam, is, you know, the Business, the sole Business of Ladies in Romances," he ironically underscores the novel's central point: in a world which restricts and limits female agency in debilitating ways, the lure of fiction will always be incredibly strong, and the "delicious falsehoods" of imagination will intoxicate with their fantasy of empowerment. A female protagonist like Arabella will always err on the side of narcissistic, imaginative self-deception, allying herself with "Heiresses of great and powerful Empires, the Daughters of valiant Princes, and the Wives of renowned Monarchs" (381; 372), rather than realistically viewing herself as an isolated dependent, disenfranchised by the conditions of her father's will, for whom an overdetermined marriage is the sole option. In Jane Austen's *Emma*, the "imaginist" heroine works at improving her illegitimate protégé Harriet Smith, "the natural daughter of somebody," whom she hopes to enhance as a candidate on the marriage market.[42] Emma Woodhouse's fantasies of amorous control and the threat that these illusions pose to her friend's future again illustrate the dual threat that marriage ideology poses to women: imaginative overreaching on the one hand, vulnerability to poverty and social disapprobation on the other. Marginal characters like Harriet Smith do not merely reflect the social reality of bastardy so prominent in the eighteenth century; they demonstrate Nekayah's argument for the superfluity of institutionalized marriage in a world in which there is "no danger that the present generation should omit to leave successors behind them" (106). The consummate portrayer of marital dysfunction, Austen memorably illustrates in her opening chapter of *Pride and Prejudice* Nekayah's point that mature marriages are no happier than youthful unions. The Bennets, an older couple, talk past rather than to each other, demonstrating conjugal stalemate and impasse to be the telos to which the novel's multiple marriage plots will move. The mother of five daughters subject to a male-biased world, Mrs. Bennet is in medias res, scheming for her daughters' matrimonial futures. The famed reference to the marriage quest as a "truth universally acknowledged"[43] as she plots her daughters' nuptials conflates two of Johnson's *Dictionary* definitions of imagination: an "unsolid and fanciful opinion" and a "scheme" or "contrivance." These novels dramatize Imlac's register of illusion, demonstrating how the fantasy world of marriage-oriented courtship erodes female reason. They bear Johnson's direct imprint, showing us how close the lexicographer, literary critic, editor of Shakespeare, and poet was to the century's most popular form—not surprising, perhaps, considering his intimacy with and influence on many of its practitioners.

William Walker's engraving of Doyle's *A Literary Party at Sir Joshua Reynolds's* is the perfect visual representation of Boswell's *Life of Johnson*. The literary icon is surrounded by massive figures of cultural authority:

A Literary Party at Sir Joshua Reynolds's. From an engraving by William Walker of an 1851 painting by James E. Doyle. From left to right the figures depicted are Boswell, Johnson, Joshua Reynolds, David Garrick, Edmund Burke, Paoli, Charles Burney, Thomas Warton and Oliver Goldsmith. Reproduced courtesy of the Trustees of Dr. Johnson's House.

Reynolds, Burke, Garrick, Paoli, Burney, Thomas Warton, and Goldsmith seem to be satellites in orbit around Johnson, with Boswell in the background at a slight distance, appearing only to record the moment. The realms of male patronage are well represented; the art world, politics, the theater, the military, the arenas of music and poetry. But we must remember that the biographer envisioned here as a mere recorder of events was actually a skillful manipulator of fact and mood who created the mystique of a purely male literary brotherhood. Walker's representation gives us only a partial truth. Its appropriate complement is the image of a very different Johnson painted by James Barry on a wall of the Royal Society for the Encouragement of Arts, Manufactures, and Commerce, and unveiled in 1783 (see frontispiece). Here Johnson peers from behind the figures of two women, the Duchess of Devonshire, a poet and novelist as well as a burgeoning patron of female authors, and the Duchess of Rutland. This image emblematizes Johnson's involvement with the community of eighteenth-century women writers and his relationship to their chief literary artifact, the novel, a genre about which he wrote little but to which he had profound connections.

Notes

The author would like to thank Marcia Geller for her support of this and other scholarly projects.

1. The anecdote is cited by Isobel Grundy, "Samuel Johnson as Patron of Women," *AJ* 1 (1987): 66. Grundy makes reference to Richardson's letter to Sarah Fielding of 7 December 1756.

2. For an account of such responses see James G. Basker's "Myth Upon Myth: Johnson, Gender, and the Misogyny Question," *AJ* 8 (1997): 175–87.

3. Blanford Parker, *The Triumph of Augustan Poetics: English Literary Culture from Butler to Johnson* (Cambridge: Cambridge University Press, 1998), 12.

4. See for instance Jane Spencer's *The Rise of the Woman Novelist: From Aphra Behn to Jane Austen* (Oxford: Blackwell, 1986).

5. Joseph Reed, "Boswell and Women: Convivial Hilarity," a paper delivered at the Tenth International Conference on the Enlightenment, University College, Dublin, 31 July 1999, provides the following assessment of Boswell's vexed relationship to women: "To say he was a feminist would be an absurd stretch. To say he could think sympathetically with women would be an understatement. He was attracted to strong women and they to him. He didn't take their part: empathetically he didn't really know it. He frequently was heard to confess he failed because he couldn't master their way of thinking or understand completely what they freely said to him. This brings us to a conundrum: not to put too fine a point on it, Boswell was a sexist pig."

6. See for instance Greg Clingham, *Boswell: The Life of Johnson* (Cambridge: Cambridge University Press, 1992), 22–29, and Annette Wheeler Cafarelli, "Johnson and Women: Demasculinizing Literary History," *AJ* 5 (1992): 61–114.

7. See A. M. Broadley, *Dr. Johnson and Mrs. Thrale* (New York: John Lane, 1909), 44–45; 101, Joseph Wood Krutch, *Samuel Johnson* (New York: Henry Holt, 1944), 407; 410, and John Wain, *Samuel Johnson* (New York: Viking Press, 1974), 233; 315.

8. Wheeler Cafarelli, "Johnson and Women," 75.

9. James G. Basker, "Dancing Dogs, Women Preachers and the Myth of Johnson's Misogyny," *AJ* 3 (1990): 63–90.

10. Wheeler Cafarelli, "Johnson and Women," 61.

11. Blanford Parker views Boswell as a late participant in the Augustan project, an initiative which responded to the violence of post-Reformation religious factionalism by creating a neutral observer whose quality of superior judgment separated him from the cultural pathologies of his age. See his *Triumph of Augustan Poetics*.

12. See "Extracts from Sir John Hawkins's Life of Johnson," *Miscellanies*, 2:99–100: "One evening at the club, Johnson proposed to us celebrating the birth of Mrs. Lenox's first literary child, as he called her book, by a whole night spent in festivity. . . . The place appointed was the Devil tavern, and there, about the hour of eight, Mrs. Lenox and her husband, and a lady of her acquaintance, now living, as also the [Ivy Lane] club, and friends to the number of near twenty, assembled. Our supper was elegant, and Johnson had directed that a magnificent hot apple-pye should make a part of it, and this he would have stuck with bay-leaves, because, forsooth, Mrs. Lenox was an authoress, and had written verses; and further, he had prepared for her a crown of laurel, with which, but not till he had invoked the muses by some ceremonies of his own invention, he encircled her brows."

13. Susan Goulding, "Placing a Claim: Women Writers and Literary Tradition in Eighteenth-Century England," Diss., New York University, 1995, 140–1; 136.

14. For the relationship between Johnson and Frances Reynolds, see Helen Ash-

more, " 'Do Not, My Love, Burn Your Papers': Samuel Johnson and Frances Reynolds: A New Document," *AJ* 10 (1999): 165–94.

15. See Christopher Hibbert, *The Personal History of Samuel Johnson* (London: Longman, 1971), 258, and Grundy, "Patron of Women," 63. Johnson reportedly compared Burney favorably to Henry Fielding, praising one of the suitors in *Evelina*: " 'Oh, Mr. Smith, Mr. Smith is the Man!' cried he, Laughing violently. Harry Fielding *never* drew so good a Character!' " See *The Streatham Years: Part 1—1778–1779*, vol. 3 of *The Early Journals and Letters of Fanny Burney*, ed. Lars E. Troide, et al., 3 vols. (Oxford: Clarendon Press, 1988–94), 90.

16. Burney, *The Early Journals and Letters of Fanny Burney*, 3:151.

17. Wheeler Cafarelli, "Johnson and Women," 86.

18. For Johnson's encouragement of "Susy," see part 5 (1782) of *The Diary and Letters of Madame D'Arblay*, ed. "by her Niece" (Charlotte Barrett), 7 vols. (London: Henry Colburn, 1854), 2:176–77; for Burney's discussions of Shakespeare with Johnson, see part 8 (1784) of the *Diaries*, 2:273–75.

19. Grundy, "Patron of Women," 67–68.

20. *Thraliana: The Diary of Mrs. Hester Lynch Thrale, 1776–1809*, ed. Katharine C. Balderston, 2 vols. (Oxford: Clarendon Press, 1942), 1 (1776–84): 195. When, after Johnson's death, Mrs. Thrale's second husband encouraged her to add her name to the list of people who had undertaken to write a "Life," she notes: "and so I would; but that I think my Anecdotes too few." See *Thraliana*, 2 (1784–1809): 625.

21. For commentary on Johnson's relationship with Mrs. Thrale, see Grundy, "Patron of Women," 63; 73. On Johnson's letter to Queeney quoted here, see Robert DeMaria, Jr., *The Life of Samuel Johnson: A Critical Biography* (Oxford: Blackwell, 1993): "The advice is both general and specifically directed to Queeney, who evidently tended to be cool. The tone of the letter is more than avuncular and suggests a kind of courtly civility that was already antique at the time. Such courtliness marks Johnson's relations with the Thrales to the end" (299).

22. Cf. Paul Fussell's observation, in *Samuel Johnson and the Life of Writing* (London: Chatto and Windus, 1972), that Johnson "instinctively denies that conception of the letter which would hold that it constitutes an opportunity for natural self-expression" (116).

23. Gerda Lerner, *The Creation of Feminist Consciousness: From the Middle Ages to Eighteen-seventy* (New York: Oxford University Press, 1993), 229–46.

24. Ibid., 230.

25. William Godwin, *Memoirs of the Authoress of A Vindication of the Rights of Women*, ed. Gina Luria (New York: Garland, 1974), 45. I highlight this omission not as an indictment of Boswell's text but because it seems significant that Johnson embarked upon a friendship with the first feminist theoretician to contextualize demands for female equality within a broader liberationist argument and the first thinker to develop a secular feminist analysis. Given Wollstonecraft's emphasis on educational disadvantaging at the heart of female subordination and Johnson's apparent belief in women's access to education, we should perhaps not be surprised that he invited her back.

26. W. H. Craig, *Doctor Johnson and the Fair Sex: A Study in Contrasts* (London: Sampson Low, Marston, 1895), 2–3.

27. Ibid., 1.

28. For Anna Seward see Letter 2, 29 October 1784, *The Letters of Anna Seward written between the years 1784 and 1807*, 6 vols. (London, 1811), 1:7–8: "I have lately been in the almost daily habit of contemplating a very melancholy spectacle. The great Johnson is here, labouring under the paroxysms of a desease, which must speedily be fatal. He shrinks from the consciousness with the extremest horror. It is by his repeatedly ex-

pressed desire that I visit him often: yet I am sure he neither does, nor ever did feel much regard for me; but he would fain escape, for a time, in any society, from the terrible idea of his approaching dissolution. I never would be awed by his sarcasms, or his frowns, into an acquiescence with his general injustice to the merits of *other* writers; with his national, or party aversions; but I feel the truest compassion for his present sufferings, and fervently wish I had power to relieve them." For further commentary on Seward's opinion of Johnson's literary views, see the essay by Mason and Rounce, *post.* For Burney, see *Diaries,* 2:273–75.

29. See Goulding, "Placing A Claim," Spencer, *Rise of the Woman Novelist,* and Janet Todd, *The Sign of Angellica: Women, Writing, and Fiction, 1660–1800* (New York: Columbia University Press, 1989).

30. Samuel Johnson, *A Dictionary of the English Language,* 2 vols. (London, 1755).

31. The astronomer cites as a symptom and cause of his misery the absence of female friendship. Here, female companionship is a grounding force, an antidote to discontent and intellectual folly, as Kathleen Nulton Kemmerer and others have noted. Kathleen Nulton Kemmerer, *"A Neutral Being Between the Sexes": Samuel Johnson's Sexual Politics* (Lewisburg, Pa.: Bucknell University Press, 1998), 111–12.

32. Nancy Armstrong, *Desire and Domestic Fiction: A Political History of the Novel* (New York: Oxford University Press, 1987), 73.

33. For accounts of the emergence of a companionate marriage ideal in the eighteenth century see John Gillis, *For Better, For Worse: British Marriages, 1600 to the Present* (New York: Oxford University Press, 1985), and Lawrence Stone, *The Family, Sex and Marriage in England: 1500–1800* (New York: Harper and Row, 1977).

34. Stone, *The Family,* 190.

35. "By marriage, the husband and wife are one person in law; that is, the very being or legal existence of the woman is suspended during the marriage, or at least incorporated and consolidated into that of her husband; under whose wing, protection, and *cover,* she performs everything. . . ." Quoted in James Trager, *A Woman's Chronology* (New York: Henry Holt, 1994), 190.

36. "It is striking, as one looks over the lists of women from different countries, spanning over 1300 years, who have developed some aspect of feminist thought, how many of them lived what today we would call woman-focused lives. Whether by choice or for want of alternative, they removed themselves from the marriage market and focused their most intense activity on abstract thought. Most of them did their significant work in a single state, either prior to marriage, during widowhood or as women who, by choice, remained single. And further, for most of them what mattered most was the existence of some female audiences or support network" (Lerner, *Feminist Consciousness,* 224). Nekayah's plans appear to create the social conditions necessary for the evolution of feminist theory.

37. See Joseph Allen Boone, *Tradition Counter Tradition: Love and the Form of Fiction* (Chicago: University of Chicago Press, 1987).

38. See Basker, "Dancing Dogs, Women Preachers," and Wheeler Cafarelli, "Johnson and Women."

39. Fanny Burney, *Evelina,* ed. Edward A. Bloom (Oxford: Oxford University Press, 1968), 353.

40. For an account of the legal disenfranchisement of illegitimates effected by Hardwicke's Marriage Act, see Eve Tavor Bannet, "The Marriage Act of 1753: 'A most cruel law for the Fair Sex,' " *ECS* 30 (spring 1997): 233–54.

41. Charlotte Lennox, *The Female Quixote or the Adventures of Arabella,* ed. Margaret Dalziel (Oxford: Oxford University Press, 1989), 70–76. Subsequent references are cited parenthetically in the text.

42. Jane Austen, *Emma*, ed. Fiona J. Stafford (London: Penguin, 1996), 21.
43. Jane Austen, *Pride and Prejudice*, ed. Vivien Jones (London: Penguin, 1996), 5.

BIBLIOGRAPHY

Armstrong, Nancy. *Desire and Domestic Fiction: A Political History of the Novel*. New York: Oxford University Press, 1987.

Ashmore, Helen. " 'Do Not, My Love, Burn Your Papers': Samuel Johnson and Frances Reynolds: A New Document," *AJ* 10 (1999): 165–94.

Austen, Jane. *Emma*. Edited by Fiona Stafford. London: Penguin, 1996.

———. *Pride and Prejudice*. Edited by Vivien Jones. London: Penguin, 1996.

Basker, James G. "Dancing Dogs, Women Preachers and the Myth of Johnson's Misogyny." *AJ* 3 (1990): 63–90.

———. "Myth Upon Myth: Johnson, Gender, and the Misogyny Question." *AJ* 8 (1997): 175–87.

Boone, Joseph Allen. *Tradition Counter Tradition: Love and the Form of Fiction*. Chicago: University of Chicago Press, 1987.

Boswell, James. *Boswell's Life of Johnson*. 6 vols. Edited by George Birkbeck Hill. Revised by L. F. Powell. Oxford: Clarendon Press, 1934–64.

Broadley, A. M. *Dr. Johnson and Mrs. Thrale*. New York: John Lane, 1909.

Burney, Fanny. *The Diary and Letters of Madame D'Arblay*. 7 vols. Edited "by her Niece" (Charlotte Barrett). London: Henry Colburn, 1854.

———. *The Early Journals and Letters of Fanny Burney*. 3 vols. Edited by Lars E. Troide et al. Oxford: Clarendon Press, 1988–1994.

———. *Evelina*. Edited by Edward A. Bloom. Oxford: Oxford University Press, 1968.

Clingham, Greg. *Boswell: The Life of Johnson*. Cambridge: Cambridge University Press, 1992.

Craig, W. H. *Doctor Johnson and the Fair Sex: A Study in Contrasts*. London: Sampson Low, Marston, 1895.

DeMaria, Robert, Jr. *The Life of Samuel Johnson: A Critical Biography*. Oxford: Blackwell, 1993.

Gillis, John. *For Better, For Worse: British Marriages 1600 to the Present*. New York: Oxford University Press, 1985.

Godwin, William. *Memoirs of the Authoress of A Vindication of the Rights of Women*. Edited by Gina Luria. New York: Garland, 1974.

Goulding, Susan. "Placing a Claim: Women Writers and Literary Tradition in Eighteenth-Century England." Ph.D. diss., New York University, 1995.

Grundy, Isobel. "Samuel Johnson as Patron of Women." *AJ* 1 (1987): 59–77.

Hibbert, Christopher. *The Personal History of Samuel Johnson*. London: Longman, 1971.

Hill, George Birkbeck, ed. *Johnsonian Miscellanies*. 2 vols. Oxford: Clarendon Press, 1897.

Johnson, Samuel. *A Dictionary of the English Language*. 2 vols. London: 1755.

———. *Poems*. Edited by E. L. McAdam, Jr. and George Milne. Vol. 6 of The Yale Edition of the Works of Samuel Johnson. New Haven and London: Yale University Press, 1964.

―――. *Rasselas and Other Tales*. Edited by Gwin J. Kolb. Vol. 16 of The Yale Edition of the Works of Samuel Johnson. New Haven and London: Yale University Press, 1990.

Kemmerer, Kathleen Nulton. *"A Neutral Being Between the Sexes": Samuel Johnson's Sexual Politics*. Lewisburg, Pa.: Bucknell University Press, 1998.

Krutch, Joseph Wood. *Samuel Johnson*. New York: Henry Holt, 1944.

Lennox, Charlotte. *The Female Quixote or The Adventures of Arabella*. Edited by Margaret Dalziel. Oxford: Oxford University Press, 1989.

Lerner, Gerda. *The Creation of Feminist Consciousness: From the Middle Ages to Eighteen-seventy*. New York: Oxford University Press, 1993.

Parker, Blanford. *The Triumph of Augustan Poetics: English Literary Culture from Butler to Johnson*. Cambridge: Cambridge University Press, 1998.

Piozzi, Hester Thrale. *Thraliana: The Diary of Hester Lynch Thrale, 1776–1809*. 2 vols. Edited by Katharine C. Balderston. Oxford: Clarendon Press, 1942.

Reed, Joseph. "Boswell and Women: Convivial Hilarity." Paper presented at the Tenth International Conference on the Enlightenment. Dublin, July 1999.

Seward, Anna. *The Letters of Anna Seward written between the years 1784 and 1807*. 6 vols. London: 1811.

Spencer, Jane. *The Rise of the Woman Novelist: From Aphra Behn to Jane Austen*. Oxford: Blackwell, 1986.

Stone, Lawrence. *The Family, Sex and Marriage in England: 1500–1800*. New York: Harper and Row, 1977.

Tavor Bannet, Eve. "The Marriage Act of 1753: 'A most cruel law for the Fair Sex.' " *ECS* 30 (spring 1997): 233–54.

Todd, Janet. *The Sign of Angellica: Women, Writing, and Fiction, 1660–1800*. New York: Columbia University Press, 1989.

Trager, James. *A Woman's Chronology*. New York: Henry Holt, 1994.

Wain, John. *Samuel Johnson*. New York: Viking Press, 1974.

Wheeler Cafarelli, Annette. "Johnson and Women: Demasculinizing Literary History." *AJ* 5 (1992): 61–114.

Thinking of Italy, Making History: Johnson and Historiography

DANIELLE INSALACO

JOHNSON THE MONOLITH, JOHNSON THE CURMUDGEON, JOHNSON the omniscient, and especially Johnson the "antihistorical": in how many cases are the resulting stereotypes that flow from these common-places simply wrong? The most valuable starting point in dismantling the misconceptions about Johnson is his own work, particularly those writings which are frequently disregarded or overlooked. For instance, many assume Johnson held disrespectful views on history and histori-ography, an opinion substantiated mainly through his comments to Boswell, but most of his major writings touch on the value of history in some way. This is a key issue for modern scholarship, currently en-trenched in the historicism debate. But now that we have "returned to history," various new theoretical constructs can be applied. My sugges-tion in this essay is that one way that Johnson's historical writings an-ticipated modern conceptions of history was by focusing on "local history" and "microhistory." Moreover, while Johnson is often viewed as an insular, even xenophobic man, he actually loved to travel and was interested in other cultures and lands. In particular, Johnson, like many other writers in the period, was intrigued and inspired by conceptions of Italy. By reference to one neglected instance of this international per-spective, Johnson's "Life of Paul Sarpi," I should accordingly like to draw attention to Johnson's writings concerning Italy, and to John-son's cosmopolitanism as an aspect of his historiographical ideology.

JOHNSON AND HISTORY

One of the reasons why critics tend to discount the "historical John-son" may be that his views on history were never expressed at length in any of his most famous texts. They instead appear piecemeal in works as varied as the periodical essays, *Rasselas*, and the *Lives of the Poets*. Taken together, though, such views represent a sustained reaction to problems that have continued to play a role in historiographical thought. Moreover, when Johnson was recorded by Boswell in the *Life* criticizing specific works such as Robertson's *History of Scotland*, at the time he may have been "talking for victory." He told Boswell and Reynolds that the *History of Scotland* "is not history, it is imagination. . . . You must look upon Robertson's work as romance, and try it by that standard" (*Life*, 2:236–37). But his comments would later be taken at face value. For this reason many critics came to believe that Johnson was dismissive of political-historical thinking altogether: Macaulay declared in the nineteenth century that Johnson "loved biography, literary history, the history of manners; but political history was positively distasteful to him."[1] In fact, most other critics have merely described the *anti*historical: what Johnson did *not* consider history, what he did not like about contemporary history, and why he purportedly did not or could not write history. Jean Hagstrum went so far as to qualify Johnson's distrust of history as "the opposition of a man of fact to speculation," and going beyond Macaulay he suggested that Johnson "was himself extremely chary of expressing in his own works any philosophy of literary history."[2]

In common with John Vance, the only critic in the last forty years to address Johnson's "sense of history" in a full-scale treatment, my suggestion points in a quite different direction. While Godfrey Davies, in 1948, was the first to give credence to the historical aspect of Johnson's work, it was not until eleven years later that William Keast created appropriate categories in which to place Johnson's various treatments of history.[3] Keast distinguished between Johnson's dislike of the historical writing of his day in the way that it utilized the past, and the kind of history he did appreciate and admire. He believed that Johnson's most complete statement on history was made in *Rasselas*, where Imlac remarks that: "To judge rightly of the present we must oppose it to the past; for all judgment is comparative, and of the future nothing can be known" (112). Yet despite their value, those very studies of Johnson which highlight his historical interests are exclusionary in their own way. None of them, even Vance, seeks to read Johnson in terms of current theories of historiography. Although such scholars acknowledge the humanistic and conjectural beliefs Johnson shared with the philosophical historians, they rarely engage with recent theoretical approaches as the interpretive key to Johnson's work.

We might begin by unpacking Johnson's 1755 *Dictionary* entry for "history" as "a narration of events and facts delivered with dignity."[4] By "narration," Johnson undoubtedly meant "narrative," or writing history as story, a form which became increasingly popular in the eighteenth century. Today's narrativists believe that it is the historian's language—not the organization of historical events themselves—that gives coherence to the past. Johnson himself was dismayed with histories that read like romances—the explanation behind his quip about the author of the *History of Scotland*: "I love Robertson, but I will not talk of his book" (*Life*, 2:53). In the *Dictionary* he cites Pope to underscore his attempt to distinguish between history and fiction: "Justly Caesar scorns the poet's lays; / It is to history he trusts for praise." Johnson tries to equate narration with objectivity, but he also knew that the historian had to "employ all his powers in arranging and displaying" his materials for an attractive presentation (*Rambler* 122, 4:288).

Johnson's concern with "facts" in the *Dictionary* entry reflects his near-obsession with ascertainable truth and a concept of factuality which is sometimes at odds with his appreciation of what he calls elsewhere "the colourings of history," and his worries that too many facts will spoil the soup, as it were: "Between falsehood and useless truth there is little difference," he writes in *Idler* 84 (2:262). Johnson always was interested in the style of historical writing, one whose "dignity," as he calls it in the *Dictionary*, might be impaired either by too much detail or by a lack of moral imperative. The brief definition he wrote for the lexicon points to the possibility that, as early as the 1750s, Johnson had developed what we should feel comfortable calling a "theory of history."

However the text in which Johnson attempts most explicitly to reconcile narrativity with truth-telling is (as cited above) *Rambler* 122. Here he bemoans writers who "cloud the facts" in their historical narratives, when, as far as he is concerned, "no writer has a more easy task than the historian." Supposedly "the happy historian has no other labour than that of gathering what tradition pours down before him" (4:288). However, in this instance Johnson complicates the issue of narration when he claims that the historian "records treasure for his *use*." What use could a writer have for facts unless he wanted to place a particular slant on them? Bolingbroke declared that "history is philosophy teaching by examples," and in many instances Johnson apparently shared this view.[5] Johnson demonstrates in *Adventurer* 99 that a moralist may deliver his sentiments by adopting historical examples (2:429–35), and in this essay he uses Catiline, Caesar, Xerxes, Columbus, Charles XII, and Peter the Great to show how heroes are both virtuous and fortunate. In *Rasselas*, meanwhile, Imlac supposes that "example is always more efficacious than precept. A soldier is formed in war, and a painter must copy pictures" (113). From this perspective, the success of a historical document would seem to correspond to the quality of its lessons.

Aside from the use of history for moral purposes, Johnson is concerned with its form. In 1743 he wrote to Edward Cave that history is that which "ranges facts according to their dependence on each other, and postpones or anticipates according to the convenience of narration" (*Letters*, 1:34). But in *Rambler* 122 he declares that most historians write mere "chronological memorials, which necessity may sometimes require to be consulted, but which fright away curiosity, and disgust delicacy" (4:288). Like later writers on the principles of history, Johnson wants to distinguish between mere chronicle and history. For Collingwood, in the twentieth century, chronicle is "the body of history from which the spirit has gone; the corpse of history,"[6] and such statements as these may seem to reiterate Johnson's struggle with what Damrosch calls the "fictions of reality," the recognition that "even the most abstract and logical modes of thought are inseparable from invention." Damrosch quotes Raymond Williams, who had indicated that since the Romantic period, *literature* implies "an even firmer separation between imagination and reality, fiction and fact," a distinction thought not to be made in the eighteenth century.[7] Objectivity could rarely be reconciled with narrativity, and for the sake of narrative continuity, facts sometimes had to be rearranged or amplified. Johnson's sense of history, then, was developed and demonstrated throughout his career. It is now opportune to examine how far we might situate Johnson's ideas in the context of modern historiographical theory.

LOCAL AND MICROHISTORY

Thirty years ago Alan McKillop recognized the "local attachment" and "citizen of the world" motifs present in eighteenth-century literature from Addison to Akenside.[8] Today we can better theorize such motifs through Clifford Geertz's idea of local knowledge and Jurgen Habermas's public cosmopolitanism, but must ask, at the same time, why (and on what theoretical grounds) Johnson should be excluded from this debate. Johnson wrote the last lines of Goldsmith's *The Traveller*, a poem which embodies the conflict between local knowledge and universality. In his own writings, both a sense of locality and a sense of the larger world often existed side by side in the same text, and such qualities seem to prefigure today's valuation of local knowledge. Johnson recognized that narrative plays an important role in the definition of knowledge, but also realized that the overt "metanarratives" of his period (a term he did *not* use, though a concept he understood) did not necessarily reflect the heterogeneity of the real world.

Writing as a recent advocate of the goal of local historical knowledge, Geertz turns away from "trying to explain social phenomena by weaving them into grand textures of cause and effect to trying to explain them by placing them in local frames of awareness."[9] Johnson's motives for a local historiography, not surprisingly, were more practically based. On the one hand, the quotidian elements of human life are preferable when the aim of the historian is to engage and retain the reader's attention. On the other hand, "[h]istories of the downfall of kingdoms, and revolutions of empires, are read with tranquility" since they are so far removed from normal human experience (*Rambler* 60, 3:322). The local, as it is more familiar, more intimate, and more easily identifiable, allows lessons to be more easily learned. Although Johnson was still interested in universal principles, he found them most often available in local history, and tried to utilize local detail in the service of his humanistic epistemology. Johnson's position corresponds with what Geertz entertains when he writes that "the shapes of knowledge are always ineluctably local, indivisible from their instruments and their encasements."[10]

Local history might seem like an unusual option for a resident of London during the Enlightenment, a time when the public sphere was "transformed" and the cosmopolitan was a mainstay of intellectual society. But Johnson is careful to distinguish between worthless detail and local knowledge: "The general and rapid narratives of history, which involve a thousand fortunes in the business of a day, and complicate innumerable incidents in one great transaction, afford few lessons applicable to private life" (*Rambler* 60, 3:319). The "innumerable incidents" which are cited merely to complicate "one great transaction" are simply an unnecessary embellishment. This is not to suggest that they are not important, as Johnson points out in *Idler* 84: "The examples and events of history press, indeed, upon the mind with the weight of truth." The problem is, rather, that "they are oftener employed for show than use, and rather diversify conversation than regulate life" (2:262). Detail becomes knowledge when it is used appropriately; if lessons are gleaned from it, a history book becomes a guide to life.

Closely related to the idea of local history is the construct of microhistory, essentially a microscopic analysis of social systems, and here too, Johnson is prescient of modern patterns and conceptions of knowledge and enquiry. In a microhistorical approach, even the smallest action reveals much about a large-scale system. Thus Giovanni Levi—who has written an admirable introduction to the subject of microhistory—gives the example of how "somebody going to buy a loaf of bread, actually encompasses the far wider system of the whole world's grain markets."[11] Here, the task of local historians and microhistorians alike is to validate the particular both in its own terms and by inferring the universal from it. A second example might be the work of the social and educational theorist Pierre Bourdieu, who has utilized aspects of microhistory in which Johnson was interested. The notion of a "reflexive sociology"—closely connected to the conception of microhistory that Johnson had valued—was embraced by Bourdieu as a method of analyzing society. Bourdieu found that by studying the unique historical properties of a given microcosm—whether it was the French academy or the Algerian working class—he could uncover "the universal laws that tendentially regulate the functioning of all fields."[12] Often, though, to the dismay of many observers, the universal is also "the common and the average."[13] We can see that Johnson was a precursor of Bourdieu to the extent that his writings recommend a local-universal sequence. Johnson's *Rambler* and *Idler* personae were dedicated to reflecting on the common aspects of everyday society which were also of general significance.

For Bourdieu, as he discovered when researching *Homo Academicus*, "reflexive sociology" is an effective method in the study of one's own environment. The best examples of this type of microhistory in Johnson are found in his "Historical Memoirs" published in the *Literary Magazine*. The first number of the *Literary Magazine*, in April 1756, contained Johnson's "Introduction to the Political State of Great Britain." There, in an important historical essay, Johnson uncovers two hundred years of European history to find the causes of the current conflict between England and France that would soon become the Seven Years' War. He shows how Great Britain shared in the "great scene of European ambition," the discovery and settlement of the Americas, and how England became a great naval power which enabled it to mount the European stage with confidence (*Politics*, 130). He explains that European commerce, even when outside European shores, was the driving force of many political skirmishes. Donald Greene calls the essay "a piece of substantial and serious historiography, with a concern for careful documentation much closer to that of the better historians of the twentieth century than to those of his own day" (*Politics*, 126). But this is also an example—one of many in Johnson's writings—of the kind of "reflexive sociology" that interested Bourdieu. Johnson peers into the corners of his own society to demonstrate universal desires for power and glory and he spent a lot of time dissecting "little England," for example in his analyses of the casket letters of Mary, Queen of Scots. What calls for more attention now is Johnson's application of the techniques of microhistory to foreign affairs, as for instance his contributions to the "Foreign History" column of the *Gentleman's Magazine*.

Now that scholars are beginning to turn their attention more fully to microhistory and local history—indeed, to historicize the historiographies themselves—they are able to appreciate with greater clarity the contribution of their exponents and originators in earlier periods. Thus David Simpson can call the Romantic poets local historians, as when Wordsworth extols the virtues of Grasmere and Tintern Abbey.[14] Johnson, whose concept of the value of the "local" is written into his idea of literary history in the *Lives of the Poets*, had called Denham the "originator of local poetry" where "some particular landscape [is] to be poetically described, with the addition of such embellishments as may be supplied by historical retrospection or incidental meditation" (*Lives*, 1:77). As a practicing literary historian, Johnson in the *Lives* successfully blends an appreciation of the English poets' contact with their immediate locale with a perspective that includes the value of Shakespearean "general nature," where "particular manners can be known to few" (*Shakespeare*, 7:61).

ITALY IN HISTORY AND IMAGINATION: "THE LIFE OF SARPI"

In 1768, Johnson notes that the writing of local histories "prevails much in many parts of the Continent." "I have been told," he continues, "that scarcely a village of [Italy] wants its historian" (*Letters*, 1:311). Italy presents an imaginative and historical challenge to Johnson, for although he never traveled there, according to E. S. de Beer, the country would have provided "a far richer field than the Hebrides for literary association and moral reflexion, the pursuits in which Johnson's heart and mind were most fully and actively engaged."[15] Despite his advanced age, in 1776 his lifelong dream was closest to realization: he and Baretti were to go to Italy with the Thrales. (When their son died, the trip was postponed indefinitely.) They had planned a typical Grand Tour route, with stops in Turin, Genoa, Milan, Bologna, Rome, and Tuscany as well as other European cities such as Paris and Geneva. "The grand object of travelling," Johnson told Boswell in 1776, "is to see the shores of the Mediterranean" (*Life*, 2:424). Yet throughout his life, Johnson listened wistfully to the anecdotes of those who had been on the Grand Tour. He also remarked to Boswell that "A man who has not been in Italy, is always conscious of an inferiority, from his not having seen what it is expected a man should see" (3:458).

Johnson could thus turn to Italian texts as a substitute for the land he probably would never see, and read voraciously the histories, poems, and travelogues of Italy. Among his readings were texts as varied as Machiavelli's *History of Florence* and the epics of Ariosto and Dante, as well as Brydone's *Tour through Sicily and Malta* and Addison's *Remarks on Several Parts of Italy*. He clearly esteemed Italian literature, as evidenced by the prefaces he wrote for Baretti's *Italian Library* and *Intro-*

∂uction to the Italian Language.[16] He wondered to Ramsay at one point whether any other nation had done as much for the literature and scholarship of Europe as the Italians and the French: "Paris was the second city for the revival of letters: Italy had it first, to be sure. What have we done for literature, equal to what was done by the Stephani and others in France?" (*Life*, 3:254). As we shall now see, however, Johnson's own contributions to the growing body of work on Italy in the eighteenth century demonstrate both his love for the Italian nation and a pertinent development of his historiographical consciousness and techniques.

Johnson's discussion of Italy in the "Life of Milton" reveals his knowledge, while his description of Milton's tour of Italy reflects his reading of travel guides: "At Rome, as at Florence, [Milton] staid only two months; a time indeed sufficient if he desired only to ramble with an explainer of its antiquities or to view palaces and count pictures, but certainly too short for the contemplation of learning, policy, or manners" (*Lives*, 1:95). Johnson treated Milton's visit romantically: "From Florence he went to Siena, and from Siena to Rome, where he was again received with kindness by the learned and the great" (94). But Milton's controversial religious positions were cause for some alarm in Italy, and Johnson spends several paragraphs detailing the fears his friends had for his well-being, emphasizing the tyranny of the Roman Catholic Church. Nevertheless, it is clear from the passage that Johnson was closely interested in the particulars of the itinerary of Milton's travels, not least for the poetry—both Milton's and several encomiums by other poets in return—that resulted from it. An Italian journey was an inspiration and an achievement for English writers. Even when his unfulfilled trip to Italy was still in the planning stage, Johnson considered writing a book about his experiences upon his return.

But Johnson had planned to write about Italy even earlier in his career. A translation of Paolo Sarpi's *History of the Council of Trent*, begun in 1737, was one of his first historical projects. For Johnson, an English edition of Sarpi could have been the key to literary and professional success: a demonstration of his erudition, recognition, and acceptance by the educated public, and the potential to attract the attention of Queen Caroline, who was interested in intellectual theology. The seventeenth-century account was essentially a detailed attack by a Venetian cleric on the Catholic Church, its leaders, and its failed attempt to reunify Catholics and Reformers in Europe through the Council of Trent proceedings from 1562 to 1564. The implications of this account for Venetian politics were great, as the republic and its senate had been placed under an interdict by the Pope in 1606. Sarpi saw the Council of Trent as representative of the kind of injustice and corruption in official Catholicism that contemporary Venetians faced.

As Johnson would doubtless appreciate clearly, the debacle of the Council of Trent became an effective tool for Protestant states, especially England, during the Counter-Reformation and beyond. The Venetian position—criticizing the council, practicing Catholicism on its own terms, and later being excommunicated by the Catholic Church—"seemed to corroborate the justice of England's stand against the temporal claims of the Pope," in the words of Frances Amelia Yates. Yates points out that "The affairs of Venice had been followed in England with an interest which sometimes amounted to passion, not only for their own sake but because they could be used to point various morals nearer home."[17] The recent history of Venice, then, would certainly have been of interest to Johnson, both for its own sake, and as a model, or exemplification, of how history may be written and conceived.

The genesis of, and background to, Johnson's "Life of Sarpi" may be summarized as follows. In England, James I provided major support both to Venice and to Sarpi during the interdiction period, hoping that events in the republic might pave the way for reform. James interpreted the papal bull of 1605 as an affront to his royal status, and as early as 1606, Sarpi's anti-interdiction pamphlets were smuggled to England and widely read. The manuscript of the *History of the Council of Trent* was brought to England and first printed there (in Italian) in 1619; the text was dedicated to King James. Sarpi was considered a hero not only by James but also by the clergy for his challenge to Rome. "For Anglican apologists," writes Thomas Kaminski, "Sarpi remained a representative of liberal Catholicism seeking the reunion of the Christian churches through reform."[18] Venetian Catholics also sought a return to the "origins" of the church, as did Anglicans, according to Yates,[19] and even a century later, priests in Europe were following Sarpi's lead. One of these, Pierre François Le Courayer, fled France for England after writing a defense of the Anglican Church, and was welcomed by many, including Queen Caroline, who suggested a translation of Sarpi into French. As "one of the last major expressions of the republican culture of the Italian Renaissance," the *History*, according to William Bouswma, would appeal to Englishmen on both sides of the republic-empire debate.[20] Johnson knew that he could situate himself in this debate through careful consideration of Venice's independence before and after the interdiction.

Confident in his abilities, Johnson contacted the printer Edward Cave about the translation. His proposal included translating the Italian and preparing scholarly notes and a commentary. But the original text was a folio of over eight hundred pages; the Le Courayer translation had been published only recently, and had already reached a wide audience, considerations that made Cave wary of the project. But although he eventually agreed, the translation was never completed: Johnson's own procrastination, followed by the announcement of a rival English translation, would be the final blows to the project in 1737.

Though the translation of the *History* was eventually abandoned, Johnson retained an interest in its author, and a year later published the "Life of Father Paul Sarpi" in Cave's *Gentleman's Magazine*. Although it is one of Johnson's earliest forays into biography, and is translated in part from Le Courayer's *Vie de Sarpi*,[21] it bears the classic marks of Johnson's biographical style: pointed description, comprehensive judgments, an assessment of the subject's claim on posterity. Equally significant, however, is the conceptualization of history that arises from the biographical text. Johnson's method is consonant with Valerie Ross's contention that biographies ought to be called "historiographies of the subject."[22]

Johnson begins by providing the memorable, even sensational details that sometimes characterize Johnsonian "Lives" that are much better known: Sarpi "was born for study, having a natural aversion to pleasure and gaiety, and a memory so tenacious, that he could repeat thirty verses upon once hearing them."[23] He lingers briefly on instances of the child prodigy, but introduces political controversy by making a point of the "great zeal" of Sarpi's family against his decision to enter the priesthood. Sarpi disregarded his family's wishes, took orders at the age of fourteen, and became a priest at twenty-two; along the way, according to Johnson, he "left no branch of knowledge untouched" (12:5). However, Johnson moves very quickly in the "Life of Sarpi" from the particulars of Father Paul's rising career in the Catholic Church to a dramatic scene of religious and political controversy in seventeenth-century Venice, the details of which are only peripheral to Sarpi's personal life. He launches into a discussion about Pope Paul V's bull of 1606, which decried what Johnson terms "some decrees of the senate of Venice that interfered with the *pretended* rights of the church" (12:6, my emphasis).[24] Granted, Sarpi did contribute to the essays published in protest against the papal bull, but Johnson does not even discuss them. Instead, he moves away from Sarpi and focuses on the Pope's arguments for excommunication of the Venetians.

Johnson lists the Pope's claims in a manner which highlights the reflexive and literary nature of his biographical-historical text. But his goal here seems to be not to delve into the personal experience of Sarpi for its own sake so much as to explore the historical events of the period in order to develop his own views on the activities of the Catholic Church:

The propositions maintained on the side of Rome were these: That the Pope is invested with all the authority of heaven and earth. That all princes are his vassals, and that he may annul their laws at pleasure. . . . That he may depose kings without any fault committed by them, if the good of the church requires it. . . . That the Pope cannot err. . . that the Pope is God upon earth; [and] that his sentence and that of God are the same.

Johnson calls these "maxims equally shocking, weak, pernicious, and absurd," and almost as an aside, qualifies them as points which "did not require the abilities or learning of Father Paul, to demonstrate their falsehood, and destructive tendency" (12:7). He thus digresses from the biographical flow in the interests of historical speculation. While Richard Ellmann has noted that biography may be "intrusive" in history, here, history intrudes on biography.[25] Biographical and historical narrative are linked through a common moral purpose in Johnson's hands.

Similarly, Johnson passes judgment on the literary abilities of the Pope's advocates, who "defended the papal claims with great scurrility of expression, and very sophistical reasonings," which, in Johnson's opinion, "were confuted by the Venetian apologists in much more decent language, and with much greater solidity of argument" (12:6). It was that literary failure, Johnson claims, that forced the Pope to "conclude the affair by treaty" (12:8). Johnson's own efforts to narrate the Venetian side of the story are marked with elements of those "arrangements" and "colourings" that Johnson admitted were necessary to bring history alive. For instance, when describing the assassination attempt on Sarpi, he tells a romantic, almost gothic moral tale: "The murderers fled for refuge to the nuncio, and were afterwards received into the Pope's dominions, but were pursued by divine justice, and all, except one man who died in prison, perished by violent deaths" (12:8). The episode is recounted not because we need to know what happened to the assassins, but because it reflects papal vengeance and because it allows Johnson to retain the heightened sense of drama he established in the earlier sections of the "Life."

Not surprisingly, the "Life of Sarpi" contains echoes of, and influences from, the same historical techniques used by Sarpi himself in his *History of the Council of Trent.* For like Sarpi, at this point in his career, Johnson was free from the obligation to represent the official view of the church or its enemies. The parallelism between Sarpi's historiographical practice and Johnson's resonates throughout the "Life." The Venetian believed in history as empirical exploration undertaken to tell the truth about the past, and according to Bouswma, "he considered knowledge of history potentially useful and occasionally urgent; historical composition was to be judged above all by its utility for the purposes of men." Like Johnson, Sarpi sought impartiality and pragmatism, and Venetian historiography, as Bouswma elsewhere suggests, "was admired because of its capacity to get at and effectively to reveal the truth."[26]

Despite its brevity and occasional quality, Johnson's "Life of Sarpi" shows that we may not have been looking for history in the right places in Johnson's works, and it helps us begin to understand the wide range of Johnson's interests in European history. For it may be that in contrast to many eighteenth-century Englishmen—Gray, Thomson, Gibbon—Italy in Johnson's mind and imagination was not an end in itself; it was merely the instance of a much larger subject: the history of Europe as a whole. Such a view is in keeping with the philosophical historians of the period such as Hume and Bolingbroke, who were proponents of exemplary history. Events in Italy could serve as a model, as well as a cautionary tale, for other Europeans, and, in this case, English readers.

Like so much of Johnson's thought, then, his view of European history is bifurcated: on the one hand, thinking of Italy would be a medium of expression for his cosmopolitan outlook and a metaphor for the universal human condition. (See the essay by Clement Hawes earlier in this volume.) On the other, Johnson was drawn to provincial, local idiosyncrasies, the particular events and individuals responsible for historical change. In the "Life of Sarpi," Johnson is at once local and international, and like Bourdieu he shows that "the opposition between the universal and the unique, between nomothetic analysis and idiographic description, is a false antimony."[27] Johnson never wrote an extended historical study like Hume's *History of England*, Gibbon's *Decline and Fall*, or Robertson's *History of Charles V*. But Johnson's "idea of history," inferred here from one overlooked avenue of his biographical work, can nevertheless take its place among the innovative historical thought of his period.

NOTES

1. Thomas Babington Macaulay, *The Complete Works of Lord Macaulay*, 12 vols. (New York: Longmans, Green, 1898), 10:481.

2. Jean Hagstrum, *Samuel Johnson's Literary Criticism* (Minneapolis: University of Minnesota Press, 1952; Chicago: University of Chicago Press, 1967), 23.

3. Godfrey Davies, "Dr. Johnson's History," *HLQ* 12 (1948): 1–21; William Keast, "Johnson and Intellectual History," in *New Light on Johnson*, ed. Frederick Hilles (New Haven: Yale University Press, 1959), 247–56; John Vance, *Samuel Johnson and the Sense of History* (Athens: University of Georgia Press, 1984).

4. The second definition is "Narration; relation," and the third "The knowledge of facts and events."

5. Henry St. John, Viscount Bolingbroke, *Letters on the Study and Use of History*, in *Historical Writings*, ed. Isaac Kramnick (Chicago: University of Chicago Press, 1972),

9. Note, though, that Bolingbroke was clearly against local knowledge for its own sake: "we must rise from particular to general knowledge" (25).

6. R. G. Collingwood, *The Idea of History* (Oxford: Clarendon Press, 1946), 203.

7. Leo Damrosch, *Fictions of Reality in the Age of Hume and Johnson* (Madison: University of Wisconsin Press, 1989), 3, 7; Williams, *Politics and Letters* (London: NLB, 1979), 325–26.

8. Alan McKillop, "Local Attachment and Cosmopolitanism: The Eighteenth-Century Pattern," in Frederick Hilles and Harold Bloom, *From Sensibility to Romanticism* (New York: Oxford University Press, 1965), 191–218. The phrase "local attachment" comes from eighteenth-century sources themselves: for example, Richard Polwhele, *The Influence of Local Attachment with Respect to Hume* (London, 1790).

9. Clifford Geertz, *Local Knowledge* (New York: Basic Books, 1983), 6.

10. Ibid., 4.

11. Giovanni Levi, "On Microhistory," in *New Perspectives on Historical Writing*, ed. Peter Burke (University Park, Pa.: Pennsylvania State University Press, 1992), 96.

12. Pierre Bourdieu and Loic J. D. Wacquant, *An Invitation to Reflexive Sociology* (Chicago: University of Chicago Press, 1992), 75.

13. Ibid., 72.

14. David Simpson, *The Academic Postmodern and the Rule of Literature* (Chicago: University of Chicago Press, 1995), 137–45.

15. E. S. de Beer, "Johnson's Italian Tour," in *Johnson, Boswell, and Their Circle: Essays Presented to Lawrence F. Powell*, ed. M. Lascelles, James L. Clifford, J. D. Fleeman, and J. P. Hardy (Oxford: Clarendon Press, 1965), 169.

16. See Allen T. Hazen, *Samuel Johnson's Prefaces and Dedications* (New Haven: Yale University Press, 1937). In the *Prefazioni al Dizionario delle lingue italiana e inglese* (London, 1760), Baretti reprints the English grammar Johnson included in his *Dictionary*. See Baretti, *Prefazione e polemiche*, ed. Luigi Piscioni (Bari: Laterza e Figli, 1911).

17. Frances Amelia Yates, *Renaissance and Reform: The Italian Contribution* (London and Boston: Routledge, 1983), 194; 192.

18. Thomas Kaminski, *The Early Career of Samuel Johnson* (New York: Oxford University Press, 1987), 68.

19. "In Venice, Englishmen saw a living representative of the old Catholic world, to which they themselves claimed still to belong, joining with them for a brief moment in protest against 'Popery' " (207).

20. William Bouswma, *Venice and the Defense of Republican Liberty* (Berkeley: University of California Press, 1968), 572.

21. See Walter Jackson Bate, *Samuel Johnson* (New York: Harcourt Brace Jovanovich, 1977), 219; Donald Greene, *The Politics of Samuel Johnson*, 2nd ed. (Athens: University of Georgia Press, 1990), 109.

22. Valerie Ross, "Too Close to Home: Repressing Biography, Instituting Authority," in *Contesting the Subject*, ed. William H. Epstein (West Lafayette, Ind.: Purdue University Press, 1996), 135–66.

23. "Life of Paolo Sarpi," in *The Works of Samuel Johnson*, ed. Arthur Murphy, 12 vols. (London, 1810), 12:7. Subsequent references are cited by volume and page number parenthetically in the text.

24. Note that Johnson misdates the interdict of 1606 as 1615.

25. See Richard Ellmann, *Golden Codgers: Biographical Speculations* (New York: Oxford University Press, 1973). I am grateful to Susan Goulding for this observation.

26. William Bouswma, "Venice and the Political Education of Europe," in *Renaissance Venice*, ed. J. R. Hale (Totowa, N.J.: Rowman and Littlefield, 1973), 593; 460.

27. Bourdieu, *Reflexive Sociology*, 75.

BIBLIOGRAPHY

Baretti, Giuseppe. *Prefazione e polemiche*. Edited by Luigi Piscioni. Bari: Laterza e Figli, 1911.

Bate, Walter Jackson. *Samuel Johnson*. New York: Harcourt Brace Jovanovich, 1977.

Bolingbroke, Henry St. John. *Letters on the Study and Use of History*. In *Historical Writings*. Edited by Isaac Kramnick. Chicago: University of Chicago Press, 1972.

Boswell, James. *Boswell's Life of Johnson*. 6 vols. Edited by George Birkbeck Hill. Revised by L. F. Powell. Oxford: Clarendon Press, 1934–64.

Bourdieu, Pierre, and Loic J. D. Wacquant. *An Invitation to Reflexive Sociology*. Chicago: University of Chicago Press, 1992.

Bouswma, William. *Venice and the Defense of Republican Liberty*. Berkeley: University of California Press, 1968.

———. "Venice and the Political Education of Europe." In *Renaissance Venice*. Edited by J. R. Hale. Totowa, N.J.: Rowman and Littlefield, 1973.

Collingwood, R. G. *The Idea of History*. Oxford: Clarendon Press, 1946.

Damrosch, Leo. *Fictions of Reality in the Age of Hume and Johnson*. Madison: University of Wisconsin Press, 1989.

Davies, Godfrey. "Dr. Johnson's History." *Huntington Library Quarterly* 12 (1948): 1–21.

de Beer, E. S. "Johnson's Italian Tour." In *Johnson, Boswell, and Their Circle: Essays Presented to Lawrence F. Powell*. Edited by M. Lascelles, James L. Clifford, J. D. Fleeman, and J. P. Hardy. Oxford: Clarendon Press, 1965.

Geertz, Clifford. *Local Knowledge*. New York: Basic Books, 1983.

Greene, Donald J. *The Politics of Samuel Johnson*. 2nd ed. Athens: University of Georgia Press, 1990.

Hagstrum, Jean H. *Samuel Johnson's Literary Criticism*. Minneapolis: University of Minnesota Press, 1952; Chicago: University of Chicago Press, 1967.

Hazen, Allen T., ed. *Samuel Johnson's Prefaces and Dedications*. New Haven: Yale University Press, 1937.

Johnson, Samuel. *A Dictionary of the English Language*. 2 vols. London: 1755.

———. *Johnson on Shakespeare*. Edited by Arthur Sherbo. Vol. 7 of The Yale Edition of the Works of Samuel Johnson. New Haven and London: Yale University Press, 1968.

———. *The Letters of Samuel Johnson*. 5 vols. Edited by Bruce Redford. Princeton: Princeton University Press, 1992.

———. *The Lives of the English Poets*. 3 vols. Edited by George Birkbeck Hill. Oxford: Clarendon Press, 1905.

———. *Rasselas and Other Tales*. Edited by Gwin J. Kolb. Vol. 16 of The Yale Edition of the Works of Samuel Johnson. New Haven and London: Yale University Press, 1990.

———. *The Works of Samuel Johnson*. 12 vols. Edited by Arthur Murphy. London: 1810.

Kaminski, Thomas. *The Early Career of Samuel Johnson*. New York: Oxford University Press, 1987.

Keast, William. "Johnson and Intellectual History." In *New Light on Johnson*. Edited by Frederick Hilles. New Haven: Yale University Press, 1959.

Levi, Giovanni. "On Microhistory." In *New Perspectives on Historical Writing*. Edited by Peter Burke. University Park, Pa.: Pennsylvania State University Press, 1992.

Macaulay, Thomas Babington. *The Complete Works of Lord Macaulay*. 12 vols. New York: Longmans, Green, 1898.

McKillop, Alan. "Local Attachment and Cosmopolitanism: The Eighteenth-Century Pattern." In *From Sensibility to Romanticism*. Edited by Frederick Hilles and Harold Bloom. New York: Oxford University Press, 1965.

Ross, Valerie. "Too Close to Home: Repressing Biography, Instituting Authority." In *Contesting the Subject*. Edited by William H. Epstein. West Lafayette, Ind.: Purdue University Press, 1996.

Vance, John. *Samuel Johnson and the Sense of History*. Athens: University of Georgia Press, 1984.

Williams, Raymond. *Politics and Letters*. London: NLB, 1979.

Yates, Frances Amelia. *Renaissance and Reform: The Italian Contribution*. London and Boston: Routledge, 1983.

Ironies of the Critical Past: Historicizing Johnson's Criticism

PHILIP SMALLWOOD

> Emphatically may it be said of the Poet, as Shakespeare hath said
> of man, 'that he looks before and after.' He is the rock of defence
> for human nature; an upholder and preserver, carrying everywhere
> with him relationship and love. . . . [T]here can be little doubt but
> that more pathetic situations and sentiments, that is, those which
> have a greater proportion of pain connected with them, may be en-
> dured in metrical composition. . . . This opinion may be further illus-
> trated by appealing to the Reader's own experience of the
> reluctance with which he comes to the re-perusal of the distressful
> parts of Clarissa Harlowe, or the Gamester; while Shakspeare's
> writings, in the most pathetic scenes, never act upon us, as pathetic,
> beyond the bounds of pleasure.
>
> —William Wordsworth, preface to *Lyrical Ballads*

IN HIS NOTES TO HIS EDITION OF SHAKESPEARE OF 1765, JOHNSON
confessed how he had once felt when coming to the end of a famous
Shakespearean tragedy:

> Cordelia, from the time of Tate, has always retired with victory and felicity.
> And, if my sensations could add any thing to the general suffrage, I might
> relate, that I was many years ago so shocked by Cordelia's death, that I
> know not whether I ever endured to read again the last scenes of the play
> till I undertook to revise them as an editor. (*Shakespeare*, 8:704)

In a century which has concluded with F. R. Leavis (in the 1940s) that
Johnson's criticism is "not for direct instruction in critical thinking,"
with Jean Hagstrum (in the 1950s) that "[Johnson's] example is not
one to be followed in our day," and with John Wain (in the 1970s) that
Johnson's mind "was not a modern mind" whose views "are not, and
in most respects never can be, our views,"[1] this momentary glimpse into
the private depths of Johnson's emotional consciousness—quoted and
discussed by Greg Clingham in the opening essay of this volume—has
been often remarked, puzzled over, or simply dismissed.[2] Yet Johnson's

114

at once strained, intimate, and curiously self-opening statement points to the presence of a critical past that can still disturb us after almost 250 years. In what follows I will touch on some of the questions about the quality of Johnson's critical relationship to the present of criticism that are raised by the historicizing claim that Johnson's views "never can be" ours and that his criticism is "not for direct instruction in critical thinking." To set such statements in context, and provide a foil to the discussion of Johnson's own distinctively different historicization of the critical past, I will first give an account of how Johnson has fared in twentieth-century representations of eighteenth-century criticism written within the historical mode. On what "principles of history" are histories of this kind conceived?

DETERMINIST REPRESENTATIONS OF JOHNSON'S CRITICISM

Readers who looked for information on Samuel Johnson in major histories of criticism written in the twentieth century—volume two of George Saintsbury's *A History of Criticism and Literary Taste* of 1902, the first volume of René Wellek's *History of Modern Criticism, 1750–1950* of 1955, and the recently published volume four of the *Cambridge History of Literary Criticism* of 1997[3]—might be less concerned to gain "direct instruction in critical thinking" from the critical past than to discover a number of plausibly ascertainable facts; yet if modern historiographical theory as developed by Michel Foucault, Hayden White, or Paul Ricoeur is correct, the "facts" of history are conditioned by the textuality, the inescapable fictionality of historical composition.[4] Other twentieth-century theorists of history have examined the pervasiveness of treatments of the past where ultimate power is exerted by "causes largely beyond the control of individuals." In this connection Isaiah Berlin has explained how determinist theories of history have one common characteristic—"the implication that the individual's freedom of choice . . . is ultimately an illusion."[5] The particular "entity" or "spiritual organism" (in Berlin's terms) to which the most influential representations of eighteenth-century criticism are committed is "neoclassicism." This "larger unit" is seen by historians of criticism to have imposed a cast-iron set of initial assumptions upon individual critics. The continuing presence of "neoclassicism" as an organizational motif for the history of eighteenth-century criticism leads to two observations: (1) the extraordinary *inertia* of historical accounts of past literary criticism—with all the differences of cultural situation and contemporary context that hold them apart, a history published in 1997 can be found using an interpretive framework substantially similar to that of histories published in 1902 and 1955; (2)

the tendency of historians of criticism, like intellectual historians, to conceive their material in terms of *ideas*. Such a tendency has critical implications for the historians' conception of their logical subject: by the organization of classificatory units into narrative chains, historians of criticism are able to locate the work of an earlier critic such as Samuel Johnson at a conceptually more primitive stage in the development of this subject than they are. Yet while no one can blame a historian for selecting and interpreting his facts (the notion of bare facts untainted by interpretation or arrangement is—as Berlin reminds us—equally mythological),[6] we shall see that there comes a point where the historical patterning of Johnson's significance offends too deeply against the canons of verification which we ordinarily apply to what does not change whoever is looking at it, and where what is left out of the account seems too elementary.

Using the rubric of "Eighteenth-Century Orthodoxy" to claim that Johnson's "general critical attitude" was one of rigidity which he could never entirely evade, George Saintsbury's verdict on Johnson was as follows:

> [I]n the four great documents of *The Rambler*, *Rasselas*, the Shakespeare *Preface*, and the *Lives*, we see it in the two first rigid, peremptory, in the *Preface*, curiously and representatively uncertain, in the last conditioned by differences which allow it somewhat freer play, and at some times making a few concessions, but at others more pugnacious and arbitrary than before. (480)

The tendency of this intellectual context is reinforced by interest in the defects of Johnson the Man. Saintsbury (like Macaulay before him) constructs a caricature based on Johnson's variously alleged physical and temperamental eccentricities and ailments. Johnson approached the task of criticism with his mind made up, with a natural Toryism and a "transcendental scepticism."[7] Being nearsighted, he was "entirely insensible to the beauties of nature." He "liked human society in its most artificial form—that provided by towns, clubs, parties." He had no ear for poetry except for "an extremely regular and almost mathematical beat of verse" (478–79). Saintsbury's loquacious tale of cheerful inconsistency and dogmatism in Johnson creates a comic persona where Toryism and visual or aural impairment are logically linked. His *History* thereby accommodates Johnson to the terms of a certain kind of phony, sentimentalist national past. In this conception, Johnson's tastes and attitudes are confined to the patrimonial or English heritage Johnson, the literary critic of olden, golden times.

Wellek's account some half a century later is darker in tone. Johnson is now a transitional mind in turmoil. He is suspended at midpoint between the fixed statutes of neoclassical theory and the freedoms of a romantic aesthetic. His consciousness is the site of a cultural schizophrenia. The field of conflict is Johnson's mentality and the inner narrative a tragedy of psychic incoherence. Like Saintsbury, however, Wellek is also inclined to award Johnson marks according to his freedom from neoclassic rules: "While Johnson . . . is liberal in the matter of decorum in characterization, he holds firmly to neoclassical views about decorum in language" (90). Once again, Johnson's critical attitudes are explained by early influences: "Dr Johnson's ear must have been early attuned only to the heroic couplet, whose niceties and differences he was obviously very well able to perceive and to describe," so that "Johnson is . . . firmly rooted and even enclosed in the taste of his own age" (92–93). Wellek goes on to explain how, in certain respects, Johnson conceptually lagged behind the times in which he lived: he "seems hardly touched by two of the new motifs of 18th-century criticism: aesthetics and cosmopolitanism" (93).[8]

Johnson's sense of the want of sincere emotion in some metaphysical poems, or in Milton's *Lycidas*, is for Wellek a sign of the limited vision that is the *inevitable* accompaniment of the neoclassical mind. To Johnson's criticism of *Lycidas*, for example, that "It is not to be considered as the effusion of real passion" (*Lives*, 1: 163), Wellek's response is that "Johnson does not realize that the requirement of sincere grief in the poet himself, though justifiable by Horatian or even Aristotelian precepts . . . introduces the standard of the individual experience of the author, which is both indeterminable and aesthetically false" (80–81). From this assessment of Johnson's role in the historical structure, and the deficit view of "neoclassical" tradition on which it depends, it follows that the modern historian can stand in a position of superior modernity to Johnson which makes even his praise seem faint:

> Johnson's concept of poetic justice is not always so obtusely literal minded . . . it is impossible to dismiss him as a mere moralist or expounder of a realistic view which confounds art and life. . . . He recognizes that realism is not enough. . . . Johnson correctly grasps what modern aestheticians would call "aesthetic distance." (83, 84, 85, 89)

According to Wellek, Johnson struggles with only partial success to conceive with all the powers at his command what we, apparently without any undue effort, can simply suppose. Wellek stresses the difficulty Johnson found in reconciling concepts that there is no evidence he actually used as critical terms. Johnson deals with "realism," "moralism," and "abstractionism," writes Wellek, "apparently without a clear consciousness that these criteria lead to very different conclusions about the nature of art and the value of particular works of art" (87). Try harder, Dr. Johnson.

Within these assumptions, Wellek can then conclude that Johnson's conception of genius has "*none* of the romantic connotations" (96, my emphasis). Johnson "cannot show *any* interest in the new theory of the creative imagination" (96, my emphasis again). But in making such claims, Wellek's account is representative of a central problem in the historicization of Johnson's criticism—and criticism of the eighteenth century more generally perhaps—that deserves some closer attention at this point. This is the fact that most histories of criticism in which Johnson is discussed have tended to impose a template upon their view of the critical past that has very specific sympathies within history itself. For reasons I shall now attempt to explain, this template calls into question both the *accuracy* of the history and the reliability of the readings of the texts of criticism upon which history is based.

The constituent of criticism that this representation seems most consistently to suppress, I would argue, finds its epitome in Johnson's emotionally charged response to *King Lear*. When this example is recalled, Wellek's textual underpinning for his judgments does not seem to justify the confidence of his critical interpretation of Johnson, or the larger historical conclusions concerning the relations of eighteenth and nineteenth centuries to which these tend. Wellek does not allude to Johnson's striking enthusiasm for "the current of the poet's imagination" in *King Lear*:

> The tragedy of Lear is deservedly celebrated among the dramas of Shakespeare. There is perhaps no play which keeps the attention so strongly fixed; which so much agitates our passions and interests our curiosity. The artful involutions of distinct interests, the striking opposition of contrary characters, the sudden changes of fortune, and the quick succession of events, fill the mind with a perpetual tumult of indignation, pity, and hope. There is no scene which does not contribute to the aggravation of the distress or conduct of the action, and scarce a line which does not conduce to the progress of the scene. *So powerful is the current of the poet's imagination, that the mind, which once ventures within it, is hurried irresistibly along.* (*Shakespeare*, 8:702–3, my emphasis)

The implication that Johnson does not comprehend "the new theory of the creative imagination" emphasizes by contrast the mechanistic idea of drama, and the rigid notion of moral purpose, in Johnson's conception of Shakespeare—the thought that Johnson wanted Shakespeare to follow the "rules." Wellek does not foreground Johnson's extraordinary praise of Shakespeare's moral power in the "Preface" or his sensitivity to questions of right and wrong in his notes, but instead observes that Johnson complained of "Shakespeare's lack of morality" (84).[9] This observation seems to be based on the belief that "Johnson . . . frequently required poetical justice" (83). Yet the evidence of the text (as distinct from the historical narrative it is made to support) suggests that Johnson's position cannot be confined by this term. Johnson's use of "poetical justice" is *either* descriptive and cursory (as in his "General Observation" on Shakespeare's *Hamlet*: "The poet is accused of having shewn little regard to poetical justice, and may be charged with equal neglect of poetical probability" [*Shakespeare*, 8:1011]) *or* confutational, as in his "Life of Addison": "He [Dennis] then condemns the neglect of poetical justice. . . . The stage may sometimes gratify our wishes; but, if it be truly the *mirror of life*, it ought to shew us sometimes what we are to expect" (*Lives*, 2:134–35). In his note on *King Lear*, a play we have seen is *praised* by Johnson for the "aggravation of the distress," Johnson *reports* Dennis's complaints about the discrediting of "poetical justice" by the *Spectator* at the time of Tate's alteration, but refers himself to Shakespeare having suffered the virtue of Cordelia to perish in a just cause "contrary to the *natural* ideas of justice" (my emphasis). Just as "all reasonable beings naturally love justice," Johnson goes on to say that "I cannot easily be persuaded, that the observation of justice makes a play worse; or, that if other excellencies are equal, the audience will not always rise better pleased from the final triumph of persecuted virtue" (*Shakespeare*, 8:704).[10] In the general criticism on the "faults" of Shakespeare in his "Preface to Shakespeare" of 1765, he writes of "justice," but not "poetical justice." His *exact* words are these:

> His first defect is that to which may be imputed most of the evil in books or in men. He sacrifices virtue to convenience, and is so much more careful to please than to instruct, that he seems to write without any moral purpose. . . . he carries his persons indifferently through right and wrong, and at the close dismisses them without further care, and leaves their examples to operate by chance. This fault the barbarity of his age cannot extenuate; for it is always a writer's duty to make the world better, and justice is a virtue independant on time or place. (*Shakespeare*, 7:71)

With the phrase "natural ideas of justice," and the proviso that Shakespeare "*seems* to write without any moral purpose," we can recall that Johnson had also drawn attention earlier in the same essay to Shakespeare's "wide extension of design" and that from this "so much instruction is derived" (62). Johnson had elevated Shakespeare to the supreme position within the canon of European literature as "the poet of nature" (62), while in *King Lear*, Shakespeare was the poet whose imagination expressed "nature," not by gratifying our wishes, *or* showing us "what we are to expect," but by exciting a "perpetual tumult of indignation, pity, and hope." It is precisely the "genius" and "imagination" of Shakespeare, such textual "facts" might suggest, which provoke "indignation" and emotional pain when the justice demanded by reasonable beings is outraged. Despite the lapses of care, morally, in some of the plays, or in all of the plays for some of the time, it seems to be this which gives Shakespeare the presiding moral importance that Johnson allows him.

Wellek's failure to appreciate the centrality of Shakespeare to the construction of Johnson's idea of "genius" in turn leads to an overestimate of the value Johnson was able to place on the movement toward "nature" made by the "genius" of Dryden and Pope, and it enables Wellek to regard the operations of "genius" and the test of "nature" as necessarily opposed. The conception of "genius" is not limited by Johnson's conception of Shakespeare. Fifteen years after the "Preface" and the notes to Shakespeare, Johnson describes Dryden's compositions in the *Lives of the Poets* as "the effects of a vigorous genius operating upon large materials" ("Life of Dryden," *Lives*, 1:457), while Pope, according to Johnson, had "in proportions very nicely adjusted to each other, all the qualities that constitute genius" (*Lives*, 3:247). Johnson had earlier and memorably written in the "Life of Pope" of "genius" as "a mind active, ambitious, and adventurous, always investigating, always aspiring; in its widest searches still longing to go forward, in its highest flights still wishing to be higher; always imagining something greater than it knows, always endeavouring more than it can do" (217). For Johnson, as he thinks of Pope, "genius" is "that power which constitutes a poet; that quality without which judgement is cold and knowledge is inert; that energy which collects, combines, amplifies and animates" (222).[11]

But in the course of his narrative Wellek seems to believe that it was in versification and diction that Johnson viewed his own time as the "pinnacle of perfection" (92), while his commentary at this point seems to pass over the many severely qualifying judgments of Pope's and Dryden's poetry in the *Lives*—his highlighting of the shortcomings of the *Essay on Man*, for example, which as Mason and Rounce note in this volume's concluding essay, is "not the happiest of Pope's performances" and where the subject is "not very proper for poetry" (*Lives*, 3:242), the extravagance and inhumanity of many of Dryden's heroic plays, or the more general account of Dryden's poetical limits in the conclusion to the "Life": "With the simple and elemental passions, as they spring separate in the mind," wrote Johnson of Dryden, "he seems not much acquainted" (*Lives*, 1:457). Some of the poems taken by the twentieth century to represent Dryden at his characteristic best are somewhat coldly regarded by Johnson. The criticism he has of Dryden's *Absalom and Achitophel*, for example, is that the treatment of its subject is ultimately one-track. The poem "admitted little imagery or description, and a long poem of mere sentiments easily becomes tedious; though all the parts are forcible and every line kindles new rapture, the reader, if not relieved by the interposition of something that sooths the fancy, grows weary of admiration, and defers the rest" (*Lives*, 1:437). Such judgments not only raise the question of what Johnson actually says about Dryden, Pope, and Pope's influence in the eighteenth century, but suggest the implications of his estimate of Dryden and Pope for the kind of historical narrative that can be made plausible in a history of criticism.

In the passage on the language of Pope's translation of Homer, Johnson had written that:

> There is a time when nations emerging from barbarity, and falling into regular subordination, gain leisure to grow wise, and feel the shame of ignorance and the craving pain of unsatisfied curiosity. To this hunger of the mind plain sense is grateful; that which fills the void removes uneasiness, and to be free from pain for a while is pleasure; but repletion generates fastidiousness, a saturated intellect soon becomes luxurious, and knowledge finds no willing reception till it is recommended by artificial diction. (*Lives*, 3:239)

In determining that the eighteenth-century development shows (in Johnson's conception) "a progress of English poetry toward an ideal technical norm attained especially by Pope" (103), Wellek necessarily turns his back on the inferences to be drawn from "fastidiousness," "saturated" and "luxurious" as they inflect the phrase "artificial diction." But in undervaluing the subtlety of Johnson's judgment of Pope, with its weighing of praise and blame, Wellek also commits himself to a type of historical narrative that underplays some of the more obvious and explicit continua between Johnson's criticism and the romantic critics. In the first place, Wellek is typical of critical historians of Johnson in sliding over the historical survivals of Johnsonian criticism of Shakespeare in Hazlitt, Coleridge, and Schlegel. Schlegel, not unlike Wellek himself in the twentieth century, complained of Johnson that he had confused art and life, but his appeal to the concept of the "romantic drama" as "neither tragedies nor comedies in the sense of the ancients," where "all contrarieties . . . are blended together in the most intimate combination,"[12] is clearly reminiscent of what Johnson had said, one-half century earlier, on the "mingled drama" of Shakespeare: "Shakespeare's plays are not in the rigorous and critical sense either tragedies or comedies, but compositions of a distinct kind; exhibiting the real state of sublunary nature, which partakes of good and evil, joy and sorrow, mingled with endless variety of proportion and innumerable modes of combination. . . ." (*Shakespeare*, 7:66).[13]

Hazlitt complained of Johnson that he "might cut down imagination to matter-of-fact, regulate the passions according to reason, and translate the whole into logical diagrams and rhetorical declamation,"[14] but his criteria are in no fundamental sense distinguishable from the ones that Johnson had used in praise of Shakespeare. "The characters in Shakespear," wrote Hazlitt, "do not declaim like pedantic school-boys, but speak and act like men, placed in real circumstances."[15] For Johnson:

> It will not easily be imagined how much Shakespeare excells in accommodating his sentiments to real life, but by comparing him with other authors. It was observed of the ancient schools of declamation, that the more diligently they were frequented, the more was the student disqualified for the world, because he found nothing there which he should ever meet in any other place. The same remark may be applied to every stage but that of Shakespeare. (*Shakespeare*, 7:63)

The consequence of such omissions is that Wellek is able to exaggerate the Johnsonian commitment to Dryden's and Pope's perfecting of versification and diction, and thus to obscure the means whereby Johnson was able to prepare the way, however unknowingly, for a more open and thoroughgoing attack on the work of Dryden, Pope, (and Johnson himself) by Wordsworth. This is what Wordsworth—somewhat less equivocally than Johnson—was later to say of Pope's influence on poetry in the appendix to *Lyrical Ballads* first published in 1802:

> The earliest poets of all nations generally wrote from passion excited by real events; they wrote naturally, and as men: feeling powerfully as they did, their language was daring, and figurative. In succeeding times, Poets, and Men ambitious of the fame of Poets, perceiving the influence of such language, and desirous of producing the same effect without being animated by the same passion, set themselves to a mechanical adoption of these figures of speech, and made use of them, sometimes with propriety, but much more frequently applied them to feelings and thoughts with which they had no natural connection whatsoever. A language was thus insensibly produced, differing materially from the real language of men in *any situation*. . . . Poets, it is probable, who had before contented themselves for the most part with misapplying only expressions which at first had been dictated by real passion, carried the abuse still further, and introduced phrases composed apparently in the spirit of the original figurative language of passion, yet altogether of their own invention, and characterised by various degrees of wanton deviation from good sense and nature. (1:160–61)[16]

In order to expose the defects of the tradition of Pope, Wordsworth writes of "the real language of men." Hazlitt, in order to distinguish the Shakespearean from the artifice dominant in other kinds of drama, was to claim (in 1818) that the characters in Shakespeare's plays "are real beings of flesh and blood; they speak like men, not like authors."[17] But it was in 1779 that Johnson had criticized "a voluntary deviation from nature in pursuit of something new and strange" in the metaphysical poets ("Life of Cowley" [*Lives*, 1:35]),[18] and in 1765 that Johnson had written that "Addison speaks the language of poets, and Shakespeare, of men" [*Shakespeare*, 7:84]). Wordsworth's challenge to the later ages of poetry echoes the sequence of transitions from nature to art that can be found in the following passage from the "Preface to Shakespeare":

> It may be observed, that the oldest poets of many nations preserve their reputation, and that the following generations of wit, after a short celebrity, sink into oblivion. The first, whoever they be, must take their sentiments and descriptions immediately from knowledge; the resemblance is therefore just, their descriptions are verified by every eye, and their sentiments acknowledged by every breast. Those whom their fame invites to the same studies, copy partly them, and partly nature, till the books of one age gain such authority, as to stand in the place of nature to another, and imitation, always deviating a little, becomes at last capricious and casual. Shakespeare, whether life or nature be his subject, shews plainly, that he has seen with his own eyes; he gives the image which he receives, not weakened or distorted by the intervention of any other mind. (*Shakespeare*, 7:89–90)

Both Johnson and Wordsworth place the emphasis on the genuineness of "true passion" whose discriminations, in Johnson's phrase, are "the colours of nature." Both write of the poet conversing with "general nature" and of the "permanent" and the "durable" in their congruence with what Johnson called "the uniform simplicity of primitive qualities" (*Shakespeare*, 7:70), and Wordsworth in his prefaces of 1800 and 1850 "the primary laws of our nature" (1:122–23). Wordsworth was to affirm that "our elementary feelings co-exist [with each other and with nature] in a state of greater simplicity, and, consequently, may be more accurately contemplated, and more forcibly communicated" (1:125).[19] Both criticize the effect upon the traditions of poetry of such eighteenth-century departures from "nature" evident in the poetry of Gray, who (for Johnson) "thought his language more poetical as it was more remote from common use" (*Lives*, 3:435), and who (for Wordsworth) "was more than any other man curiously elaborate in the structure of his own poetic diction" (1:133). From correspondences of this kind it is apparent that there is an irony of consequence in the history of critical approaches to "artificial diction" which Wellek, qua historian, neglects to bring out. The extent of the overlap, resting as it does on key terms central to the priorities of both Wordsworth and Johnson, shifts the historical narrative of "classic to romantic" toward a different kind of story.

Wellek's *History* is now nearly half a century old. Yet there seems to be no essential difference, one could also point out, between the "certainties" of Wellek's account of Johnson's "neoclassical" commitments and what can be confidently said (surprisingly in the light of the efforts made by later Johnsonian scholarship) in the *Cambridge History* of 1997. While the deviation from what is ascertainable through the canons of verification is now without the excuse of an early work, the concept of "the real language of men" as used by Wordsworth in the passage quoted above, can be better explained in the *Cambridge History* by reference to the continental and romantic theories of Herder and Sulzer rather than to Johnson (139). At another point in this *History* there is evidence of a narrative of liberation from the past's bondage and enchainment that is very similar to Wellek's: "although Johnson lends his authority to the challenge to the unities," writes John Osborne, "he foregoes the appeal to imaginative participation in dramatic illusion which was to be so essential to those younger dramatists and critics who came to see themselves as renewers of the Shakespearean tradition":

> In other respects . . . [Johnson's] criticism tended to adhere to neo-classical principles of generic purity, decorum and poetic justice which had been dominant over the extended period he had devoted to the work of editorship, and which continued to play a part in dramatic criticism, alongside the various innovations, until the end of the century. (206)

On this occasion such comment lacks reference to (or apparent knowledge of) "facts" of history that could scarcely be missed in a reading of the Johnsonian text not hopelessly fettered by an overdetermined context of contemporary theory. Johnson's contempt for the "petty cavils of petty minds," his famous praise of "mingled drama," and his pointed attack on decorum of character all come to mind:

> His adherence to general nature has exposed him to the censure of criticks, who form their judgments upon narrower principles. Dennis and Rhymer think his Romans not sufficiently Roman; and Voltaire censures his kings as not completely royal. . . . But Shakespeare always makes nature predominate over accident; and if he preserves the essential character, is not very careful of distinctions superinduced and adventitious. His story requires Romans or kings, but he thinks only on men. (*Shakespeare*, 7:65)[20]

The phrase "poetic justice" (as opposed to the "poetical justice" considered above) is used by Johnson at *no* point in his printed writings.

Unless, then, the words that Johnson *actually* uses have some resonance within the deep structure of today's critical theory, historical
writing on criticism will always tend to distort the place of Johnson's
criticism in history, and detract from the possibilities of Johnson's historical relations with the critical present—in this case through the successful transformation of Johnson into a critic of the last age by the
Romantic Movement. To summarize the argument so far: history may
make past critical minds seem simple. But a narrative composed only of
simple minds does not make history make sense. With their tendency to
manipulate or objectivize the past, or to explain the present in terms of
a line of progression, twentieth-century histories are too familiar and
have been written in the same way too many times. As far as their diminished assumptions about the nature of past criticism point to Johnson's underdevelopment (or arrested development) as a critic, their
historical certainties seem premature. Reductivist assumptions inter-
vene at too early a stage to short-circuit the process of historicization
when more circumspection with regard to what we do not know about
past critical minds is required.

"MOTION WITHOUT PROGRESS": JOHNSON'S HISTORICAL CONCEPTUALIZATION OF LITERARY CRITICISM

Johnson planned but never wrote a history of criticism. Yet his own
work is richly suggestive of the ways that critics and criticism are ironically located in time. This we can see if we move the emphasis from
what critics and historians have said of Johnson, to Johnson's own "literary" view of this past as it appeared to him from the perspective of
1765 in his work as a practicing critic of Shakespeare. One especially
pertinent passage that lends itself to evaluation within twentieth-century literary-historiographical terms is a poignant act of self-historiciza-
tion:

> It is no pleasure to me, in revising my volumes, to observe how much
> paper is wasted in confutation. Whoever considers the revolutions of learn-
> ing, and the various questions of greater or less importance, upon which wit
> and reason have exercised their powers, must lament the unsuccessfulness
> of enquiry, and the slow advances of truth, when he reflects, that great part
> of the labour of every writer is only the destruction of those that went before
> him. The first care of the builder of a new system, is to demolish the fabricks
> which are standing. The chief desire of him that comments an authour, is to
> shew how much other commentators have corrupted and obscured him. The
> opinions prevalent in one age, as truths above the reach of controversy, are
> confuted and rejected in another, and rise again to reception in remoter

times. Thus the human mind is kept in motion without progress. Thus sometimes truth and errour, and sometimes contrarieties of errour, take each others place by reciprocal invasion. The tide of seeming knowledge which is poured over one generation, retires and leaves another naked and barren; the sudden meteors of intelligence which for a while appear to shoot their beams into the regions of obscurity, on a sudden withdraw their lustre, and leave mortals again to grope their way. (*Shakespeare*, 7:99)

Such a passage is a rhapsody of vibrant imagery drawn from physical rhythms and celestial nature. Who could read it and not appreciate Johnson's representation of the past of criticism (apt, one might think, in the light of modern theorists' accounts of the "literary" force of historical writing) as a transcendent *aesthetic* achievement?[21] One might observe the balance of the phrasing—the rise and fall of the prose, the pith of the short first sentence compared with the rolling surge and descent of the second; then the sequence of brief direct statements (with their double "thus") leading to the desolate and frightening finale. Noticeable, too, is the vocabulary—the great weight of personal effort that is compressed into Johnson's linkage of the work of the critical commentator not with joy or delight but with "labour"; the embodied abstractions at perpetual war in the persons of "truth" and "errour"; the decorousness and grace of the "retiring" tide of knowledge and the chill farewell whereby the meteors of intelligence without warning "withdraw" their luster; the contrast between the paired Latinate terms, "corrupted and obscured," "confuted and rejected," and the Anglo-Saxon "grope" of the final sentence.

Like many modern critics, Johnson elsewhere could see the ever-accumulating weight of the past as a burden. The dead are dead but the living must be perpetually on their guard against their encroachments: "had all the dead been embalmed," reflects Imlac, "their repositories must in time have been more spacious than the dwellings of the living" (*Rasselas*, 169). But here the resistance of a critic against his own past has none of the noble resonance of the Wordsworthian revolt, and despite the correlations of Johnson and Wordsworth referred to above, Johnson, unlike the romantics, does not suggest that the past is *justly* and rationally consigned to history. Nor is there any evidence of a pre-Darwinian biology of criticism spiraling upwards from its primitive forms. Johnson, by contrast, sees the telos revealed by History within Criticism as persistently delusive. The motion is "without progress." The change in critical atmosphere or "opinions prevalent" seems casual, unsystematic, or arbitrary. The primary causes of alteration are for Johnson temperamental and individual rather than grandly epistemic.

Yet because the fluctuations are viewed from inside the self (this being an aspect of Johnson's personal sense of bleak futility combined with Christian hope), the process seems coherent. It is part of nature. It attains a psychological plausibility. Johnson appeals to the *necessary* misapprehension which accompanies change. In terms of today's theories of poetical revision and revolt, this may suggest a form of Bloomian "misprision." But we may also recall that Johnson preferred the mingled dramas of Shakespeare to the inexorable movement of Greek tragedy. The rhythms of the Johnsonian past are accordingly linked to the reverses of a world where "the loss of one is the gain of another; . . . in which the malignity of one is sometimes defeated by the frolick of another; and many mischiefs and many benefits are done and hindered without design" (*Shakespeare*, 7:66). This is less the oedipal "anxiety of influence"[22] than the kind of critical play that modern critics like to refer to as "carnivalesque." So far as it is "neoclassical," it recalls Plato's *Timaeus*, the flux of Lucretius, Ovid, or Montaigne.[23] Johnson's imaginative participation in the pathos of editorial commentary on Shakespeare collapses the gulf between the historian and the material of history to produce something close to what Collingwood once called history as "self-knowledge of the mind."[24]

HISTORICAL CONSCIOUSNESS AND THE VALUE OF JOHNSON AS CRITIC

Saintsbury's Johnson of 1902 is a figure from eighteenth-century costume drama. His tale of criticism, running to three large volumes, is a rambling picaresque. Wellek's Johnson, who makes his appearance in the first volume of Wellek's magnum opus, is the psychiatric patient of 1955. The *Cambridge* historians in turn supply the decomposed and decentered subject of 1997. But what seems lost in the epiphenomena of all three histories is a sense of the historical significance of critical moments which seem to fall outside the scope of the history of criticism as a history of ideas (and any kind of narrative development based on this). Histories may have a foot in the storytelling tradition, and in the making, maintenance, and exploitation of myths; they may present their "objects" and "events" according to a complex system of textual transformation, interpolation, illustration, and inference. They may be elements in the creative translation of this past, and respond to cultural needs in their own time and place. They may instate a role for the past as a barrier to cultural egotism and self-universalization. But a more developed historical consciousness than has proved possible in formal histories seems to be needed to restore attention to the unvarnished (textual) evidence of what criticism was in the hands of a man who lived, wrote, and died before us. Only then, it seems, can the past of criticism reveal the possibilities of criticism that the present has failed to realize. Historical representation might then do more to accommodate John Stuart Mill's exhortation—praised in "humanist" terms by Berlin—to tolerate rather than respect contrary views. Mill, wrote Berlin:

> once declared that when we deeply care, we must dislike those who hold opposite views. He preferred this to cold temperaments and opinions. He asked us not necessarily to respect the views of others—very far from it— only to try to understand and tolerate them; only tolerate; disapprove, think ill of, if need be mock or despise, but tolerate. . . . [25]

It seems evident from the treatment of Johnson's "opposite views" in modern historical accounts (such as the readings by twentieth-century historians which stifle or dismiss out of hand Johnson's criticism of Shakespeare) that the tendency of historians is to place the Johnsonian past and the critical present in separate compartments. Clearly, such doctrines as the "reception aesthetics" of Hans Robert Jauss, with its notion of a "fusion of the horizon of expectations" as the model for a new kind of literary history, have failed to remold the history of literary criticism in any significant way. Yet Jauss's ideas, in common with Collingwood's or Gadamer's "re-constructive" (or dialectical) concept of the relation between the present and the past, would seem to suggest the theoretical objections that must be raised against a present and a past of criticism that are *simply* opposed. Equally to the point, from a resonantly "postmodern" perspective, would be Michel de Certeau's Freudian sense of the present's systematic repression of the past (as "other") in the "pretty line of progress," and the possibilities of this repression being overcome:

> In their respective turns, each "new" time provides the *place* for a discourse considering whatever preceded it to be "dead," but welcoming a "past" that had already been specified by former ruptures. . . . But whatever this new understanding of the past holds to be irrelevant—shards created by the selection of materials, remainders left aside by an explication—comes back, despite everything, on the edges of discourse or in its rifts and crannies: "resistances," "survivals," or delays discreetly perturb the pretty order of a line of "progress" or a system of interpretation.[26]

My suggestion would be that overcoming the resistance to Johnson's critical "survival" evident from the twentieth-century historical perspective requires a more generously accommodating consciousness of what we have learnt from Johnson's critical "sensations" as a necessary precondition of *our* reading of him—a clearer awareness of the irony of "what one will not have been able to think without him" that Jacques Derrida has appreciated in "a Hegel."[27]

With the continuing tendency to represent the past of criticism in terms of ideas, and to write the history of criticism within the frameworks of a specifically *intellectual* paradigm, Johnson's critical commitment to the world of feeling—crucially located in his comments on *King Lear*—is a legacy of emotional agency that is lost to the present. At the same time, ironically enough, such a value could not continue to be experienced as a value if Johnson's confession of "shock" had not obliterated historicity. Wain may therefore be correct *in a sense* to say that Johnson's is not a "modern mind." The qualifying consideration may however reside in the fact that such critics as Arnold and Eliot were also right. "Their first value," wrote Eliot of Johnson's *Lives of the Poets*, "is a value which all study of the past should have for us: that it should make us more conscious of what we are, and of our own limitations, and give us more understanding of the world in which we now live."[28] Within this alternative "idea of history," one that evokes Michel de Certeau's belief that the past is able to "menace our knowledge," Johnson's reaction to Cordelia's death is a recollection of the terrible injustices of this world that always have seemed and always will seem outside "nature" and beyond "reason" to "reasonable beings." As Johnson's feelings informed him, such injustices cannot be accommodated to the mere technicalities of a "poetical justice" or an evidently redundant instinct for order or rules. They are, in the Wordsworthian terms from which we began, "beyond the bounds of pleasure."

To apply Johnson's own words to the historical situation of Johnson's criticism, "To judge rightly of the present we must oppose it to the past; for all judgment is comparative" (*Rasselas*, 112). Compared with the major twentieth-century histories of literary criticism, bound as they are to a position of assumed cultural superiority to Johnson, such a conceptualization of the past of criticism would open to question whether "progress" in criticism from the eighteenth to the twentieth century is actually made, recording what is lost alongside what is altered or improved, the "turning round" as well as the "going forward" that punctures "the conceit of modern enlightenment." The terms on which it is worth taking Johnson seriously as a critic today challenge the periodization of historical narrative, as indeed the whole progressivist historical outlook on literature and criticism from the romantic to the postmodern. They do so since it is the fact of his critical value—and not the other way round—which makes Johnson a historical character worth writing about.

NOTES

See *The Prose Works of William Wordsworth*, ed. W. J. B. Owen and J. W. Smyser, 3 vols. (Oxford: Clarendon Press, 1974), 1:141; 147. Subsequent references to this edition are included parenthetically in the text.

1. F. R. Leavis, "Johnson as Critic," *Scrutiny* 12, no. 3 (1944): 187; J. H. Hagstrum, *Samuel Johnson's Literary Criticism* (Minneapolis: University of Minnesota Press, 1952; Chicago: University of Chicago Press, 1967), xvii; John Wain, introduction, *Johnson as Critic* (London: Routledge and Kegan Paul, 1973), 55–56.

2. See, for example, Norman Holland, "How Can Dr. Johnson's Remarks on Cordelia's Death Add to My Own Response?" in *Psychoanalysis and the Question of the Text*, ed. Geoffrey H. Hartman (Baltimore: Johns Hopkins University Press, 1978), 18–44. Holland asks whether "we can get beyond simply saying that Johnson was 'wrong' in his verdict on the ending of *King Lear*" (30), arguing for the need for readers to pass through or try on alternative readings to avoid subtracting and thinning out the possibilities of response (42).

3. See George Saintsbury, *From the Renaissance to the Decline of Eighteenth-Century Orthodoxy* (1902), vol. 2 of *A History of Criticism and Literary Taste in Europe from the Earliest Texts to the Present Day*, 3 vols. (Edinburgh and London: Blackwood, 1900–1904); René Wellek, *The Later Eighteenth Century* (1955), vol. 1 of *A History of Modern Criticism, 1750–1950*, 8 vols. (New Haven and London: Yale University Press, 1955–92); *The Eighteenth Century* (1997), ed. H. B. Nisbet and Claude Rawson, vol. 4 of *The Cambridge History of Literary Criticism* (Cambridge: Cambridge University Press, 1989). Subsequent references to these histories are cited parenthetically in the text.

4. See Michel Foucault, *The Archaeology of Knowledge*, trans. A. M. Sheridan Smith (1972; London: Routledge, 1995), Hayden White, part one of *Metahistory: The Historical Imagination in Nineteenth-Century Europe* (Baltimore and London: Johns Hopkins University Press, 1973), and Paul Ricoeur, *Time and Narrative*, trans. Kathleen Blamey and David Pellauer, 3 vols. (Chicago: University of Chicago Press, 1984–88), 3 (1988), 143.

5. See "Historical Inevitability" (1954), *Four Essays on Liberty* (Oxford: Oxford University Press, 1969), 45, 58.

6. Ibid., 89–100.

7. Cf. Thomas Babington Macaulay, "Boswell's Life of Johnson," *Edinburgh Review* 54, no. 107 (September 1831): 1–38.

8. Cf. Clement Hawes' discussion of Johnson's "cosmopolitanism" *ante*.

9. For a discussion of Johnson on Shakespeare's moral power see my essay, "Shakespeare: Johnson's Poet of Nature," *The Cambridge Companion to Samuel Johnson*, ed. Greg Clingham (Cambridge: Cambridge University Press, 1997 and 1999), 143–60. I argue that Johnson was in fact more sensitive than we are to Shakespeare's moral implications.

10. The fallacy about how old, dead critics hold or maintain or espouse supposedly standardized concepts (as if they were historically no different from the most wooden of modern academicians or historians of ideas) is not, of course, confined to designedly historical writing, but is a routine characteristic of writing on Johnson's "critical theory." See, for example, Greg Clingham's discussion of the failure of historical and theoretical subtlety in his review of Charles Hinnant's *"Steel for the Mind": Samuel Johnson and Critical Discourse* (1994), *AJ* 7 (1996): 480–85.

11. Both definitions of "genius" are discussed more fully by Tom Mason and Adam Rounce in the essay which follows.

12. A. W. Schlegel, "Lecture 22," *A Course of Lectures on Dramatic Art and Literature*, trans. John Black (revised ed. 1809; London: Bohn's Standard Library, 1846), 340–42.

13. In 1812, Henry Crabbe Robinson reported Coleridge as saying that "Shakespeare imitates life, mingled as we find it with joy and sorrow." See *Diary* (1811–12), in *Coleridge's Shakespearean Criticism*, ed. T. M. Raysor, 2 vols. (London: Constable, 1930), 2:212.

14. William Hazlitt, preface to *The Characters of Shakespear's Plays* (1817), in *The Complete Works of William Hazlitt*, ed. P. P. Howe, 21 vols. (London and Toronto: Dent, 1930), 4: 176. For a subtle and compelling discussion of Coleridge's, Schlegel's, and Hazlitt's "making common cause against Johnson," see G. F. Parker, *Johnson's Shakespeare* (Oxford: Clarendon Press, 1989).

15. William Hazlitt, "Mr. Kean's Macbeth," *The Champion* (13 November 1814), reprinted in *A View of the English Stage*, *Works*, 5:205.

16. While the appendix was first published in 1802, this quotation includes the minor amendments from the text of 1850 adopted in *The Prose Works of William Wordsworth*.

17. See William Hazlitt, "Lectures on The English Poets: Lecture 3, On Shakspeare and Milton" (1818), *Works*, 5:50.

18. In his "Essays on Epitaphs," Wordsworth objects to the portrayal of the deceased in details "minutely and scrupulously pursued" (*Prose Works*, 2:58). "All the power of description," Johnson had written of the metaphysical poets, "is destroyed by a scrupulous enumeration" (*Lives*, 1:45).

19. This quotation is taken from the 1850 text of the preface to *Lyrical Ballads*. The 1800 text had stated that such elementary feelings, rather than "co-exist," simply "exist" (1:124).

20. For further discussion of this point, see Philip Smallwood, review of *The Cambridge History of Literary Criticism*, vol. 4: *The Eighteenth Century*, in *AJ* 10 (1999): 392–99.

21. The comparison suggested on these grounds is with Johnson's preface to *A Dictionary of the English Language*, 2 vols. (London, 1755). There, by an act of self-fashioning, Johnson had lifted the drudgery of compiling and introducing a dictionary above the mundane. Here too, in a different context, we can recall what Hayden White might term the tragic or the ironic rhetorical mode. White writes of the "Ironic mode of conceiving history" in "The Historical Achievement of the Enlightenment," *Metahistory*, 65, and claims that "the historiography of the age was necessarily impelled toward a purely Satirical mode of representation, in the same way that the literature of the age in general was" (66).

22. Harold Bloom, *The Anxiety of Influence: A Theory of Poetry* (1973; 2nd ed. New York and Oxford: Oxford University Press, 1997). David Perkins, *Is Literary History Possible?* (Baltimore and London: Johns Hopkins University Press, 1992) includes Bloom among the theorists of "immanent change" in literary history, where there is "the desire or necessity of writers to produce works unlike those of previous writers" (161), and where influence takes place "not by reading but by misreading, by 'misprision' or misunderstanding the texts of the past" (169).

23. In Montaigne, see, for example, "Of Experience," *Essays of Michael Seigneur de Montaigne*, trans. Charles Cotton, 2nd ed., 3 vols. (London, 1693), 3, esp. 468–87; 510–11.

24. See "Human Nature and Human History," in R. G. Collingwood, *The Idea of History*, ed. Jan van der Dussen (1946; Oxford: Oxford University Press, 1993), esp. 226–27. Recent developments in Collingwood scholarship, including the first publication of the lost manuscript of Collingwood's *Principles of History*, reinforce the importance of this concept in twentieth-century British historiography and the value that it may now have as a tool fitted to unlock the history of literary criticism from its positivist models. See R. G. Collingwood, *The Principles of History and Other Writings in Philosophy of History*, ed. W. H. Dray and W. J. van der Dussen (Oxford: Oxford University Press, 1999).

25. See *Autobiography and Literary Essays* (1981), ed. John M. Robson and Jack Stillinger, *Collected Works of John Stuart Mill*, 33 vols. (Toronto and London: University of Toronto Press and Routledge, 1963–91), 1: esp. 53. Cf. Isaiah Berlin, "John Stuart Mill and the Ends of Life," *Four Essays on Liberty*, 184.

26. Michel de Certeau, *The Writing of History*, trans. Tom Conley (New York: Columbia University Press, 1988), 4. Other references are to H. R. Jauss, "Literary History as a Challenge to Literary Theory," *Toward an Aesthetic of Reception*, trans. Timothy Bahti (Minneapolis: University of Minnesota Press, 1982), 3–45; R. G. Collingwood, *The Idea of History* (1946, 1993); Hans-Georg Gadamer, *Truth and Method*, trans. Joel Weinsheimer and Donald G. Marshall (London: Sheed and Ward, 1989).

27. Jacques Derrida, *Glas*, translated by John P. Leavey, Jr. and Richard Rand (Lincoln and London: University of Nebraska Press, 1986), 1.

28. T. S. Eliot, "Johnson as Critic and Poet" (1944), in *On Poetry and Poets* (London: Faber and Faber, 1957), 192. See also Matthew Arnold, preface to *The Six Chief Lives from Johnson's "Lives of the Poets"* (London, 1879).

BIBLIOGRAPHY

Arnold, Matthew. *The Six Chief Lives from Johnson's "Lives of the Poets."* London, 1879.

Berlin, Isaiah. *Four Essays on Liberty*. Oxford and New York: Oxford University Press, 1969.

Bloom, Harold. *The Anxiety of Influence: A Theory of Poetry*. 1973. New York and Oxford: Oxford University Press, 1997.

Certeau, Michel de. *The Writing of History*. Translated by Tom Conley. New York: Columbia University Press, 1988.

Collingwood, R. G. *The Idea of History*. 1946. Revised edition by Jan van der Dussen. Oxford and New York: Oxford University Press, 1993.

———. *The Principles of History and Other Writings in Philosophy of History*. Edited by W. H. Dray and W. J. van der Dussen. Oxford: Oxford University Press, 1999.

Derrida, Jacques. *Glas*. Translated by John P. Leavey, Jr. and Richard Rand. Lincoln and London: University of Nebraska Press, 1986.

Eliot, T. S. "Johnson as Critic and Poet." 1944. In *On Poetry and Poets*. London: Faber and Faber, 1957.

Foucault, Michel. *The Archaeology of Knowledge*. Translated by A. M. Sheridan Smith. 1972. London: Routledge, 1995.

Gadamer, Hans-Georg. *Truth and Method*. Translated by Joel Weinsheimer and Donald G. Marshall. London: Sheed and Ward, 1989.

Hagstrum, Jean H. *Samuel Johnson's Literary Criticism*. Minneapolis: University of Minnesota Press, 1952; Chicago: Chicago University Press, 1967.

Hazlitt, William. *The Complete Works of William Hazlitt*. 21 vols. Edited by P. P. Howe. London and Toronto: Dent, 1930.

Jauss, Hans Robert. "Literary History as a Challenge to Literary Theory." In *Toward an Aesthetic of Reception*. Translated by Timothy Bahti. Minneapolis: University of Minnesota Press, 1982.

Johnson, Samuel. *Johnson on Shakespeare*. Edited by Arthur Sherbo. Vols. 7–8 of The Yale Edition of the Works of Samuel Johnson. New Haven and London: Yale University Press, 1968.

————. *The Lives of the English Poets*. 3 vols. Edited by George Birkbeck Hill. Oxford: Clarendon Press, 1905.

————. *Rasselas and Other Tales*. Edited by Gwin J. Kolb. Vol. 16 of The Yale Edition of the Works of Samuel Johnson. New Haven and London: Yale University Press, 1990.

Leavis, F. R. "Johnson as Critic." *Scrutiny* 12, no. 3 (1944): 187–200.

Macaulay, Thomas Babington. "Boswell's Life of Johnson." *Edinburgh Review* 54, no. 107 (September 1831): 1–38.

Mill, John Stuart. *Autobiography and Literary Essays*. 1981. Edited by John M. Robson and Jack Stillinger. Vol. 1 of *Collected Works of John Stuart Mill*. 33 vols. Toronto and London: University of Toronto Press and Routledge, 1963–91.

Nisbet, H. B., and Claude Rawson, eds. *The Eighteenth Century*. 1997. Vol. 4 of *The Cambridge History of Literary Criticism*. 8 vols. Cambridge: Cambridge University Press, 1989–.

Ricoeur, Paul. *Time and Narrative*. 3 vols. Translated by Kathleen Blamey and David Pellauer. Chicago: Chicago University Press, 1984–88.

Saintsbury, George. *From the Renaissance to the Decline of Eighteenth Century Orthodoxy*. 1902. Vol. 2 of *A History of Criticism and Literary Taste in Europe from the Earliest Texts to the Present Day*. 3 vols. Edinburgh and London: Blackwood, 1900–1904.

Schlegel, A. W. *A Course of Lectures on Dramatic Art and Literature*. Translated by John Black. Revised ed. 1809. London: Bohn's Standard Library, 1846.

Wain, John, ed. *Johnson as Critic*. London: Routledge and Kegan Paul, 1973.

Wellek, René. *The Later Eighteenth Century*. 1955. Vol. 1 of *A History of Modern Criticism, 1750–1950*. 8 vols. New Haven and London: Yale University Press, 1955–92.

White, Hayden. *Metahistory: The Historical Imagination in Nineteenth-Century Europe*. Baltimore and London: Johns Hopkins University Press, 1973.

Wordsworth, William. *The Prose Works of William Wordsworth*. 3 vols. Edited by W. J. B. Owen and J. W. Smyser. Oxford: Clarendon Press, 1974.

"Looking Before and After"? Reflections on the Early Reception of Johnson's Critical Judgments

TOM MASON AND ADAM ROUNCE

JOSEPH WARTON'S EDITION OF THE POEMS OF ALEXANDER POPE, which was first published in 1797, contains (as a commentary on a personified description of the Thames in line 350 of Pope's *Windsor Forest*) the following footnote:

> Whenever the river Thames is mentioned, I am afraid the disgraceful and impotent criticism of Dr Johnson on a passage in Gray's Odes, will recur to the mind of the reader. I heartily wish, for the sake of the author, who had more strong sense than a just relish for true poetry, that this strange and unwarrantable remark of his, could be sunk into oblivion.[1]

Warton appears to be thinking of Johnson's comment, in the 1781 "Life of Gray," on the lines in the "Ode on a Distant Prospect of Eton College" where Gray, pondering the innocence of childhood and taking a retrospective look at his schooldays, addresses the spirit of the Thames as he watches the schoolboys swimming, catching birds, chasing hoops, and playing cricket:

> Say, Father Thames, for thou hast seen
> Full many a sprightly race
> Disporting on thy margent green
> The paths of pleasure trace,
> Who foremost now delight to cleave
> With pliant arm thy glassy wave?
> The captive linnet which enthrall?
> What idle progeny succeed
> To chase the rolling circle's speed,
> Or urge the flying ball?
>
> (lines 21–30)

The strange remark that Warton heartily wished might be sunk into oblivion is one in which Johnson appears almost brutally literal-minded:

134

The *Prospect of Eton College* suggests nothing to Gray which every beholder does not equally think and feel. His supplication to father Thames, to tell him who drives the hoop or tosses the ball, is useless and puerile. Father Thames has no better means of knowing than himself. (*Lives*, 3:434–35)

Warton's comment, however, is itself strange — and almost unwarrantable as a commentary on *Pope's* line. The oddity lies in the contrast between Warton's conviction that Johnson's criticism is both "disgraceful" and "impotent" on the one hand, and his supposition, on the other, that Johnson's remark will "recur to the mind of the reader" (any reader?) *whenever* the River Thames is mentioned. Warton seems to want to cast into oblivion a passing irrelevant inanity that he nevertheless believes to be omnipresent in the minds of his readership. He appears to be writing under the conviction that Johnson's derision will, somehow, follow Gray's poem throughout its afterlife, with the efficiency of an omnipresent commentary, indelibly coloring every reader's thoughts.[2]

Warton's supposition, mad as it may seem, appears not to have been entirely without foundation. A great many readers (both during Johnson's life and for many years after his death) wrote as if they had fragments of his critical judgments active and working in their minds — often, it appears, as some kind of irritant.[3] Many hostile comments on Johnson's criticism share some of the features of Warton's complaint. In many cases, the paradox that presents itself is the same. Why, if Johnson's judgments were obviously contemptible, was it necessary to decry them in and out of season? (Strange, unwarrantable, disgraceful, and impotent critical remarks, it might be thought, require no refutation.)

One peculiarity common to many of the more virulent attacks on Johnson is the copresence of an intense concentration on the particularity of Johnson's formulations, and an apparent unwillingness or inability to allow for variations in Johnson's tone, stance, or degree of solemnity. In his footnote on Gray, for example, Joseph Warton refuses to allow the possibility that Johnson's discussion of Father Thames in the "Eton Ode" presents the mind with a playful, almost comic image. (Gray asks the reverend river for the names of current scholars circa 1742. Father Thames refers Gray back to the school register.) William Kenrick's book-length assault on Johnson's 1765 edition of Shakespeare, perhaps the most virulent of all attacks on Johnson's criticism, shows a similar refusal to permit Johnson the occasional joke. When coming across Johnson's footnote to a speech in *The Winter's Tale* (act 4, scene 4, 20–22) where Perdita fears that her father, "by some accident" will discover Prince Florizel in his peasant clothing "O the

Fates! / How would he look, to see his work, so noble, / Vilely bound up?" Kenrick complains that "Dr. Johnson has found Shakespeare tripping again. — Hear what he says":

> '*His work so noble, &c.*] It is impossible for any man to rid himself of his profession. The authorship of Shakespeare has supplied him with a metaphor, which, rather than he would lose it, he has put, with no great propriety, into the mouth of a country maid. Thinking of his own works, his mind passed naturally to the binder. I am glad he has no hint at an editor.'
>
> We have here also, another aukward attempt of our editor at wit and pleasantry. But why wilt thou, Dr. Johnson, persist thus in playing the bob-cherry, when the prize hangeth so high above thine head, and such a weight of lead is incumbent in thy heels? . . . why, Dr. Johnson, art thou glad that Shakespeare hath no hint at an editor? Dost thou think he would have thrown out any censures that might reach *thee*? — No — that incomparable bard was, as thou sayest, the poet of nature, and drew his characters from the life: and nature had not produced in that age so arrogant, and at the same time so dull an animal, as the present commentator on Shakespeare. . . . A modern editor of Shakespeare is . . . a fungus attached to an oak; a male agaric of the most astringent kind, that, while it disfigures its form, may last for ages to disgrace the parent of its being.[4]

The heat of Kenrick's fury appears inexplicable — particularly since he too appears to believe that Johnson's joke will adhere to Shakespeare's text like an "astringent" fungus that will not only "disfigure" the "form" of the work to which it is attached but "last for ages," all the while bringing the text into further "disgrace."

In Kenrick's case, and in many other instances, it seems likely that literary critical antagonism colluded with personal animus. Objections to Johnson's judgments slide easily (or uneasily) into animadversions on Johnson's politics, pension, or personality. (Warton may be a case in point.)[5] And yet, while some of those who accuse Johnson of writing out of envy may be open to a similar charge themselves, personal dislike of Johnson appears very rarely to be an adequate explanation for the warmth of hostile reactions to his work. In a great many cases the hostility appears to arise from the discrepancy between Johnson's phrasing and the particulars of the poem at which Johnson directed his animadversions. It was not so much that Johnson wrote silly things, but that he wrote silly things about poems or passages that his readers loved and revered.[6] He obtruded coarse witticism where, as his detractors saw it, angels should fear to tread.

Implicit in many attacks on Johnson's critical judgments is the assumption that the reading public at large is in need of disabusement. It may have seemed to Johnson's contemporaries as it seemed to Lawrence Lipking: "sooner or later all conversations come round to him. Listening to eighteenth-century colloquy on the arts, sooner or later we listen to his voice."[7] And it does appear to be the case that the warmth of Johnson's detractors was at least matched by that of his admirers — and that, for them too, Johnson's critical judgments were closely connected to the works to which they referred. For Frances Burney this was literally the case. When she was offered the choice of the amended proof sheets of the *Lives of the Poets* "without hesitation, the choice was Pope," partly because the proof sheets included Pope's corrections to his *Iliad*, and Johnson's emendations to his own texts so that she was able to obtain at once "on the same page, the marginal alterations and second thoughts of that great author, and of his great biographer."[8]

Burney saw Johnson as Pope's peer. The clergyman and occasional reviewer Edmund Cartwright, welcoming the first volumes of *The Lives of the English Poets* in 1779, described the criticism of *Paradise Lost* in the "Life of Milton" as displaying as distinctive a mind as Milton's and as equaling the best offered by the ancient world:

> Of this truly excellent analysis and criticism, it is scarcely hyperbolical to affirm that it is executed with all the skill and penetration of Aristotle, and animated and embellished with all the fire of Longinus. It is every way worthy of its subject: the *Paradise Lost* is a poem which the mind of Milton only could have produced; the criticism before us is such as, perhaps, the pen of Johnson only could have written.[9]

Cartwright's criticism of, and Burney's pleasure in, the *Lives* might be said to represent the response of (more or less) general readers. Cartwright's terms of reference and the height of his praise for the "skill" and "penetration" shown in the *Lives*, are, however, strikingly similar to the commendation bestowed upon parts of Johnson's criticism by Edmond Malone, perhaps the deepest-read literary scholar of his time, and one who had deep reservations about Johnson's biographical (and occasionally editorial) techniques. At the conclusion of the "Life of Dryden" that he provided for his edition of Dryden's prose (1800), Malone remarked that "a critical examination of the merits and defects" of Dryden's "various productions formed no part" of his "undertaking":

> and indeed may be well dispensed with, after Dr. Johnson's elaborate and admirable disquisition on his writings than which a more beautiful and judicious piece of criticism perhaps has not appeared since the days of Aristotle.

Malone added in a footnote that:

> With that incomparable work should be read his exquisite parallel of Dryden and Pope, in the Life of the later poet . . . in which 'the superiority of

genius,—that power which constitutes a poet; that quality without which judgment is cold and knowledge is inert; that energy which collects, combines amplifies and animates; is, with some hesitation' attributed to Dryden.[10]

There appears to be, that is, a strange correspondence between the reactions of those who admired and those who despised Johnson's critical judgments. Both are specific and immoderate—even passionate. Johnson's critical writings, it seems safe to say, were not things about which it was possible to be coolly neutral. Whether deferred to (as by Malone) as representing definitive truth, or decried (as by Warton) as "strange and unwarrantable," Johnson's critical formulations seem to have become, in the minds of many readers for many years, inextricably attached to the works which Johnson had praised or blamed. (It is remarkable, for example, how widely Johnson's judgments are suffused throughout Walter Scott's critical writings, and how many of Coleridge's comments on Shakespeare formulate themselves as corrections to Johnson's remarks. There is, in this respect, small difference in the attitudes of succeeding generations. Malone's respect for Johnson's criticism is equaled by Scott's. The general objections to Johnson's criticism of Shakespeare by Coleridge and Hazlitt are sometimes similar to those of Johnson's personal physician.)[11]

In his preface to *The Plays of William Shakespeare*, Johnson considered it "proper to inquire" by "what peculiarities of excellence" Shakespeare had "gained and kept the favour of his countrymen" (*Shakespeare*, 7:61). The corresponding question in Johnson's own case might be to ask what were the peculiar qualities of his critical judgments that aroused (and to some extent kept), if not the favor, at least the passionate interest of his countrymen. Why did Johnson's criticism continue to operate as a stimulus or an irritant in the minds of so many readers for so long? Why, it might be asked in particular, were his judgments not *successfully* dismissed as merely personal and eccentric by his more hostile contemporaries? Why was he not *successfully* classified into innocuousness by his adversely critical successors? It is worth asking, that is, why Johnson's judgments were not "sunk into oblivion" in correspondence with the wishes of Warton and many other literary commentators, and what the durability of Johnson's criticism might suggest about present and future understanding of Johnson's literary criticism.

Such questions are not easy to answer. Various explanations were offered by Johnson's detractors. Kenrick will allow Johnson *nothing*. For him, and a very few others, Johnson was simply an egregious ass.[12] Most objectors to Johnson's critical remarks, however, seem to derive the strength of their feeling from a sense of the *discrepancy* among Johnson's judgments. How is it, they seem to ask, that a mind displaying such critical acuity in the appreciation of one work should be blind to the obvious beauties of another? One answer was to suppose that Johnson's mind exhibited "strong sense" rather than a "just relish for true poetry" (as Warton had it), or for the more lyrical and passionate forms of verse. This common observation, was often (though not necessarily) associated with a contention that Johnson was envious of the poetical success of others, or with a belief that his tastes were formed early in life by a particular kind or species of poetry—that written by himself, or by, say, Dryden and Pope—and that his mind, so indelibly formed, was incapable of understanding or appreciating more recent work. These notions come in various forms, in various combinations, and with various emphases.

So William Cowper, who in his epitaph on Johnson described him as one "Whose prose was Eloquence, by Wisdom taught, / The graceful vehicle of virtuous thought" (lines 3–4), wrote in a letter that he "could thresh" Johnson's "old jacket" till he "made his pension jingle in his pocket" on account of the critical judgments in the "Life of Milton."[13] And in a letter of 1782, Cowper wondered that "the boys and girls" did not "tear this husky, dry commentator limb from limb" in "resentment" of the injury "done to their darling poet" by Johnson's account of Matthew Prior's *Henry and Emma*:

> I admire Johnson as a man of great erudition and sense; but when he sets himself up as a judge of writers upon the subject of love, a passion which I suppose he never felt in his life, he might as well think himself qualified to pronounce upon a treatise on horsemanship, or the art of fortification.[14]

For Cowper, Johnson's "great erudition and sense" seem almost to *necessitate* a corresponding lack of "passion."[15]

A similar combination of dissonant opinions appears to have coexisted in the mind of Anna Seward, the "Swan of Lichfield." She had a high, unwavering, and unshakable opinion of what she described in a poem as Johnson's "lofty rhyme" and "moral thought sublime," but some of the *Lives* convinced her that Johnson was essentially a "philistine critic." Johnson there displayed "party-prejudice," "malignant spleen," "literary envy," "sophist reasoning," and "detractive powers." Yet in the same poem, Seward described Johnson's "mighty mind" as "pious, liberal, kind," and as possessing a kind of "Truth." In another poem she compared Thomas Warton's edition of Milton's shorter poems with Johnson's *Lives* as works that display the "glow / That Talent sheds, or Judgement can bestow." Johnson's *Lives*, however, are stained with "Envy's fell blight" and "Party's stormy rage." And she ended her sonnet "On the Posthumous Fame of Dr. Johnson" with the concluding paradox that "A radiant course did Johnson's glory run, / But large the spots that darken'd on its sun."[16]

Some sense of the particular disagreements underlying and fueling Seward's general remarks can be gathered from a footnote to the sonnet "On Dr. Johnson's Unjust Criticisms in his *Lives of the Poets*," where she listed her critical dissensions:

> When Johnson's idolaters are hard pressed concerning his injustice in those fallacious though able pages;—when they are reminded that he there tells us the perusal of Milton's Paradise Lost is a task, and never a pleasure;—reminded also of his avowed contempt of that exquisite Poem, the Lycidas;—of his declaration that Dryden's absurd Ode on the death of Mrs Anne Killegrew, written in Cowley's worst manner, is the noblest Ode in this language;—of his disdain of Gray as a lyric poet; of the superior respect he pays to Yalden, Blackmore, and Pomfret;—When these things are urged, his adorers seek to acquit him of wilful misrepresentation by alledging that he wanted ear for lyric numbers, and taste for the higher graces of Poetry.

The last charge against Johnson is one that was frequently repeated, and one that, in a slightly modified form, has been influential in the present century. Seward, however, will have none of it:

> it is impossible so to believe, when we recollect that even his prose abounds with poetic efflorescence, metaphoric conception, and harmonious cadence, which in the highest degree adorn it, without diminishing its strength.[17]

Her letters further the impression that Johnson's judgments constantly obtruded themselves into her thoughts, and she offers various explanations for their aberrant nature. Her leading thought was that Johnson was motivated by malignant envy. Another, however, was that his capacities to read poetry atrophied at an early age. In a letter of 1797, Seward summarized her theory explaining Johnson's condemnation of his contemporaries:

> After Johnson rose himself into fame, it is well known that he read no other man's writings, living or dead, with that attention without which public criticism can have no honour, or, indeed, common honesty. If genius flashed upon his maturer eyes, they ached at its splendour, and he cast the book indignantly from him. All his familiarity with poetic compositions, was the result of juvenile avidity of perusal; and their various beauties were stampt upon his mind, by a miraculous strength and retention of memory. The wealth of poetic quotation in his admirable Dictionary, was supplied

from the hoards of his early years. They were very little augmented afterwards.

In subsequent periods, he read verse, not to appreciate, but to depreciate
its excellence. His first ambition, early in life, was poetic fame; his first
avowed publication was in verse. Disappointed in that darling wish, indig-
nant of less than first-rate eminence, he hated the authors, preceding or contemporary, whose fame, as poets, eclipsed his own.[18]

Anna Seward saw Johnson as a critic out of step with his time. Later
commentators sometimes took the opposite view. Keats's friend, the
publisher's assistant Richard Woodhouse, in a letter of 1818, uses
Johnson as an example to demonstrate that critical taste is essentially
fashionable and therefore inevitably ephemeral. Critics and poets
"ought to write for Posterity," while those of the present "write for the
day, or rather the hour" so that "Their thoughts & Judgments are fashionable garbs":

How is the great Johnson
    'Fallen Fallen Fallen Fallen
    Fallen from his high Estate,'
by the malice, the Injustice, & envy of his criticisms in that 'Monument of
his Mortality the lives of the Poets' and his deadness to the exalted & excellent in Poetry.[19]

The notion that Johnson's tastes were formed early, and his understanding of later verse accordingly diminished, so that he was dead to
"the exalted & excellent," was commonly advanced without the admix-
ture of Seward's and Woodhouse's conception of Johnson's malevolent
envy. In this respect, the philosopher Sir James Mackintosh, in a
sketch of Johnson of 1811, is representative:

He came into the world when the school of Dryden and Pope gave the law
to English poetry. In that school he had himself learned to be a lofty and
vigorous declaimer in harmonious verse; beyond that school his unforced
admiration perhaps scarcely soared; and his highest effort at criticism was
accordingly the noble panegyric on Dryden.[20]

Mackintosh, like Seward, sees Johnson's taste as remaining intrinsi-
cally that of his youth—the "school of Dryden and Pope," beyond
which his opinions and tastes did not progress; while this taste produced the "noble panegyric" on Dryden, it also ensured that his approach to his own poetic contemporaries must be overwhelmingly
suspicious and negative. Mackintosh does not censure this aspect of
Johnson's judgments—he merely takes it for granted; Johnson's criti-

cism may result from personal passions (or the lack thereof), but its dominating and directing motive is his taste, which depends exclusively upon the standards of Dryden and Pope rather than those of the 1760s or 1780s. Johnson's criticism is representative of the "taste" of an "age," albeit an earlier one.[21]

Although this is again an explanation of Johnson's judgments that has received considerable endorsement in this century, it is not one that can survive even cursory examination.[22] For while it does seem to be the case that Johnson found much less to admire in the poetry discussed in the *Lives* than did most of his contemporaries, it is not at all clear that the relevant critical standards were derived from the poems that he read in his youth.[23] It may be significant, for example, that Mackintosh should single out the "Life of Dryden" (if that is what he is thinking of in writing of Johnson's "noble panegyrick") rather than that of Pope as an example of the peculiar strengths of Johnson's judgment. Johnson's animadversions upon and coolness toward areas of Pope's work were listed among his critical solecisms by several critics. Johnson considered *An Essay on Man*, for example, as "not the happiest of Pope's performances," and had drawn attention to what he had seen as "penury of knowledge and vulgarity of sentiment" by means of a reductive account of Pope's argument (*Lives*, 3:242–43). Joseph Warton, in his dialogue with Johnson's criticism in the footnotes to his edition of Pope, complained of the "contemptuous and degrading" terms of Johnson's "burlesque abstract," when applied to a poem "in which are so many splendid and highly finished passages" (3:162). There were even judgments in the "Life of Dryden" where Warton (and others) considered that Johnson's appreciation was deficient. Johnson's praise of the "Ode to Anne Killigrew," for example, mystified Warton (as it did most readers). And where Johnson had complained that Dryden's "Palamon and Arcite" contained "an action unsuitable to the times in which it is placed" (*Lives*, 1:455), Warton asserted that any critic "who could have leisure dully and soberly to attend to the anachronism" in a poem which contains the "blaze" of "animated poetry" by which "the mind is whirled away" in a "torrent of rapid imagery" must be "frigid and phlegmatic."[24]

One of Warton's explanations for the aberrations of Johnson's judgment was to look to Johnson's own verse rather than that of Dryden and Pope:

> Strong couplets, modern manners, present life, moral sententious writings alone pleased him. Hence his tasteless and groundless objections to the Lycidas of Milton, and to the Bard of Gray. Hence his own Irene is so frigid and uninteresting a tragedy; while his imitations of Juvenal are so forcible and pointed.[25]

Those critics of the next generation whose opinions of Johnson's poems were lower than Joseph Warton's or Anna Seward's, found themselves at a greater distance of sympathy. For Warton, Johnson's mind exhibited one kind of strength — that embodied in his "forcible and pointed" moral satires. Seward was puzzled by what seemed to her the obviously poetic qualities of Johnson's prose. For William Hazlitt, in marked contradistinction, such powers as Johnson had were entirely detrimental to his critical judgments. In the preface to *The Characters of Shakespear's Plays* (1817), he implied that Johnson's critical abilities were overwhelmed by his mistaken notions and incorrigible habits of style:

> We do not say that a man to be a critic must necessarily be a poet: but to be a good critic, he ought not to be a bad poet. Such poetry as a man deliberately writes, such, and such only will he like. Dr. Johnson's Preface to his edition of Shakespear looks like a laborious attempt to bury the characteristic merits of his author under a load of cumbrous phraseology, and to weigh his excellences and defects in equal scales, stuffed full of 'swelling figures and sonorous epithets.' Nor could it well be otherwise; Dr. Johnson's general powers of reasoning overlaid his critical sensibility.[26]

Johnson is here the dull, plodding reasoner who refused to countenance whatever lies outside the "given mould" of his "general powers." It is not a great distance from this position to Macaulay's 1831 review of Croker's edition of Boswell's *Life*, which appears to have had the effect of convincing successive generations that they need not read Johnson's writings at all and would be better off with Boswell's creation.[27] In seeing Johnson's works as the ponderous repository of stock opinions and ideas, Hazlitt's criticism also anticipates the picture of Johnson as entirely representative of his time — the chief upholder in the second half of the century of so-called "neo-classical" or "Augustan" values. Hazlitt's Johnson, with his "measured prose," dependence on the standards of his own works, and critical narrow-mindedness, is a period-piece, unworthy of genuinely serious attention.[28]

Here again, the eighteenth and early-nineteenth-century thesis has found supporters in the twentieth. The argument, however, is again open to question on various grounds. There are, for example, very few reasons for thinking that Johnson had a high opinion of his own verse. Given that he told Boswell that he had, to some degree or other, mentally translated all except one of Juvenal's satires, it is surprising that he should have published only two.[29] Although Johnson's opinion of these particular poems is not recorded, Boswell gives an account of his estimate of his journalistic and dramatic writings that suggests that contemplating his own work caused Johnson some pain:

One day, having read over one of his Ramblers, Mr. Langton asked him, how he liked that paper; he shook his head, and answered, 'Too wordy.' At another time, when one was reading his tragedy of 'Irene' to a company at a house in the country, he left the room; and somebody having asked him the reason of this, he replied, 'Sir, I thought it had been better.' (*Life*, 4:5)

There are many reasons for thinking that comments such as these were not the expressions of false modesty or a neurotic self-loathing, but represent Johnson's best judgment. His ability to act as a severe judge on his own work seems to have been intrinsic to his process of thought. He wrote to Hester Thrale, in 1783, after suffering a stroke that deprived him of speech and caused him to fear that he was losing or had lost his mind:

> I was alarmed and prayed God, that however he might afflict my body he would spare my understanding. The prayer, that I might try the integrity of my faculties, I made in Latin verse. The lines were not very good, but I knew them not to be very good. I made them easily, and concluded myself to be unimpaired in my faculties. (*Letters*, 4:151)

Johnson's proof of possession of his own mind was not the poetic but the critical faculty. It appears, however, to be one characteristic of the operations of that faculty to appreciate merits very different from those exhibited in the *Vanity of Human Wishes* or *Irene*. To Voltaire, who had expressed his "wonder" that Shakespeare's "extravagances" had been "endured by a nation, which has seen the tragedy of *Cato*," Johnson rejoined:

> Addison speaks the language of poets, and Shakespeare, of men. We find in *Cato* innumerable beauties which enamour us of its authour, but we see nothing that acquaints us with human sentiments or human actions; we place it with the fairest and the noblest progeny which judgment propagates by conjunction with learning, but *Othello* is the vigorous and vivacious offspring of observation impregnated by genius. *Cato* affords a splendid exhibition of artificial and fictitious manners, and delivers just and noble sentiments, in diction easy, elevated and harmonious, but its hopes and fears communicate no vibration to the heart; the composition refers us only to the writer; we pronounce the name of *Cato*, but we think on Addison. (*Shakespeare*, 7:84)

It is, perhaps, impossible to gauge to what degree the distinction between Addison and Shakespeare might have involved an awareness on Johnson's part of a similar discrepancy between the "just and noble sentiments" or the "elevated and harmonious diction" of his own work and the "vigorous and vivacious offspring of observation impregnated" by the genius of Shakespeare. The speculation might be put by asking how far it is possible to imagine Johnson agreeing with the account of his poems given in William Mudford's *Critical Enquiry into the Moral Writings of Dr. Samuel Johnson* of 1802:

> Johnson's claim to poetry is very doubtful. He was too much given to reasoning and declamation ever to attain those heights of sublimity which astonish and delight. If he seldom offends by his harshness he as seldom exhilarates by his vivacity; and though he did not detract from our poetic dignity, he cannot be said to have added any thing to it. . . . It was not in his power to assume much variety, nor did he seek to improve this inability by labour; for he was, I believe, little ambitious of the title of poet; an indifference proceeding, perhaps, from a consciousness of natural disqualifications for the exercise of that exalted function. He was indeed, soon aware that his abilities did not consist in poetry; for he began it late, and abandoned it early: and it is very probable that had he been exempt from want, he never would have produced the imitations of Juvenal.[30]

Whereas it has often been said that Johnson's critical principles were derived from a contemplation (and constituted a defense) of his own writings, the opposite contention seems to be nearer the truth. Johnson's warmest praise was reserved for writing—like much of Shakespeare's or some of Dryden's—distinctly *unlike* his own.[31]

One place where Johnson's thoughts about Dryden and Shakespeare come together with his general notion of the critical endeavor is his remarks on the account of Shakespeare given by Neander in *Of Dramatic Poesy*:

> *Shakespeare* was the man who of all Modern, and perhaps Ancient Poets, had the largest and most comprehensive soul. All the Images of Nature were still present to him, and he drew them not laboriously, but luckily: when he describes any thing, you more than see it, you feel it too. Those who accuse him to have wanted learning, give him the greater commendation: he was naturally learn'd; he needed not the spectacles of Books to read Nature; he look'd inwards, and found her there. I cannot say he is every where alike; were he so, I should do him injury to compare him with the greatest of Mankind. He is many times flat, insipid; his Comick wit degenerating into clenches, his serious swelling into Bombast. But he is always great, when some great occasion is presented to him: no man can say he ever had a fit subject for his wit, and did not then raise himself as high above the rest of Poets,
> *Quantum lenta solent, inter viburna cupressi*
> [as high as cypress trees often do among the bending osiers].[32]

Johnson quoted this passage as the culmination of his own "Preface to Shakespeare" and praised it again with extraordinary warmth in his "Life of Dryden":

The account of Shakespeare may stand as a perpetual model of encomiastic criticism; exact without minuteness, and lofty without exaggeration. The praise lavished by Longinus, on the attestation of the heroes of Marathon by Demosthenes, fades away before it. In a few lines is exhibited a character, so extensive in its comprehension and so curious in its limitations, that nothing can be added, diminished, or reformed; nor can the editors and admirers of Shakespeare, in all their emulation of reverence, boast of much more than of having diffused and paraphrased this epitome of excellence, of having changed Dryden's gold for baser metal, of lower value though of greater bulk. (*Lives*, 1:412)

Johnson's claim for Dryden's encomium, that the "praise lavished by Longinus, on the attestation of the heroes of Marathon by Demosthenes, fades away before it," is surprising in that its aptness is not immediately apparent. In section 16 of his treatise *On the Sublime*, Longinus mentions the "attestation" of Demosthenes as part of a discussion of the rhetorical appropriateness and force of certain kinds of oath. Demosthenes, faced with the task of defending a policy which had led to an Athenian defeat, "fill'd as it were with sudden Inspiration, and transported by a God-like Warmth . . . thunders out an Oath by the Champions of *Greece*: 'You were not in the wrong, no, you were not I swear by those noble Souls who were so lavish of their Lives in the Field of *Marathon*.' " By means of "this figurative manner of Swearing," or "Apostrophe," Longinus claimed, Demosthenes seems:

> to have deified their noble Ancestors, at the same time instructing them, that they ought to swear by Persons, who fell so gloriously, as by so many Gods. He stamps into the Breasts of his Judges the generous Principles of those applauded Patriots; and by transferring what was naturally a Proof into a soaring Strain of the Sublime and the Pathetic, strengthened by such a solemn, such an unusual and reputable Oath, he instills that Balm into their Minds which heals every painful Reflexion, and assuages the smart of Misfortune. . . . In short, by the sole Application of this Figure, he violently seizes the Favour and Attention of his Audience, and compels them to acquiesce in the Event. . . .[33]

Johnson praised Dryden's criticism generally as being "the criticism of a poet; not a dull collection of theorems, nor a rude detection of faults . . . but a gay and vigorous dissertation where delight is mingled with instruction, and where the author proves his right of judgement, by his power of performance" (*Lives*, 1:412). Johnson is apparently praising Dryden on the same grounds that Pope had praised Longinus in *An Essay on Criticism*: "Whose *own Example* strengthens all his Laws, / And *Is himself* that great *sublime* he draws" (lines 679–80).[34]

The "comprehensiveness" of Dryden's criticism and the "comprehensiveness" of Shakespeare's "soul" have in common the power to bring a great deal into a little space, to rise to a great occasion, and to carry all hearers along. According to Longinus, Demosthenes had invented a "soaring Strain of the Sublime," endowed with the passion and the power of conviction. A "comprehensive soul," it seems, was closely associated with the sublime both by the ancient and the modern writer. In the "Life of Cowley," Johnson defined the "sublime" as "that comprehension and expanse of thought which at once fills the whole mind, and of which the first effect is sudden astonishment, and the second rational admiration," arguing that "sublimity is produced by aggregation, and littleness by dispersion" since "great thoughts are always general, and consist in positions not limited by exceptions, and in descriptions not descending to minuteness." For Johnson "comprehensiveness" seems to issue in "images"—images of "Nature." The "metaphysical" poets "broke every image into fragments, and could no more represent, by their slender conceits and laboured particularities the prospects of nature or the scenes of life, than he who dissects a sunbeam with a prism can exhibit the wide effulgence of a summer noon" (*Lives*, 1:20–21), but when Shakespeare "describes any thing," as Dryden put it, "you more than see it, you feel it too."

In all these cases, the emphasis seems to rest on the operations of "Mind." In Longinus' description of Demosthenes those operations might be dismissed as mere skill, but in Dryden's account of Shakespeare, as in Johnson's account of Dryden, the emphasis appears to be on "that comprehension and expanse of thought which at once fills the whole mind." Johnson's suggestion seems to be that Dryden "*Is himself that great sublime* he draws." If that is the case, Johnson may be hinting that as Demosthenes transformed his audience into gods, so Dryden made a line of Virgil "sublime": "no man can say he ever had a fit subject for his wit" (force of mind) "and did not then raise himself as high above the rest of Poets":

Quantum lenta solent, inter viburna cupressi.

The line which Dryden borrowed to express his sense of the enormous difference between Shakespeare at his best and the best of any other poet occurs in Virgil's "First Pastoral." A shepherd is expressing his astonishment at the size of Rome. "Fool that I was," he says in Dryden's own version, "I thought Imperial *Rome* / Like *Mantua*, where on Market-days we come." His mistake, he now realizes, is that "the Great I measur'd by the Less." He sees now that "Country Towns, compar'd with her, appear / Like Shrubs, when lofty Cypresses are near" (lines

34–35). It may be that Dryden, as Johnson read him, resembled Demosthenes in filling the mind with a sense of *disparate greatness* — presented as an image of the enormous disparity between a shrub and a towering cypress. If that is the case, Johnson's admiration for Dryden's passage may have involved an element of *recognition*. The immense divergence between the supreme achievements of any writer and their staple, as between the achievements of great authors and those unread and unreadable authors (who, as he saw it, constituted the norm of any age of literature), is a theme that recurs so often in Johnson's criticism that Robert Folkenflik has suggested that an "awareness of the possibility of intellectual tasks followed by the realisation of the impossibility of their ideal attainment forms the diastole and systole of Johnson's thought."[35]

The metaphor is appropriate, in that there are many reasons for thinking that the very circulation of Johnson's critical blood, so to speak, depended upon an alternation between the possible and the impossible, between necessary aspiration and inevitable failure (a variant of the opposition that appears to underpin much of Johnson's creative writings, from the searches for "proper objects" for "hope and fear" in the *Vanity of Human Wishes*, to the balancing of enjoyment and endurance in *Rasselas*). In *Idler* 88 Johnson described the reasons why human retrospection must always be painful:

> He that compares what he has done with what he has left undone will feel the effect which must always follow the comparison of imagination with reality; he will look with contempt on his own unimportance, and wonder to what purpose he came into the world; he will repine that he shall leave behind him no evidence of his having been, that he has added nothing to the system of life, but has glided from youth to age among the crowd, without any effort for distinction.

However, he argues that such feelings depend on a "mistaken notion of human greatness" and anyone should be consoled by the thought that "a little more than nothing is as much as can be expected from a being who, with respect to the multitudes about him is himself little more than nothing." Furthermore:

> He that has improved the virtue or advanced the happiness of one fellow-creature, he that has ascertained a single moral proposition, or added one useful experiment to natural knowledge, may be contented with his own performance, and, with respect to mortals like himself, may demand, like Augustus, to be dismissed at his departure with pleasure. (*Idler* 88, 2:274–75)[36]

This conclusion is at once capacitating and levelling. The comparisons of the achievements with the possibilities of human attainment place every mortal on a par with Augustus, who, for all his power, is subject to the laws of life and the nature of things.

There are few reasons to doubt that the generalities of the *Idler* were grounded in Johnson's personal experience. In the preface to the *Dictionary*, he restated his notion of the essential difficulty facing anyone with "comprehensive views":

> To have attempted much is always laudable, even when the enterprise is above the strength that undertakes it. To rest below his own aim is incident to every one whose fancy is active, and whose views are comprehensive; nor is any man satisfied with himself because he has done much, but because he can conceive little.

However, since whatever can be done will never be enough, all that remains is the self-injunction to bear inevitable imperfection in patience:

> I may surely be contented without the praise of perfection which, if I could obtain, in this gloom of solitude, what would it avail me? I have protracted my work till most of those whom I wished to please have sunk into the grave, and success and miscarriage are empty sounds: I therefore dismiss it with frigid tranquillity, having little to fear or hope from censure or from praise.[37]

The ceaseless (but necessary) struggle between (and mutual interdependence of) hope and failure is extended in the "Preface to Shakespeare" to the "unsuccessfulness of enquiry" and the "slow advances of truth" in literary study—where the "great part of the labour of every writer is only the destruction of those that went before him," with the corollary that the "opinions prevalent in one age, as truths above the reach of controversy, are confuted and rejected in another, and rise again to reception in remoter times" so that "the human mind is kept in motion without progress." For Johnson, on this occasion, the universality of this generality appears to have been consoling rather than depressing:

> These elevations and depressions of renown, and the contradictions to which all improvers of knowledge must for ever be exposed, since they are not escaped by the highest and brightest of mankind, may surely be endured with patience by criticks and annotators, who can rank themselves but as the satellites of their authours. How canst thou beg for life, says Achilles to his captive, when thou knowest that thou art now to suffer only what must another day be suffered by Achilles? (*Shakespeare*, 7:99)

Again Johnson encapsulated his thought in an image. Pope had described the moment in the twenty-first book of the *Iliad* where Lycaon sues (in vain) for mercy from Achilles as "a speaking Picture" of which he believes "every one perceives the Beauty."[38] Johnson's impression of the passage appears to have been identical with that of Pope, who discovered "an Air of Greatness in the Conclusion of the Speech of Achilles," which, he added, "strikes me very much": "He speaks very unconcernedly of his own Death, and upbraids his Enemy for asking for Life so earnestly, a Life that was of so much less Importance than his own":

> Talk not of Life, or Ransom, (he replies)
> *Patroclus* dead, whoever meets me, dies . . .
> Die then, my Friend! what boots it to deplore?
> The great, the good *Patroclus* is no more!
> He, far thy Better, was fore-doom'd to die,
> 'And thou, dost thou, bewail Mortality?'
>
> (8:425; 426)[39]

Johnson both admits the necessity of critical ambition and deconstructs its possibilities. His critical judgments are offered in the knowledge that they are subject to the same temporal constraints and vicissitudes as befall all mortal endeavors, including those of Lycaon, Patroclus, and even Achilles. The critical humility that he suggests as a necessary bulwark against the depressive conclusion of "motion without progress" is no panacea, given the weight placed throughout Johnson's writings on the dangers of complacency, of standing still, of stagnation. One impression left by Johnson's writing is its remorseless questioning of its own nature, and conviction that, despite this questioning, something must be done, some sort of resolution must ensue from the endless conflict between hope and failure.

In this light it is perhaps significant that the widely-admired "Life of Dryden" should consist, for much of its length, of a record of comparative *failure*. Dryden's plays are largely dismissed. Johnson is noticeably less impressed by Dryden's satires than most twentieth-century readers. He was, as we have seen, at variance with most of his contemporaries over Dryden's *Fables*. It is not always easy to see the connections between any particular work and Dryden's profound effects on the course of poetry. Boswell is not the only commentator to have suggested that the inwardness of the "Life of Dryden" might be attributed to Johnson's perceiving some natural affinity between his subject and himself (*Life*, 4:45). There would indeed appear to be many reasons for applying Johnson's description of Dryden's criticism to Johnson's own writings:

His criticism may be considered as general or occasional. In his general precepts, which depend upon the nature of things and the structure of the human mind, he may doubtless be safely recommended to the confidence of the reader; but his occasional and particular positions were sometimes interested, sometimes negligent, and sometimes capricious. (*Lives*, 1:413)

It is perhaps significant that the passages from Johnson singled out by Malone as equaling the criticism of Aristotle include the "exquisite parallel" between Pope and Dryden, which is substantially a description of the "structure" of two different minds—minds that are irreconcilable, and therefore blest with different kinds of relative success and doomed to different kinds of relative failure. If Johnson's formulations stuck in the minds of his readers (as exhibited in either their praise or their censure), partly because of their qualities as literature, and in particular through their power to present the mind with an image, the passages that most impressed included those where Johnson's literary powers were applied to descriptions of the structure of the *poetic* mind.

Johnson had three sustained attempts at the definition of the mind of the ideal poet—the tenth chapter of *Rasselas*, the "Preface to Shakespeare," and his general account of Pope, particularly in comparison with Dryden. Johnson leads into this comparison through his description of Pope's "intellectual character," of which "the constituent and fundamental principle was Good Sense, a prompt and intuitive perception of consonance and propriety" (*Lives*, 3:216). In writing this, Johnson, as Birkbeck Hill suggested, may have been following Pope himself in the *Epistle to Burlington* where he argues that good taste is dependent upon another faculty—"Sense":

> Good Sense, which only is the gift of heav'n,
> And tho' no science, fairly worth the seven.[40]

In using the term "fundamental," Johnson may indeed have been recalling Pope's footnote to the 1736 edition of his poems, describing the subject of this passage: "That the first principle and foundation of all Taste, is Good Sense." As Johnson defines it, "Good Sense" might be a gift from heaven because its operation as a perception of "propriety" is *intuitive*. The word "propriety" seems to be used here as might be expected, indicating "fitness, appropriateness, aptitude, suitability; appropriateness to the circumstances or conditions; conformity with requirement, rule, or principle; rightness, correctness, justness, accuracy" (*OED* 6). "Consonance," however, is something of an odd word for Johnson to use at such a juncture since its primary associations were with correspondence of sounds. (Johnson first defines "Consonancy" in his *Dictionary* as "accord of sound," and he was to use it as such in his "Life of Gray": "The ode is finished before the ear has learned its measures, and consequently before it can receive pleasure from their consonance and recurrence" [*Lives*, 3: 438–39].) As applied to Pope's good sense, the relevant meaning would appear to be Johnson's second definition, where it is linked with "consonancy" to suggest "consistency; congruence; agreeableness." Pope's intuitive perception of consonance and propriety gives him a kind of instinctive self-judgment: "He saw immediately, of his own conceptions, what was to be chosen, and what to be rejected; and, in the works of others, what was to be shunned, and what was to be copied." Johnson's analysis of Pope's powers of combination and assimilation recalls Dryden's description of Plutarch:

> And as he was continually in Company with Men of learning, in all professions, so his memory was always on the stretch, to receive and lodge their discourses; and his Judgement perpetually employ'd in separating his notions, and distinguishing which were fit to be preserv'd, and which to be rejected.[41]

Joseph Warton had asserted that good sense was Pope's *defining* quality:

> We do not, it should seem, sufficiently attend to the difference there is, betwixt a MAN OF WIT, a MAN OF SENSE, and a TRUE POET. Donne and Swift, were undoubtedly men of wit, and men of sense, but what traces have they left of PURE POETRY? . . . all I plead for, is, to have their several provinces kept distinct from each other; and to impress on the reader, that a clear head, and acute understanding are not sufficient, alone, to make a POET; that the most solid observations on human life, expressed with the utmost elegance and brevity, are MORALITY, and not POETRY.[42]

Johnson, on the other hand, was at pains to claim that good sense was only the foundation of the edifice of Pope's mind. The import of his remarks is to obviate Warton's distinctions between "sense" and "true poetry" while conceding that "good sense" is not of itself (nor could be) a sufficient qualification for a poet: "good sense alone is a sedate and quiescent quality, which manages its possessions well, but does not increase them; it collects few materials for its own operations, and preserves safety, but never gains supremacy."[43] "Sedate" Johnson glosses as "calm; quiet; still; unruffled; undisturbed; serene" citing Watts ("Disputation carries away the mind from that calm and *sedate* temper which is so necessary to contemplate truth") and Dryden's *Aeneid* ("With count'nance calm and soul *sedate*, / Thus Turnus"). Again in the "Life,"

Johnson shares his vocabulary with Dryden, who in the preface to *Fables, Ancient and Modern* had ascribed "propriety" to Virgil's "sedate" poetical character, contrasting it with Homer, who was "rapid in his Thoughts, and took all the Liberties both of Numbers, and of Expression, which his Language, and the Age in which he liv'd allow'd him. *Homer's* invention was more copious, *Virgil's* more confin'd."[44]

Johnson appears to be preparing the ground for the striking suggestion (with which he concludes the "Life") that Pope was peculiarly fitted to be a translator of Homer—whose mind and verse are perpetually in motion, and whose "invention" (as Pope had it) is everywhere active. For these reasons, "good sense," a "quiescent" quality, cannot be more than the basis of the structure of Pope's poetic mind. "Quiescent" seems to have been a word borrowed from natural philosophy. In the *Dictionary*, Johnson glosses it as "resting; not being in motion; not movent; lying at repose," citing among several examples Newton's *Optics*: "Pression or motion cannot be propagated in a fluid in right lines beyond an obstacle which stops part of the motion, but will bend and spread every way into the quiescent medium, which lies beyond the obstacle."

As Johnson presents the matter, a poet whose essential faculties were "sedate" and "quiescent" could never achieve the poetic "supremacy" over the minds of contemporaries and successors wielded by Pope's works. It follows, for Johnson, that Pope *must* have possessed:

> likewise genius; a mind active, ambitious, and adventurous, always investigating, always aspiring; in its widest searches still longing to go forward, in its highest flights still wishing to be higher; always imagining something greater than it knows, always endeavoring more than it can do. (*Lives*, 3:217)[45]

Johnson's definition of "genius" here does not absolutely accord with any of the definitions given in his *Dictionary*, though it would seem to contain some elements of all: "The protecting or ruling power of men, places, or things"; "A man endowed with superiour faculties"; "Mental power or faculties"; "Disposition of nature by which any one is qualified for some peculiar employment"; "Nature; disposition." Johnson's leading distinction in the "Life" seems to be between a "sedate" and "quiescent" foundation and a coexisting restless energy and activity.

Whether the possession of "genius" is a blessing or a curse is left by Johnson for the reader to decide. Where the possessor of "good sense alone" might hope, as it were, to lead a quiet and comfortable life, the possessor of "genius" appears to be doomed by restless, aspiring ambition to a life of frustrated hopes. "Aspiring" does not appear as a headword in Johnson's *Dictionary*, but is used as a gloss for "Ambitious": "Eager to grow bigger; aspiring." (Johnson's illustration is from *Julius Caesar*: "I have seen / Th' *ambitious* ocean swell, and rage, and foam, / To be exalted with the threat'ning clouds.") The ambitious mind must always be subordinate to what it aspires to, yet in its aspiration it achieves as much as can be expected or hoped for. The works of "genius" will achieve supremacy over the works of "good sense" (which will have no greater quality than "safety"), but will also display signs of inevitable failure.

Johnson's thoughts, that is, seem at this point to be as dependent on "the nature of things" as on the "structure of the human mind." The aspirations of genius are almost to be numbered among the vanities of human wishes. The ambition of a "genius" is not, for example, entirely dissimilar from that of Lucretius' Sisyphus, whose condition is described by Dryden as Johnson described Pope's genius—by repetition of the adverb "still":

> For, still to aim at power, and still to fail,
> Ever to strive, and never to prevail,
> What is it, but, in reason's true account,
> To heave the stone against the rising mount?
> Which urged, and laboured, and forced up with pain,
> Recoils, and rolls impetuous down, and smokes along the plain.
> Then, still to treat thy ever-craving mind
> With every blessing, and of every kind,
> Yet never fill thy ravening appetite,
> Though years and seasons vary thy delight,
> Yet nothing to be seen of all the store,
> But still the wolf within thee barks for more.
> ("Against the Fear of Death," lines 206–17)

Johnson's account of "genius" is initially general rather than particular. Pope possessed that general quality which Sir Richard Blackmore — who had never "elevated his views to that ideal perfection which every genius born to excel is condemned always to pursue, and never overtake"—lacked (*Lives*, 2:253). Blackmore was, according to Johnson, not "diligent in perusing books"—or in any other poetic responsibility. By contrast, it is a peculiarity of the mind of Pope to have improved the "benefits of nature" ("good sense," "genius," "strength and exactness of memory") by "incessant and unwearied diligence." The word "unwearied" seems to be another borrowing (almost a quotation) from Pope, who had described his poetic mind as "that unweary'd Mill / That turn'd ten thousand Verses" (*The Second Epistle of the Second Book of Horace, Imitated*, lines 78–79).

"Diligence" provides the crux of Johnson's distinction between Pope and Dryden: "Pope had perhaps the judgement of Dryden; but Dryden certainly wanted the diligence of Pope." Indeed, Johnson's method is to present his initial description of the two poetic minds apparently to the detriment of Dryden, who (rather like Blackmore) "spent no time in struggles to rouse latent powers," or ever "attempted to make that better which was already good." It is not until Johnson comes to discuss intellectual capacity that the balance begins to turn the other way. Dryden's "mind has a larger range, and he collects his images and illustrations from a more extensive circumference of science" than does Pope. Although Johnson does not on this occasion link his sentences with his habitual adverbial "therefore," it seems to follow from the more extensive circumference of Dryden's knowledge that he:

> knew more of man in his general nature, and Pope in his local manners. The notions of Dryden were formed by comprehensive speculation, and those of Pope by minute attention. There is more dignity in the knowledge of Dryden, and more certainty in that of Pope. (*Lives*, 3:222)

"Dignity of knowledge" is a striking and unusual phrase, and again one that extends the language beyond that recorded in Johnson's *Dictionary*.[46] It seems to be at once more specific and more general than the remark recorded by Boswell, that "in Dryden's poetry there were passages drawn from a profundity which Pope could never reach" (*Life*, 2 85).

It is at this point that Johnson brings forth the sentence so admired by Malone: "Of genius, that power which constitutes a poet; that quality without which judgement is cold and knowledge is inert; that energy which collects, combines, amplifies, and animates—the superiority must, with some hesitation, be allowed to Dryden." It supports the present argument that Johnson's second definition of "genius" should be in terms of capacity and range. "Genius" is again active, but on this occasion is described in terms of its operations rather than aspirations. There appears to be a sequence in the poetic process—assimilation, association, and vivification. "Animates" is given a remarkable definition in the *Dictionary*, in that Johnson uses the occasion to assert one of the fundamentals of Christian belief: "to quicken; to make alive; to give life to: as, the soul *animates* the body; man must have been *animated* by a higher power." The word, however, seems to have played as large a part in his literary understanding as it does in his religious sentiments. It is used in the famous sentence from the *Rambler* accounting for the "force of poetry" in a speech from *Macbeth*, "that force which calls new powers into being, which embodies sentiment, and animates matter" (*Rambler* 168, 5:127).

At this point, having described the two dissimilar structures of writers' minds, Johnson turns to the works themselves, and then, significantly, to their effects on the mind of the reader:

> If the flights of Dryden therefore are higher, Pope continues longer on the wing. If of Dryden's fire the blaze is brighter, of Pope's the heat is more regular and constant. Dryden often surpasses expectation, and Pope never falls below it. Dryden is read with frequent astonishment, and Pope with perpetual delight. (*Lives*, 3, 223)

It is again possible that Johnson's critical vocabulary is modeled on Dryden's comparison of Homer and Virgil in the preface to *Fables, Ancient and Modern*. Dryden's suggestion was that the differing minds of the two ancient writers were reflected in the different conduct of the action of their poems, which were reflected, in turn, in a different experience of pleasure for the reader:

> the *Grecian* is more according to my Genius, than the *Latin* Poet. . . . The very *Heroes* shew their Authors: *Achilles* is hot, impatient, revengeful . . . the Action of *Homer* being more full of Vigour . . . is of consequence more pleasing to the Reader. One warms you by Degrees; the other sets you on fire all at once and never intermits his Heat. 'Tis the same Difference which *Longinus* makes betwixt the Effects of Eloquence in *Demosthenes*, and *Tully*. One persuades; the other commands. You never cool while you read *Homer*. . . .[47]

There are probably several reasons for Malone's description of Johnson's comparison as both "beautiful" and "judicious." The term "judicious" might point to the number of acute observations of the particulars of many thousand lines subsumed within Johnson's careful generalities. It is not often, however, that criticism has been described as "beautiful." The supposition of the present essay is that Johnson's criticism at its best struck its admirers as indistinguishable from literature itself. Malone may have read Johnson's comparison very much as Johnson read Dryden's account of Shakespeare, as a work *of* a poetic mind as much as a discourse *about* a poetic mind.

When Imlac's "desire of excellence" impels him to transfer his attention from books "to nature and to life," in the knowledge that nature was to be his subject, and men his auditors, he realizes that he "could not hope to move those with delight or terror whose interests and opinions" he did not understand (*Rasselas*, 41). There are reasons for thinking that Johnson would not have been at all surprised at the reception of many of his critical judgments. His speculations on the minds of poets and the minds of readers seem equally sure. Most of the passages that gave pain to readers seem deliberately or deliberatively designed to do so.[48]

At the same time, most of Johnson's animadversions, whether on Milton's earlier poems, or Gray's pindaric odes (or, indeed, most poetry written after 1730), reflect, or assume, or imply a notion of what poetic genius, in its "wider searches" and "highest flights," might be capable. Lawrence Lipking offers a pertinent speculation on the attacks on Johnson's *Lives*:

> Again and again the critics charged that Johnson's opinions were grudging, ruthless and negative. Doubtless so persistent a reaction contains a grain of truth. Yet it also reflects an insensitivity to Johnson's major loyalty, the loyalty to poetry that asks poets to strive always for the best of which they are capable.[49]

The "best" of which poetic genius was capable was found very rarely by Johnson in English poetry. He discovered it in some aspects of *Paradise Lost*, in some passages and a very few poems by Pope and Dryden, and most overwhelmingly (though intermittently) in Shakespeare. At the end of the "Life of Gray," Johnson concluded that "by the common sense of readers uncorrupted with literary prejudices, after all the refinements of subtilty and the dogmatism of learning, must be finally decided all claim to poetical honours" (Lives, 3:441). In its constant reference to the judgments of time, conceived of as a process conducted in the minds of generations of readers, Johnson's criticism is often essentially *predictive*. That which has been found durable will prove to be durable (or as he puts it in the "Life of Butler," "co-extended with the race of man" [*Lives*, 1:214]). The "pleasures and vexations" of the personages in Shakespeare's comic scenes are "communicable to all times and to all places; they are natural, and therefore durable":

> The accidental compositions of heterogeneous modes are dissolved by the chance which combined them; but the uniform simplicity of primitive qualities neither admits increase, nor suffers decay. The sand heaped by one flood is scattered by another, but the rock always continues in its place. The stream of time, which is continually washing the dissoluble fabrics of other poets, passes without injury by the adamant of Shakespeare. (*Shakespeare*, 7:70)

As Johnson presents the case, the durability of Shakespeare's "fabric" is a direct result of the comprehensiveness of his mind. It is both Johnson's belief and his experience that the products created by a comprehensive mind are "communicable to all times and to all places"; they have been ratified in the past and will continue to be ratified in the future. Johnson's critical judgment of literature appears to return again and again to whether it makes the past, the distant, or the future predominate over the present. (Shakespeare "approximates the remote, and familiarizes the wonderful" [*Shakespeare*, 7:65].)

If Johnson's "idea of poetry" was, as Hester Thrale records, "magnificent indeed," so that "very fully was he persuaded of its superiority over every other talent bestowed by heaven on man" (*Miscellanies*, 1:284–85), his accounts of poetic genius nevertheless resemble Wordsworth's in implying that the faculties of the poetic mind are those of every human mind (though in superabundance). Wordsworth (echoing Dryden's praise of Shakespeare), maintained that "a Poet" possesses "a greater knowledge of human nature, and a more comprehensive soul, than are supposed to be common among mankind."[50] When Johnson came to Hamlet's famous rhetorical question —

> What is a man
> If his chief good and market of his time
> Be but to sleep and feed? A beast, no more.
> Sure, he that made us with such large discourse,
> Looking before and after, gave us not
> That capability and godlike reason
> To fust in us unused

—he glossed the phrase "large discourse" as "Such latitude of comprehension, such power of reviewing the past, and anticipating the future" (*Shakespeare*, 8:994).

The longevity of Johnson's critical judgments may be partly explained in his own terms — in their "latitude of comprehension" demonstrated as a capacity to look before and after. Johnson, for all his engagement with contemporary debate, appears to have wished to place his critical judgments beyond the vicissitudes of time and critical practice. If his judgments resist explanation in terms of their being the expressions of his personality, the critical doctrines of the early eighteenth century or the taste of his own day, if they seem rather to rest on his sense of occasional transcendent excellence (of Shakespeare in particular) and the structure — and particularly the inevitable limitations — of the human mind, and if they attain the qualities of literature, then there might be some reason to expect that when the "tide of seeming knowledge which is poured over one generation, retires and leaves another naked and barren" (*Shakespeare*, 7:99), Johnson's criticism may count for more than it has done in our immediate past.

NOTES

1. *The Works of Alexander Pope*, ed. Joseph Warton, 9 vols. (London, 1797), 1:134.

2. Warton's strange remark perpetuates Johnson's own criticism. His comment on Johnson's comment was retained in the 1822 reprint of his edition of Pope.

3. In George Mason's 1796 edition of Thomas Hoccleve, for example, there is a similarly distracting comment on Johnson. Mason has been glossing the hard words in Hoccleve. He comes to the word "skill" which he glosses as "Reason" citing from *The Winter's Tale* the lines "You have / As little skill to fear, as I have purpose / To put you to't." Mason points out that the passage is correctly explained in Johnson's edition of Shakespeare but then observes that the passage is differently glossed in the fourth edition of Johnson's *Dictionary*. Mason suspects that "the lexicographer had not collected his authorities for himself, not even revised them when collected for him." He then appears to repent of his own asperity: "Let however his moral failings be / Interred with his bones. / Men's literary deeds live after them [here Mason continues in prose] and are proper subjects of animadversion, when an author's natural decease has entitled his literary character to an epitaph." The following page and a half are occupied with an epitaph which Mason describes in a footnote as written "very soon after Dr. Johnson's death, while Newspapers were perpetually pestering the public with idle anecdotes about him": "HERE, PEACEABLE AT LAST / ARE DEPOSITED THE REMAINS / OF DOCTOR SAMUEL JOHNSON / THE POET, / THE CRITIC. . . . THE PUBLIC TASTE, / (PATRON OF EVERY NOVELTY) / CHERISHED HIS WRITINGS FOR A WHILE, / AS MOST EXTRAORDINARY SPECIMENS / OF PEDANTIC VERBOSITY. . . . HIS POLITICAL AND POETICAL TENETS / DIFFERED WIDELY FROM EACH OTHER . . . HIS OWN FAILURES IN POETRY / RENDERED HIM A PERFECT LEVELLER / THROUGHOUT THE REGION OF THE MUSES. / INCOMPETENT CRITIC FROM HEBETUDE, / CREDULOUS RETAILER OF CALUMNIES. / ILLIBERAL IN HIS CENSURES, / CYNICAL IN HIS EXPRESSIONS, / HE ACQUIRED THE LITERARY TITLE OF / SNARLER GENERAL. / TO THE MANES OF POETS AUGUST, / WHOM JOHNSON SLANDERED IN THEIR GRAVES, / BE THIS AN EXPIATORY OFFERING." *The Poems of Thomas Hoccleve* (London, 1796), 105–7.

4. William Kenrick, *A Review of Doctor Johnson's New Edition of Shakespeare, in which the ignorance, or inattention of that editor is exposed, and the poet defended from the persecution of his commentators* (London, 1765), reprinted in *On Johnson's Shakespeare, 1765–1766* (New York and London: Garland, 1975), 87–88. Kenrick's criticism is directed as much against Johnson's recent acceptance of a pension, and his assumed standing as the leading contemporary critic, as it is against Johnson's edition in particular.

5. The long relationship between Warton and Johnson is extremely complex; it is impossible to know whether the intellectual differences of the two necessitated or resulted from a cooling of their friendship, though Warton's comments after Johnson's death are more forthright in their disagreement. For more details and examples of Warton's later antagonism to Johnson's criticism, see Joan Pittock, *The Ascendancy of Taste: The Achievement of Joseph and Thomas Warton* (London: Routledge, 1973), 161; James Allison, "Joseph Warton's Reply to Dr Johnson's 'Lives,'" *Journal of English and Germanic Philology* 51 (1952): 186–91, 190; and Hugh Reid, "'The Want of a Closer Union . . .': The Friendship of Samuel Johnson and Joseph Warton," *AJ* 9 (1998): 133–43, 138–39.

6. In some cases it was the poet rather than the poems that needed defense— Lyttelton, for example. As Boswell puts it, Johnson's "expressing with a dignified free-

dom what he really thought of George, Lord Lyttelton, gave offence to some of the friends of that nobleman. . . ." (*Life*, 4:64). One of Johnson's most controversial comments in the "Life of Lyttelton" was the application of an adjective, when speaking of the reception of Lyttelton's *Dialogues of the Dead*: "When they were first published they were kindly commended by the Critical reviewers, and poor Lyttelton with humble gratitude returned, in a note which I have read, acknowledgements that can never be proper, since they must be paid either for flattery or for justice" (*Lives* 3:452). "Poor Lyttelton" thus joins "poor Collins" and "poor Smart." In a letter to Elizabeth Montagu, Johnson's most formidable opponent over the memory of Lyttelton, W. W. Pepys related an argument between himself and Johnson over the matter, and voiced his concern: "what hurts me all the while is, not that Johnson should go unpunished, but that our dear and respected friend should . . . be handed down to succeeding generations under the appellation of poor Lyttelton." William Weller Pepys, Letter of 4 August 1781, reprinted in *Miscellanies*, 2:416–17.

7. Lawrence Lipking, *The Ordering of the Arts in Eighteenth-Century England* (Princeton: Princeton University Press, 1970), 405.

8. *Dr. Johnson and Fanny Burney; Being the Johnsonian Passages from the works of Mme D'Arblay*, ed. Chauncey Brewster Tinker (Westport, Conn.: Greenwood Press, 1911), 216.

9. Edmund Cartwright, *Monthly Review* (1779), reprinted in *Johnson: The Critical Heritage*, ed. J. T. Boulton (London: Routledge, 1971), 263.

10. *The Critical and Miscellaneous Prose Works of John Dryden*, ed. Edmond Malone, 4 vols. (London, 1800), 1:549. Malone esteemed Johnson's preface to his edition of Shakespeare no less highly. In the preface to his own edition of Shakespeare's plays (1790), he described Johnson as "one, whose extraordinary powers of mind, as they rendered him the admiration of his contemporaries, will transmit his name to posterity as the brightest ornament of the eighteenth century; and will transmit it without competition." He considered Johnson's "admirable preface" to be "perhaps the finest composition in our language": "his happy, and in general just, characters of these plays, his refutation of the false glosses of Theobald and Warburton, and his numerous explications of involved and difficult passages, are too well known to be here enlarged upon; and therefore I shall only add, that his vigorous and comprehensive understanding threw more light on his author than all his predecessors had done." Malone's preface was reprinted in *The Plays And Poems Of William Shakespeare, With The Corrections And Illustrations Of Various Commentators* (London, 1821), 244–45.

11. Coleridge referred in a letter of 1816 to "[Johnson's] strangely contradictory and most illogical Preface to Shakespear," and even Sir John Hawkins, Johnson's executor and first biographer, rather quixotically remarked that it "endeavoured to sink [Shakespeare] in the opinion of his numerous admirers." Coleridge, letter of 13 May 1816 to Daniel Stuart, in *The Letters of Samuel Taylor Coleridge*, ed. Ernest Hartley Coleridge, 2 vols. (London: Heinemann, 1895), 2:664. Sir John Hawkins, *The Life of Samuel Johnson* (1787; reprinted New York and London: Garland, 1974), 537.

12. Robert Potter, for example, gives a strident example of damning with faint praise, in closing his book-length consideration of the *Lives* by describing Johnson as a "great author, notwithstanding his Dictionary is imperfect, his Rambler pompous, his Idler inane, his Lives unjust, his poetry inconsiderable, his learning common, his ideas vulgar, his Irene a child of mediocrity, his genius and wit moderate, his precepts worldly, his politics narrow, and his religion bigoted." *The Art of Criticism; as Exemplified in Dr Johnson's Lives of the Most Eminent Poets* (London, 1789; reprinted New York and London: Garland, 1974), 194.

13. William Cowper, letter of 31 October 1779, in *The Letters and Prose Writings of*

William Cowper, ed. James King and Charles Ryskamp, 5 vols. (Oxford: Clarendon Press, 1979), 1:5.

14. William Cowper, letter of 5 January 1782, in *The Letters and Prose Writings of William Cowper*, 2:5. In a letter of 18 September 1781, Cowper said of his own poetry that "It is possible that [Johnson] may be pleased [with it], and if he should, I shall have engaged on my side one of the best trumpeters in the Kingdom. Let him only speak as favourably of me, as he has spoken of Sir Richard Blackmore, who though he shines in his poem called the Creation, has written more absurdities in Verse than any other Writer of our Country, and my success will be secured" (*Letters and Prose Writings*, 1:521).

15. Johnson had described Prior's extremely popular poem as "a dull and tedious dialogue, which excites neither esteem for the man nor tenderness for the woman" ("Life of Prior," *Lives*, 2:203).

16. "Epistle to William Hayley," *The Poetical Works of Anna Seward*, ed. Walter Scott, 3 vols. (Edinburgh, 1810), 2:147. "Verses to the Rev. William Mason, on his Silence Respecting Dr Johnson's Unjust Criticisms upon Mr Gray's Works, in the Lives of the Poets," 2:180. "To the Right Honourable the Marchioness of Donegall, with Mr Hayley's Life of Milton," 3:119. "To Charles Simpson, Esq. Barrister; With Thomas Warton's Edition of Milton's Lesser Poems," 3:57; 189.

17. Seward, *Poetical Works*, 3:188.

18. Letter of 21 December 1797, in *The Letters of Anna Seward written between the years 1784 and 1807*, 6 vols. (London, 1811), 5:31. Sir Walter Scott, in a preface to Seward's poems, speculated on her antipathy to Johnson: "Neither Dr. Darwin nor Miss Seward were partial to the great moralist. There was, perhaps, some aristocratic prejudice in their dislike, for the despotic manners of Dr. Johnson were least likely to be tolerated where the lowness of his origin was in fresh recollection" (*Poetical Works*, 1:x). Seward's complaints are not dissimilar to Joseph Warton's list of critical grievances against Johnson in his edition of Pope: "As much as I revere and respect the memory of my old acquaintance Dr. Johnson, and as highly as I think of his abilities, integrity, and virtue, yet must I be pardoned for saying, that I cannot possibly subscribe to many of his critical decisions; particularly to whatever he has said of Lycidas, Il Penseroso and Latin poems of Milton; of the Sixth Book of Paradise Lost; of Tasso's Aminta; of the Rhyming Tragedies, Ode to Killigrew, and the Fables of Dryden; of Chaucer; of the Rehearsal; of Prior; of Congreve's Mourning Bride; of Blackmore; of Yalden; of Pomfret; of Dyer; of Garth; of Lyttelton; of Fielding; of Harris; of Hammond; of Beattie; of Shenstone; of Savage; of Hughes; of Spence; of Akenside; of Collins; of Pope's Essay on Man, and imitations of Horace; and of the Odes of Gray" (*The Works of Alexander Pope*, 1:xvi). The almost comic length of this list is indicative of the strength of Warton's disagreement—it would, it might almost be thought, have been easier for him to have listed those places where he *didn't* disagree with Johnson's judgments.

19. Richard Woodhouse, letter to Mary Frogley of 23 October 1818, in *The Letters of John Keats*, ed. H. E. Rollins, 2 vols. (Cambridge: Cambridge University Press, 1958), 1:384–85. Woodhouse's quoting lines 77–78 of Dryden's then celebrated ode *Alexander's Feast, or the Power of Music* (1697) is telling, in that the "fallen fallen" image (a stock one in the eighteenth century, given the popularity of Dryden's poem) is meant to represent the degree of the decline of Johnson's critical influence, in the thirty-odd years since his death.

20. *Memoirs of the Life of Sir James Mackintosh*, ed. Robert James Mackintosh, 2nd ed., 2 vols. (London, 1836), 2:175–76. Elsewhere, Sir James remarked, "That Johnson had no science is very certain; but neither was imagination his predominant talent. Strength of understanding was his characteristic excellence. On religion and politics,

his prejudices did not allow him *fair play*; and, in polite literature, his strong sense was injured by coarse feeling" (2:104).

21. Such visions of Johnson make him representative in his inability to accommodate different kinds of writing to his taste, itself formed long ago. Variations on these positions are easy to find. M.H. Abrams, in 1959, described how Johnson "had become closely habituated to one kind of versification" suggesting that "one reason that Johnson found unpleasing much of the poetry of Milton, or Collins, or Gray, was that their numbers clashed sharply with the reading skills, the anticipations and accustomed reactions, which had been formed mainly on the numbers of Dryden and of Pope." See M.H. Abrams, "Dr. Johnson's Spectacles," in *New Light on Dr. Johnson: Essays on the Occasion of his 250th Birthday*, ed. Frederick W. Hilles (New Haven: Yale University Press, 1959), 177–87; 182.

22. For F.R. Leavis's view of the "tradition" Johnson embodied, see "Johnson and Augustanism" in *The Common Pursuit* (London: Chatto and Windus, 1952; reprinted, Harmondsworth: Penguin, 1962), 97–115. T.S. Eliot took this idea of the "representative" Johnson further. See "Johnson as Critic and Poet," in *On Poetry and Poets* (London: Faber and Faber, 1957), 162–92.

23. On the severity of Johnson's judgments in the *Lives*, Robert DeMaria has observed: "Johnson's demands on poetry are so severe that one wonders if he had not actually lost his taste for it by the time he wrote the *Lives*. He is remarkably censorious throughout, considering that his publishers must have looked on his prefaces as invitations to the reading public. He evidently considered much of English poetry puerile fiction." See *The Life of Samuel Johnson: A Critical Biography* (Oxford: Blackwell, 1993), 290.

24. Joseph Warton, *An Essay on the Genius and Writings of Pope*, 2 vols. (1756, 1782; reprinted New York and London: Garland, 1974), 2:17. In his edition of Pope, Warton defends the *Fables* further, referring to the "cold and contemptuous manner in which Dr. Johnson speaks of these capital pieces" (1:166), and complains of the omission of any notice of Dryden's version of *The Flower and the Leaf*. Robert Potter expressed similar sentiments: "Dryden is probably partial in setting 'Palamon and Arcite,' on a level with the *Eneid*; yet Chaucer was a great genius and deemed the primo-genitor of English poetry. His *Flower and Leaf*, past over by the smoak-loving Johnson, is charmingly modernized." See *The Art of Criticism; as Exemplified in Dr Johnson's Lives of the Most Eminent Poets*, 60–61.

25. Warton, *The Works of Alexander Pope*, 1:173.

26. Preface to *The Characters of Shakespear's Plays* in *The Complete Works of William Hazlitt*, ed. P. P. Howe, 21 vols. (London and Toronto: Dent, 1930), 4:174–75.

27. Thomas Babington Macaulay, "Boswell's Life of Johnson," *Edinburgh Review* 54, no. 107 (September 1831): 1–38. One of the first, and most cogent objections to the Boswellized caricature of Johnson influentially created by Macaulay was Bertrand H. Bronson, "The Double Tradition of Dr. Johnson," *ELH* 18 (1951): 90–106. For the merits or otherwise of Boswell's *Life* as literary biography, see *Boswell's Life of Johnson: New Questions, New Answers*, ed. John A. Vance (Athens: University of Georgia Press, 1985). The continuation of the argument (and the lack of likelihood of its closure) can be seen in two essays in *AJ* 9 (1998): John J. Burke's "Boswell and the Text of Johnson's *Logia*," 25–46, and the late Donald J. Greene's posthumously published reply, " 'Beyond Probability': A Boswellian Act of Faith," 47–80.

28. This became for many years the Johnson to be found in most handbooks. For example, George Saintsbury claimed that "Johnson's standards and view-points are extravagantly and exclusively of his time, so that . . . he falls into critical errors almost incomprehensible except from the historic side." See *A Short History of English Literature*

(London, 1898), 616. Andrew Lang's *History of English Literature* (London: Longmans, 1912) contains the assertion that "Johnson's critical tastes and rules are not ours, and perhaps even in his own day were falling out of fashion" (474). The account given by Louis Cazamian in the *Histoire de La Littérature Anglaise* (Paris: Hachette, 1921), translated as *The History of English Literature* (London: Dent, 1927), is much more complex (written as it is in the knowledge of the immense influence of Johnson's criticism of Shakespeare in nineteenth-century France), but nevertheless describes Johnson as "the central figure in an age of bourgeois classicism" (827). Edward Albert, *A History of English Literature* (London: Harrap, 1923), describes Johnson's *Lives* as "virile and sagacious" though "influenced by the classical school of Pope" (246). Sir Henry Newbolt considered the *Lives* to be "vitiated by political bias, and the meagre and unsympathetic account of Gray." See *A History of English Literature* (London: Nelson, 1927), 361. George Sampson's *Concise Cambridge History of English Literature* (Cambridge: Cambridge University Press, 1941) suggested that the "fashion of Johnson's mind made him incapable of appreciating the elaborated art of *Lycidas* and *The Bard*" (529). For Sampson, as for many others, however, "Johnson owes his immortality to Boswell" (530).

29. "I remember when I once regretted to him that he had not given us more of Juvenal's Satires, he said he probably should give more, for he had them all in his head; by which I understood, that he had the originals and correspondent allusions floating in his mind, which he could, when he pleased, embody and render permanent without much labour. Some of them, however, he observed, were too gross for imitation" (*Life*, 1:193). In the "Life of Dryden," Johnson maintained that it was "perhaps possible to give a better representation of that great satirist, even in those parts which Dryden himself has translated, some passages excepted, which will never be excelled" (*Lives*, 1:447).

30. Reprinted in *Johnson: The Critical Heritage*, ed. J. T. Boulton (London: Routledge, 1971), 47–48.

31. It may be significant that Shakespeare is the most and Dryden the second most quoted author in the *Dictionary*.

32. John Dryden, *Of Dramatic Poesy, an Essay* (1667), quoted by Johnson in the "Preface to Shakespeare" (*Shakespeare*, 7:112).

33. Longinus, *Dionysius Longinus on the Sublime*, trans. William Smith (London, 1739), 47–48.

34. For the relationship between Pope's thought here and Johnson's criticism, see Greg Clingham, " 'Himself That Great Sublime': Johnson's Critical Thinking," *Études Anglaises* 41, no. 2 (1988): 165–78. Clingham also discusses this matter in "Johnson on Dryden and Pope" (unpublished doctoral diss: Cambridge University, 1986).

35. Robert Folkenflik, "That Man's Scope," in *Samuel Johnson: New Critical Essays*, ed. Isobel Grundy (London and Totowa, N.J.: Barnes & Noble, 1984), 31–50, 37.

36. Johnson refers to Suetonius's account of Augustus's requesting of his friends, on his deathbed: " 'Have I played my part in the farce of life creditably enough?' adding the theatrical tag: *If I have pleased you, kindly signify / Appreciation with a warm goodbye*." "Augustus," paragraph 99 in Suetonius, *The Twelve Caesars*, trans. Robert Graves (Harmondsworth: Penguin, 1957), 106.

37. Samuel Johnson, preface to *A Dictionary of the English Language*, 2 vols. (London, 1755), 11.

38. *The Twickenham Edition of the Works of Alexander Pope*, ed. Maynard Mack et al., 11 vols. (London: Methuen, 1967), 8:423. Subsequent references to this edition are cited by volume and page number parenthetically in the text.

39. Pope's quotation marks signal his borrowing from Dryden's version of the third

book of Lucretius' *De Rerum Natura*: "Meantime, when thoughts of death disturb thy head, / Consider, Ancus, great and good, is dead; / Ancus, thy better far, was born to die, / And thou, dost thou bewail mortality?" ("Against the Fear of Death," lines 236–39).

40. *Moral Essays* 4, lines 41–44, quoted by Birkbeck Hill in *Lives*, 3:216.

41. *The California Edition of the Works of John Dryden*, ed. S. H. Monk et al. (Berkeley: University of California, 1971), 17:248.

42. Joseph Warton, *An Essay on the Genius and Writings of Pope*, 1:v.

43. In his edition of Pope's poems Warton replied: "Malignant and insensible must be the critic who should impotently dare to assert that *Pope* wanted genius and *imagination*; but perhaps it may safely be affirmed, that his peculiar and *characteristical* excellencies were good sense and judgment." See *The Works of Alexander Pope*, 1:lxx.

44. Preface to *Fables, Ancient and Modern* in *The Poems of John Dryden*, ed. James Kinsley, 4 vols. (Oxford: Oxford University Press, 1958), 4:1448.

45. For a further discussion of Pope's "genius" in relation to Dryden's, see G. F. Parker, *Johnson's Shakespeare* (Oxford: Clarendon Press, 1989), 57–58. Parker returns to some of these notions on pages 63–155.

46. Compare Johnson's contention that "whatever withdraws us from the power of our senses; whatever makes the past, the distant, or the future predominate over the present advances us in the dignity of thinking beings." See *Journey*, 148.

47. Preface to *Fables, Ancient and Modern* in *The Poems of John Dryden*, 4:1448–49. In section 12 of his treatise *On the Sublime*, Longinus had described Demosthenes as "uttering every Sentence with such Force, Precipitation, Strength and Vehemence, that it seems to be all Fire, and bears down everything before it" like a "Thunderbolt" or a "Hurricane." See *Dionysius Longinus on the Sublime*, 34.

48. Birkbeck Hill quotes Malone's recollection of Johnson saying that "we have had too many honeysuckle lives of Milton, and that his should be in another strain" (*Lives*, 1:85).

49. Lawrence Lipking, *The Ordering of the Arts in Eighteenth-Century England* (Princeton: Princeton University Press, 1970), 459.

50. Preface to *Lyrical Ballads* (1850), in *The Prose Works of William Wordsworth*, ed. W. J. B. Owen and J. W. Smyser, 3 vols. (Oxford: Clarendon Press, 1974), 1:138.

BIBLIOGRAPHY

Boswell, James. *Boswell's Life of Johnson*. 3 vols. Edited by George Birkbeck Hill. Revised by L. F. Powell. Oxford: Clarendon Press, 1934 – 64.

Boulton, J. T., ed. *Johnson: The Critical Heritage*. London: Routledge, 1971.

Burney, Fanny. *Dr. Johnson and Fanny Burney; being the Johnsonian Passages from the works of Mme D'Arblay*. Edited by Chauncey Brewster Tinker. Westport, Conn.: Greenwood, 1911.

Coleridge, Samuel Taylor. *The Letters of Samuel Taylor Coleridge*. 2 vols. Edited by Earnest Hartley Coleridge. London: Heinemann, 1895.

Cowper, William. *The Letters and Prose Writings of William Cowper*. 5 vols. Edited by James King and Charles Ryskamp. Oxford: Clarendon Press, 1979–84.

Dryden, John. *The California Edition of the Works of John Dryden*. Vol. 17. Edited by S. H. Monk et al. Berkeley: University of California Press, 1971.

———. *The Critical and Miscellaneous Prose Works of John Dryden*. 4 vols. Edited by Edmond Malone. London: 1800.

———. *The Poems of John Dryden*. Edited by James Kinsley. 4 vols. Oxford: Oxford University Press, 1958.

Grundy, Isobel, ed. *Samuel Johnson: New Critical Essays*. London and Totowa, N.J.: Barnes & Noble, 1984.

Hawkins, Sir John. *The Life of Samuel Johnson*. 1787; New York and London: Garland, 1974.

Hazlitt, William. *The Complete Works of William Hazlitt*. 21 vols. Edited by P. P. Howe. London and Toronto: Dent, 1930.

Hill, George Birkbeck, ed. *Johnsonian Miscellanies*. 2 vols. Oxford: Clarendon Press, 1897.

Hoccleve, Thomas. *The Poems of Thomas Hoccleve*. Edited by George Mason. London: 1796.

Johnson, Samuel. *A Dictionary of the English Language*, 2 vols. London: 1755.

———. *The Idler and the Adventurer*. Edited by W. J. Bate, J. M. Bullitt, and L. F. Powell. Vol. 2 of The Yale Edition of the Works of Samuel Johnson. New Haven and London: Yale University Press, 1963.

———. *Johnson on Shakespeare*. Edited by Arthur Sherbo. Vols. 7–8 of The Yale Edition of the Works of Samuel Johnson. New Haven and London: Yale University Press, 1968.

———. *The Letters of Samuel Johnson*. 5 vols. Edited by Bruce Redford. Princeton: Princeton University Press, 1992.

———. *The Lives of the Poets*. 3 vols. Edited by George Birkbeck Hill. Oxford: Clarendon Press, 1905.

———. *Rambler*. Edited by by W. J. Bate and Albrecht B. Strauss. Vols. 3–5 of The Yale Edition of the Works of Samuel Johnson. New Haven and London: Yale University Press, 1969.

———. *Rasselas and Other Tales*. Edited by Gwin J. Kolb. Vol. 16 of The Yale Edition of the Works of Samuel Johnson. New Haven and London: Yale University Press, 1990.

Keats, John. *The Letters of John Keats*. 2 vols. Edited by H. E. Rollins. Cambridge: Cambridge University Press, 1958.

Kenrick, William. *A Review of Doctor Johnson's New Edition of Shakespeare, in which the ignorance, or inattention of that editor is exposed, and the poet defended from the persecution of his commentators*. London: 1765. Reprinted in *On Johnson's Shakespeare, 1765–1766*. New York and London: Garland, 1975.

Lipking, Lawrence. *The Ordering of the Arts in Eighteenth-Century England*. Princeton: Princeton University Press, 1970.

Longinus. *Dionysius Longinus on the Sublime*. Translated by William Smith. London: 1739.

Macaulay, Thomas Babington. "Boswell's Life of Johnson." *Edinburgh Review* 54, no. 107(September 1831): 1–38.

Mackintosh, Sir James. *Memoirs of the Life of Sir James Mackintosh*. 2 vols. Edited by Robert James Mackintosh. 2nd ed. London: 1836.

Malone, Edmond. Preface to *The Plays And Poems Of William Shakespeare, With The Corrections And Illustrations Of Various Commentators*. London: 1821.

Pope, Alexander. *The Twickenham Edition of the Works of Alexander Pope*. 11 vols. Edited by Maynard Mack et al. London: Methuen, 1967.

————. *The Works of Alexander Pope*, 9 vols. Edited by Joseph Warton. London: 1797.

Potter, Robert. *The Art of Criticism; as Exemplified in Dr Johnson's Lives of the Most Eminent Poets*. London: 1789.

Seward, Anna. *The Letters of Anna Seward written between the years 1784 and 1807*. 6 vols. London: 1811.

————. *The Poetical Works of Anna Seward*. 3 vols. Edited by Walter Scott. Edinburgh: 1810.

Warton, Joseph. *An Essay on the Genius and Writings of Pope*. 2 vols. London: 1756, 1782; New York and London: Garland, 1974.

Wordsworth, William. *The Prose Works of William Wordsworth*. 3 vols. Edited by W. J. B. Owen and J. W. Smyser. Oxford: Clarendon Press, 1974.

Contributors

JAMES G. BASKER is Professor of English at Barnard College and President of the Gilder Lehrman Institute of American History in New York City. His publications include *Tobias Smollett, Critic and Journalist* (1988), *Tradition in Transition* (with Alvaro Ribeiro, S.J., 1996), and the forthcoming *Amazing Grace: Slavery in English Poetry 1660–1810*.

GREG CLINGHAM is a Professor of English at Bucknell University and author of the forthcoming *Writing Johnsonian Memory*.

JACLYN GELLER teaches English at New York University. She is currently researching the connection between formal satire and the rise of the novel, focusing on representations of marriage in British fiction and poetry. Her essays and book reviews have appeared in *Salmagundi* and *On the Issues: The Progressive Woman's Quarterly*.

CLEMENT HAWES is an Associate Professor of English at Penn State University, where he teaches eighteenth-century British literature. His publications include *Mania and Literary Style: The Rhetoric of Enthusiasm from the Ranters to Christopher Smart* (1996); the edited volume *Christopher Smart and the Enlightenment* (1999); and essays on Abiezer Coppe, John Gay, Samuel Johnson, Laurence Sterne, Christopher Smart, and Jonathan Swift. He is currently at work on a new monograph, tentatively entitled *Cannibalizing History*, and will be editing the New Riverside edition of *Gulliver's Travels*.

DANIELLE INSALACO teaches in the Department of English at New York University. Her current research focuses on representations of Italian history in British literature from Gibbon to Byron.

TOM MASON lectures in English literature at Bristol University. He is author (with David Hopkins) of *The Story of Poetry* (1992) and has published essays on Dryden and on Abraham Cowley. He is currently completing a book on the relations between poetry and literary criticism in the period from Milton to Wordsworth.

ADAM ROUNCE is Leverhulme Special Research Fellow in the Department of English at the University of Bristol. He is working on a study of eighteenth-century poetry after the death of Pope and currently contributes the "Eighteenth-Century Poetry" section to *The Year's Work in English Studies*.

PHILIP SMALLWOOD is Professor of English at the University of Central England. His writings include an edition of Johnson's *Preface to Shakespeare* (1985), and a monograph, *Modern Critics in Practice* (1990). His essays on critical and theoretical issues have appeared in American and British journals including *New Literary History* and *The British Journal of Aesthetics*. He is presently writing a book on Johnson's criticism.

Index

169